ACCESS TO COMMUNICATION

This book is dedicated to the work of the students and staff of
Harperbury Hospital School, 1981 to the present day.

Access to Communication

Developing the basics of communication with people with severe
learning difficulties through Intensive Interaction

MELANIE NIND AND DAVE HEWETT

David Fulton Publishers

London

David Fulton Publishers Ltd
Ormond House, 26–27 Boswell Street, London WC1N 3JD

First published in Great Britain by
David Fulton Publishers 1994
Reprinted 1995, 1996, 1998

Note: The right of the authors to be identified as the authors of this work has been asserted by them in accordance with the Copyright, Designs and Patents Act 1988.

Copyright © Melanie Nind and Dave Hewett

British Library Cataloguing in Publication Data

A catalogue record for this book is available from the British Library

ISBN 1–85346–283–7

Designed by ALMAC Ltd., London

Typeset by ROM-Data Corporation Ltd, Falmouth, Cornwall

Printed in Great Britain by BPC Wheatons Ltd, Exeter

Contents

Introduction   1

Chapter 1   What is Intensive Interaction?   4

Chapter 2   The Theoretical Background to Intensive Interaction   17

Chapter 3   How Knowledge of Infant Learning Helped the   44
Development of Intensive Interaction

Chapter 4   How to do Intensive Interaction   80

Chapter 5   Wider and Related Issues   163

Chapter 6   Case Studies   193

Glossary   212

Bibliography   214

Index   227

Acknowledgements

Here is a probably incomplete list of people we need to thank, for contributing to our work in so many different ways:

Mel Ainscow, Jo Allen, Paula Arnell, Andy Arnett, Rosie Augsburger, Ann Belcher, Sharon Bell, Hazel (Frances) Black, Marjorie Bocking, Nikki Bodman, Debbie Bracey, Michelle Bracey, Laura Chambers, Jenny Chaplin, Deana Collins, Angela Cutts, Bunty Davidson, Jane Dennison, Phyll Dimmock, Ali Dolan, Margaret Eady, Gary Ephraim, Andrew Ferrugia, Dorothy Foyle, Ann Garden, Sheila Glenn, Juliet Goldbart, Christina Goldie, Gaynor Goodwin, Francine Griffith, Tony Guichard, Betty Hall, Lin Hall, Mark Hand, Sue Heath, Mary Hope, David Hopkins, Sue Horne, Alice Humm, Matthew Humm, Steve Humm, Bernie Hunt, Helen Janes, Sue Kelly, Alex Kelsey, Wendy Kelsey, Christine Knight, Janet Lara, Bernadette Levoir, Steve Livingstone, Linda Miller, Sue Newton, Thomas Newton, Betty Orange, Dennis O'Regan, Yioda Panayiotou, Jez Parry, Bharti Patel, Mike Pauley, Heather Pomroy, Elaine Powell, Toniann Read, Nikki Ross, Martin Rouse, Helen Sanderson, Linda Sargent, Christine Scrase, Judy Sebba, Liz Sharpe, Sally Slater, Ian Tearle, Ron Telfer, Mandy Thackray, Rob Thompson, David Tierney, Hazel Wallis, Judith Watson, Kathy Watson, Sally Wheeldon, Tony Wigram, Lindsey Williams, Liz Williams, Rosemary Woods, Lilian Yescombe.

Introduction

This book is for anyone who works or spends time with people who have learning difficulties, especially those who do not yet use language. The focus of our work during the last eight years has been concerned with opening up the fulfilment and joy of human interaction to people who are remote from communication and companionship. We have written this book with the ambition that practitioners, relatives and friends everywhere may read it and feel more confident about offering themselves as sensitive interactors.

We are teachers, and we inevitably think about our work as teachers, but we have tried to write a book which is welcoming to people from all professions and disciplines. We frequently use the term 'practitioner' to describe all of us, from whatever discipline, who do face-to-face work. We sincerely hope that parents, relatives and friends of people with learning difficulties will also find this book friendly and helpful.

We have attempted to be as down to earth and practical as possible. This is a book about communication, particularly communication before speech. Our primary purpose is to describe an approach to helping people who are preverbal – Intensive Interaction. In particular we offer as much information as we can about what to do, minute by minute and day by day. So often we find that the theoretical outweighs the practical in publications in this field. We are often left with a feeling of having been interested by a philosophy or theory, but wondering what you actually *do*. We hope readers will not be left with that feeling after reading this; many other questions perhaps, but not fundamental ones about what you do.

Whilst dedicating ourselves to the practicalities, we have also

1

included some theory which underpins the approach. Chapter two in particular contains detailed information about research on the development of communication in early infancy. We have included many technical terms in this section, but have hopefully also managed to demystify them.

We have worked hard to keep the language we use as jargon-free as possible. This is worth doing in its own right, but is also in keeping with the essential simplicity and practicality of the approach we recommend. We have agonised over the use of certain terminology. The collective noun we use to describe people in our workplaces who have learning difficulties is a case in point. 'Clients' is the word we find used mostly by the social services staff with whom we work. It is also common in the independent sector, and used increasingly in the health service. Use of that term may risk excluding educationalists. 'Pupils' tends to refer only to school-age people, and we are concerned with people of any age. 'Students' is a word often used in education to describe learners of all ages. This term is frequently also employed in social services. We have ultimately compromised with our own composite term 'students/clients'.

We acknowledge that terminology can be an emotive subject, and that our use of it may unwittingly offend some readers with strong views. One person we consulted for advice asked us, from an assumed position of the moral high ground, what was wrong with calling them 'people'. Well, yes, nothing at all, but the text would become tedious and vexing to wade through, if every time we used the word 'people' no-one was sure to whom we were referring. It is for these reasons that we refer to 'teachers' as 'teachers'.

'Learning difficulties' is still the term used in special schools. 'Learning disability' seems to be in more common usage at the time of writing. In speech we alternate between use of the two. However, for our book we have taken the counsel of self-advocates and of 'People First' that 'people with learning difficulties' is preferred.

We have tried to break the book up into coherent, sensible chapters and sections. Nonetheless, it may be helpful to switch between chapters whilst proceeding. For instance, when reading about the practicalities of interaction in chapter four, you may have a query about general issues of physical contact. You may then like to refer to our discussion on this issue in chapter five. We include detailed contents pages, index and glossary to help with this process. Chapter two, the review of the literature, is the most technical. Some readers may find it easier to access having first read the 'how to do it' information in chapters three and four.

Whilst working with a group of social services managers in the north of England recently, we were presented with this intentionally ironic, but fundamentally accurate comment:

> 'Well we've finally done it. We've got people to come up here and train us in how to behave naturally.'

We like that observation. There is a lot of truth in it. We hope that it is reassuring, because the essentials of the approach we call 'Intensive Interaction' are styles of behaviour and interaction which seem natural to most people. We are being intellectual about it, identifying the principles and structures, documenting and recording it, calling it an approach, but its basis is natural behaviour. We sincerely hope that this will be the sensation experienced by readers as they read about it and try it.

More than anything else we hope that this book is an enjoyable read. 'Mutual enjoyment' is an essential principle of Intensive Interaction. We enjoy our work, have had a really good time writing our book, and truly hope that the enjoyment comes through to the reader.

CHAPTER 1

What is Intensive Interaction?

Background to the development of Intensive Interaction

To place Intensive Interaction in context we will describe here the development work that took place at Harperbury Hospital School from the mid-1980s. The school was for young adults with severe learning difficulties set within a long-stay hospital. Our school population comprised exclusively residents of the institution and, more specifically, those residents who were younger, who experienced the most severe learning difficulties and who, because of their behaviour or multiple disabilities, were least likely to be accommodated in other centres.

Historically, the school catered for the children living in the institution and they were offered opportunities, in an educational context, to play with sand, water, paint, to build with blocks, to thread beads, and to complete basic puzzles. The curriculum also focussed on the teaching of self-help skills; the ability to dress, eat and go to the toilet with maximum independence (see Hewett and Nind 1992).

As society's expectations of people with learning difficulties changed, children were increasingly accommodated within the community and only those young people with the most severe developmental disabilities, additional sensory and physical disabilities, and extreme behaviour, became residents of the institution. A large proportion of the emerging student group showed very limited understanding of their immediate environment; most were unable to interact with others in ways that we could find meaningful. Many of the students experienced profound and multiple difficulties in learning and in relating to others. Often their lifestyles were characterised by stereotyped, ritualistic behaviour, aggressive defence of their own isolation, and apparent total self-absorption.

These students posed massive challenges in terms of appropriate curricular provision. The historical context, however, was a time when behaviourism was in its hey-day; research had shown the successes of behavioural techniques and the approach could be readily learned and applied. In this situation, as with others, behavioural approaches and the skills analysis model (see Crawford 1980; Gardner and Crawford 1983) offered an obvious solution.

Core areas of development were subdivided into components and each component had a list of target behaviours. Very structured teaching programmes were devised with specific objectives for each student, related to how they fitted against the checklist of skills. Core areas included motor development, social skills, self-help, language, cognition, play/leisure skills and behaviour. Once the stages of a task were analysed in detail these stages were taught discretely, aided by techniques of shaping, prompting, fading and chaining as well as the use of extrinsic rewards, usually food (see Kiernan et al 1978; Gardner and Crawford 1983). In practice priority was given to the teaching of discrimination and self-help skills, partly perhaps because the subject of the teaching was tangible and lent itself to skills analysis. Similarly, in the absence of knowing anything better to do, individual teaching time was given over to the completion of superficially purposeful table-top activities which had the attraction that the teacher could physically prompt the student to make a correct response. Programmes were also devised to respond to what were perceived as aggressive and anti-social behaviours with the withdrawal of rewards, periods in 'time-out' cubicles, and exclusion.

By the mid-eighties the school curriculum had settled into a mixture of unstructured activity, highly structured teaching of discrimination and self-help skills, and behavioural programmes based largely around the use of 'time-out'. Staff turn-over had been high, with people leaving after short periods of very stressful work. There was a new staff group forming, with a large number of teachers who were largely inexperienced and in their probationary year. There was growing unease with a curriculum which seemed to produce regular failure for both the teacher and the student. There was growing discomfort also with the inflexibility of a curriculum structure which gave little scope for following up the students' interests and strengths. To summarise what was in fact a gradual and untidy process, we as a teaching staff began to question both the ethics and the effectiveness of the methods we were using. We began to recognise that much of the behaviour of our students was a response to situations that they did not understand and that they were often demonstrating communication difficulties rather than behavioural difficulties. This led us to look afresh at the students and their fundamental learning needs (see Hewett and Nind 1992).

We came to the conclusion that these needs were almost always within the realm of communication and sociability and that the existing curriculum rarely even touched upon addressing such needs. We felt that if we could begin to establish a relationship with the students, and if we could establish a basis for communication, then all other spheres of teaching and learning would become easier and more meaningful. We were conscious that our existing behavioural techniques were inadequate when addressing the complexities of communication and sociability. We knew how to prompt the use of a Makaton sign in a certain situation, but we did not know how to make this have meaningful intent, how to facilitate genuine facial expressions, or how to teach positive ways of relating to others. With the realisation that there were no readily available answers about how to teach the earliest stages of communicating and being social to young people with such learning difficulties, we began to seek a new teaching practice for ourselves. We entered a period in which practical experimentation in the classroom and theoretical inquiry complemented and informed each other, and from which new ways of working evolved.

With our interest sparked by Gary Ephraim's (1979) ideas on using 'mothering', our theoretical inquiry began with looking at the literature on caregiver-infant interaction (for example, Schaffer 1977a; Newson 1979a) where we found a model for understanding how communication and sociability develop naturally in a typical child. It became evident that usually these fundamental abilities are learned in the first year of life without being consciously taught. Analysis of videos of mothers and infants interacting has provided insights into the form that their interactive play takes and researchers have shown that this interactive play has a crucial role in ongoing development (see chapter two).

In our practice at school we began to incorporate interactive play into our daily routines. Dressing situations, for example, changed from being a non-personal and stressful routine in which skills were prompted and reinforced, into the context for a peek-a-boo type game where we were playful, offered warm physical contact, and gently narrated the action. In escorting students to different parts of the building we nagged less, and instead blended our walking rhythm with that of the student, building some mutuality based on shared timing of movement. Such changes in approach were immediately rewarding, both because the students responded positively and because our work in itself became more enjoyable.

There followed a spiralling effect of positive change. Gentler, more playful work with individual students was found to be more enjoyable and effective and so was generalised to work with other students. Rudimentary game sequences like 'I'm going to get you . . .' were repeated and developed such that students not only laughed at the game, but began to anticipate its climax and signal a desire for more. Gradually this kind of activity moved from the periphery of the school curriculum to its core. We began to use playful approaches to bring students to the table to perform a task, but the task soon diminished in importance in favour of the play itself. With many individuals we tended to stop doing table-top activities like inset puzzles in individual teaching slots, and instead engaged in free-flowing interactive play, usually without any equipment or task. With different expectations we freed ourselves to go and sit in the corner on the floor with students, where they felt safe, and to join them there in their self-absorbed world. By gently joining in with their rocking or humming rhythms we were able to capture their attention and establish some mutual pleasure; achieving this with students who had previously always rejected our approaches was really encouraging.

Without at first realising it we stopped dominating the classroom with our rules and choice of activity and began to be responsive in a very basic kind of negotiation. In allowing ourselves to use our natural teaching styles we adjusted our interpersonal behaviours with the students, which made us more interesting and accessible to them. With this and our improving abilities to read the students' signals, we were able to avoid many of the violent outbursts to which we were accustomed. The emerging calm and non-confrontational atmosphere also meant that the more anxious students were able to relax, the more active students began to slow down, and the challenging behaviours became less frequent and less challenging.

Aware of the demands of accountability we began to formalise our new curriculum. We re-wrote individual programmes with new aims and new strategies and explored ways of recording our activities and our students' progress. We addressed the growing gulf between our written curriculum and our actual practice and we looked more and more to the theoretical literature to understand and talk about the new structure of our work.

As the students made significant gains in relatively short periods of time we became aware that the work we were doing was important. We shared what we were doing with other teachers and increasingly with staff groups working in social services and health authority day centres and residential establishments, finding what was (and continues to be) great interest in the approach. We (the authors) undertook formal research projects to gain greater understanding of how the approach worked, the results of using it, and how effective it was in enhancing social and communication development.

What is Intensive Interaction?

Intensive Interaction is the name we have given to the approach which culminated from the period of curriculum innovation we have described (Davis 1985; Nind and Hewett 1988; Hewett and Nind 1989). It is an approach which was developed by a group of teachers working with pre-verbal students who were experiencing extreme difficulty in learning and in relating to others and who were demonstrating ritualistic and challenging behaviours.

Intensive Interaction makes use of the range of interactive games which have been shown to occur in interactions between infants and their primary caregivers. Some aspects of the caregiver role in such interactions are emulated by the staff member using Intensive Interaction (see chapter two). The staff member attempts to attract and hold the attention of the learner. S/he attempts to engage the learner in one-to-one interactive games with the emphasis being on pleasure first and foremost. This involves staff in modifying their usual body language, voice and face, in order to make themselves attractive and interesting to their less sophisticated partners. The intention is that the teacher and the learner become jointly focussed on each other, that they share some mutuality, and that they want to repeat this enjoyable experience. There is generally no particular task to be achieved and the focus is the quality of the activity of the two participants, often with the teacher building a game from an action, facial expression or sound made by the student. Teachers using Intensive Interaction abandon the formal pre-structured teaching role and instead employ intuitive abilities to interact at this fundamental level.

The interactions are often brief in the early stages and largely exploratory. It is the intention of the approach, however, that the interactions become longer and more sophisticated over time. The staff member facilitates the learner's increasing involvement in the games, such that the student becomes more active and the exchange becomes more mutual. With the learner's involvement in increasingly elaborate games, the process brings about the development of more complex communication abilities such as use of facial expression, anticipation and turn-taking.

As well as playfulness, sensitivity is a major theme of Intensive Interaction. The interactive sequence can be seen to be a highly sensitive response network to the signals and feedback of the learner. The staff member continuously, and largely unconsciously, adjusts her or his input to gain and maintain the student's interest and emotional arousal. With more sensitive interpersonal contact, the learner's behaviours – which may have been regarded as meaningless – can become readable cues and be treated as communications. The learner's signals of desire to change or end an interactive game are respected and staff learn 'when to initiate or respond to a variation, when to 'play safe', when to continue, and when to cool down' (Nind and Hewett 1988, p.56).

The content of the interactive sequences in Intensive Interaction varies with each pair of participants and with every occasion; what happens is spontaneous and responsive rather then pre-planned. The nature and intensity of the activity varies between, for instance, noisy rough and tumble, intense mutual face-to-face studying or simply sitting together in physical contact. Though never exactly the same, some games are repeated over and over and some have widespread popularity. We include in this the games which centre around tension and expectancy, such as peek-a-boo, 'I'm going to get you . . .' and 'round and round the garden'; games which involve shared rhythm such as rocking in unison, swinging arms as you walk, taking turns to hum; and games which involve bodily contact and movement such as blowing raspberries, jiggling on a lap, rough and tumble. Many of the learners with whom this approach is used start from a position of avoiding all contact with other human beings, therefore sharing personal space and getting involved in simple games like these are achievements in themselves.

Much of the content of Intensive Interaction will be familiar to readers who are parents, carers or practitioners working with people with severe learning difficulties; it is part of what they do in their everyday communications and good practice. Use of interactive game becomes Intensive Interaction when we give structure and deliberate progression to the interactive processes which are not normally rationalised or intellectualised (Nind and Hewett 1988). Indeed one of the challenges of the method is to retain the power of intuitive responding, whilst supplementing it with the benefits of careful analysis to maximise the potential of the interactions. Intensive Interaction facilitates the learner's progression from passivity or non-engagement in the games, through reciprocity in which the learner has an active role and is aware of this, to eventual initiation and leading of interactive games. The approach involves the participants in the kind of learning experiences and processes through which sociability and communication develop in infancy. It is the process rather than the outcome of the sequences that is central to the method.

Intensive Interaction beyond the classroom

We would like to establish from the outset that this is not just a book by teachers for teachers. It is for anyone who is in direct contact with people with severe learning difficulties who are pre-verbal. It is particularly for those who have a desire to find more effective ways of relating, who want to facilitate better communication, to enhance general development, and who want to enjoy better social contact with their clients/students/children. We hope that particular relevance will be found for readers working with, or parenting, individuals who are difficult to reach. By this we mean those people who may have a multitude of disabilities, who may be at the very earliest stages of development, or who may indicate by their behaviour that they do not want to be with you and do not understand the pleasure of social contact.

As we have explained, Intensive Interaction was developed in an educational context and we write from the standpoint of being teachers. This sometimes leads us to delve into issues of special interest to teachers, the organisation of the curriculum and record-keeping, for example. We hope that in doing this we will not exclude other readers. We have spent some years now travelling around different establishments sharing our experiences and exchanging ideas with practitioners from all disciplines. It is noteworthy that Intensive Interaction is as interesting and relevant to social workers, carers and therapists, as it is to teachers.

Perhaps one of the beauties of Intensive Interaction is that many of us already have most of the skills and abilities the approach requires.

At the crux here are the intuitive abilities that we use when we relate to infants – and we don't need to go to college for four years to learn them! Often we simply need the reassurance that these skills are what is needed. In the case of teachers in particular, we may need to unlearn other theories and practices in order to free us to use these natural abilities. Intensive Interaction is less about formal teaching, instructing or training and more about facilitating learning. Investigation of the processes of caregiver-infant interaction shows us that what the caregiver does, guided by feedback and signals from the infant, is to provide a social environment in which the infant feels safe and motivated and in which competence and understanding can develop. Providing such an environment for people with severe learning difficulties who are pre-verbal is not just a concern for teachers.

Intensive Interaction can be used, as it was at Harperbury, as the essence of what you do for the majority of the student/client group, or it can be used in part with one or two people. Some practitioners are using aspects of the approach to inform their movement sessions, to guide the quality of their caring routines, or to try to reach one individual for whom all else has failed. After adapting their interpersonal behaviours and becoming sensitive to the subtle cues of the person they are trying to reach, however, staff who begin in this small way invariably find that they do not want to (and cannot) limit this to a particular client or a particular slot in the day. Intensive Interaction can be taken up in different ways, but it does have its own momentum.

The practical guidelines and case studies later in the book will illustrate that interactive games can take place anywhere; a spontaneous sequence whilst preparing food together can be just as worthwhile as anything happening in a classroom. The fact that this approach does not entail pre-planning or structure in the usual rigid sense, actually makes the classroom a less ideal environment than the living room or kitchen. Classrooms of course can change to become more secure and relaxed. From our experience at Harperbury the classrooms became less formal as the interactive games and tranquil, fun-filled atmosphere prevailed (see Nind and Hewett 1988).

Intensive Interaction affects the quality of the interaction between the person with learning difficulties and other people with whom s/he comes into contact. Relationships with staff or carers, ability to communicate, and understanding of others will all be affected. With this the person's quality of life will also be affected. It is likely that the person will actually enjoy life more and engage in new experiences more readily. These developments are clearly not just an issue for education in its narrowest sense, they are likely to be relevant beyond the classroom and of interest to most practitioners working with this client group.

Who is Intensive Interaction for?

In its beginnings Intensive Interaction was for a very specific client group. This group consisted of learners who had in common a level of development such that their social and communication abilities were not as advanced than those of infants of less than one year old. They also shared a reluctance to explore and experiment with their physical and social environment, a tendency to remain within very familiar and ritualised patterns of behaviour, and some inability to relate to or trust others. They were all living in an institution and had been for some time.

Perhaps because of the nature of our hospital setting, we worked with a concentration of learners at this level. It is more usual, however, to find a workplace which has just one or two individuals for whom nothing seems relevant, or a small group who don't quite fit in and benefit from the usual range of activities. Whatever the reason, the concentration of students with such fundamental learning needs focussed our minds wonderfully on the endeavour to find an approach which would be relevant and basic enough.

Even with these things in common, however, our student group was as diverse as any other. Some of the students had physical disabilities, some had additional sensory impairments, some carried diagnoses of autism or mental illness, some of the students were aggressive, some injured themselves, some were very active and some were very passive. Intensive Interaction was developed for all of these people and is highly relevant for them.

We do not advocate the use of Intensive Interaction for everyone. There are plenty of people with severe learning difficulties who have no need for this intensity of approach at this level. They may have good use of verbal communication, or use some symbolic communication system combined with good use of eye contact and idiosyncratic signal systems. They may relate well to others and enjoy their company and they may respond to other teaching strategies in order to learn new skills. It is likely that some of the principles of Intensive Interaction could be usefully applied with these learners, indeed we will argue later that there are certain generalisable truths that can be applied to learners of all abilities. The content of the interaction will be different, however, and the approach readily replaceable by many others.

Intensive Interaction, as described in this book, is an approach which is relevant for people who may be pre-verbal, not at a stage of using or understanding verbal or symbolic communication. It may also be relevant for the people we meet who have some spoken language but who do not use it to communicate. Their speech may be accompanied by a sense of remoteness and lack any facial expression, eye contact or pauses for the other person's turn. It is for people who have few, or limited, communication behaviours and who lack the skills needed for being social with other people. They may have ritualistic, aggressive, self-involved or self-injurious behaviour which excludes other people.

Intensive Interaction is about reaching those learners who remain untouched by traditional approaches. It is for those people who do not yet know that being with another human being can be pleasurable or can be under their control. Their general tempo of living may be very different and they may be withdrawn. It is for those people whose signals we do not understand and whom we may have difficulty in perceiving as being social and communicative.

How does Intensive Interaction fit with other approaches?

When reviewing the literature in chapter two we will look at how Intensive Interaction fits into a wider spectrum of approaches for people with profound learning difficulties, for people who demonstrate stereotyped or challenging behaviours and for people with autism. While not wishing to pre-empt this, we would like at this stage to orientate the reader to Intensive Interaction in the general context of other approaches.

Educational approaches for people with learning difficulties can be viewed as spanning a continuum with teacher or product-centred approaches at one end and student- or process-centred approaches at the other, though this is obviously a simplification. With product-centred approaches we would include the behavioural methods and skills analysis model which we described as part of Harperbury School's history. We include teaching which is based on the teacher's idea of what should be learned and how, when and at what pace it should be taught. Associated here are notions that the person with learning difficulties should act according to a pre-specified idea of what is acceptable and appropriate. We include the various types of dominance and compulsion likely to be used to achieve this.

At the opposite end of the continuum pre-specified objectives are seen as unnecessary and as a hindrance. In process-centred teaching the activity lacks structure in the traditional sense, the learning is not compartmentalised or approached in small steps. Much consideration is given to the learning environment and to the stimulation which is offered, but what happens will depend very much on the student, following her/his interests and lead. In this way the teaching is seen less as technology and more as art. The outcomes and end-products of the sessions are seen as less important that the process itself. The emphasis is on the exploring, the doing, the discovery. It is the understandings that come as part of this active process that the teacher aims to promote.

As will already be obvious to the reader, Intensive Interaction lies towards the process and student-centred end of this continuum. The teaching style is interpretative rather than directive and the power base of the learning is shared between the teacher and the learner during interaction sequences. We would stress, however, that Intensive Interaction is not a laissez-faire approach to education or development. It is highly purposeful and analytical and it contains its own structure. We will return to a further discussion of this philosophical and curricular debate in chapter five.

Although different language is used in other contexts such as social services day centres and residential settings, a similar diversity of approach exists. Workplaces vary. At one extreme there is rigid structuring of activity and a dedication to constant intervention in the clients' behaviour. The opposite extreme may show unstructured activity and much more freedom for the clients to express themselves in their behaviour. Some settings provide behavioural environments and some more therapeutic environments. More often what is offered is somewhere in between. Intensive Interaction would fit well with the more therapeutic approaches offering a gentle way of facilitating development in those clients who are more challenging. It also sits well within the self-advocacy movement and would provide a way of developing self-determination and giving control to those adults with more severe learning difficulties.

The philosophical basis of Intensive Interaction

We have placed Intensive Interaction within the context of other approaches, within the context of its psychological basis and within the context of the development work at Harperbury Hospital School. Before we move on we would like to say something about our values and outlook with regard to Intensive Interaction.

Valuing the process

We have referred to Intensive Interaction as being process-based rather than outcomes-based. We reiterate our commitment to this. Part of the inspiration for developing our way of working at Harperbury School was a desire to bring quality to everything we did with our students. We were concerned just as much with the quality of what we were doing on a day to day basis as with the overall aim of developing fundamental communication and sociability. Indeed, we saw the two as intertwined. If we aim to make every interaction a mutually enjoyable and satisfying experience then we are likely to promote positive social development. If we aim to respond sensitively to each behaviour as an initiation or communicative act we are likely to help our learners to become communicators.

With some approaches – Holding Therapy (Welch 1983) perhaps – the end seems to be used to justify the means. Often the stages of natural development are worked towards using processes which bear no relation to the natural model of teaching and learning seen in caregiver-infant interaction. There is no sense of this in Intensive Interaction, the process of learning about sociability and communication is valued in itself.

Respect, negotiation and participation

Intensive Interaction is essentially an approach which is respectful of the individual. It is based on valuing the pre-verbal person with learning difficulties as a social and communicative being whose behaviours are worthwhile. When using this approach there is no element of eradicating parts of a person's behavioural repertoire which don't make sense to us. There is no sense of taking away what a person feels safe and comfortable with, and imposing what might seem comfortable and appropriate for us. Intensive Interaction is about accepting the person and offering her/him new opportunities. It is about making these opportunities understandable and achievable.

The philosophy underlying our work sees people as individuals. We do not regard people with severe learning difficulties as a homogenous group for whom we know best. We avoid the prescriptive stance of the strict age-appropriateness school of thought, for instance, in which there is a doctrine that all people of a certain age should behave in a certain way. We certainly respect adult status, but we also respect individuality. Ways forward for individual learners will vary according to many factors and will need to take into account the person's emotional maturity and ability to understand, as well as our ability to understand them. Intensive Interaction is offered as a framework for an array of individual practice which might be useful for the people with whom you work.

Intensive Interaction is concerned with negotiation and participation as opposed to dominance and compliance. Part of valuing the learner on an equal basis is not imposing on her/him our agenda for action, our style and pace of working, and our needs. What we do and how we go about it can and should be negotiated whatever the person's abilities and difficulties. The process of starting with the learner's own behaviour and preferred place is part of this 'negotiation'. The ongoing process of looking for and responding to each person's signals and feedback is also crucial to this. The fact that you respond to the other person's signals of desire to initiate, maintain or terminate an interaction gives that person the negotiating powers to which she/he is entitled.

The central theme of mutual pleasure is linked with the philosophy of participation. If the learner is taking part for reasons other than that they want to, they are likely to be complying rather than participating. If the motivation and participation are absent, then communication and sociability are likely to be absent also. It is vital to this approach that people are involved in interactions because they want to be.

The practice of Intensive Interaction is, and should be, inextricably linked with attitudes of respecting and valuing the learner and the process of communicating and being social. We believe that sociability and communication cannot be taught to the pre-verbal learner without a commitment to both the learner and the learning. It cannot be done coldly from a professional-seeming distance. We need to really get to know the learner and to get a feel for what it is like to be social and communicative with that person primarily on that person's terms. We believe that some warmth and solidarity with the learner are needed for facilitating the development of sociability and communication. We recommend the book *Gentle Teaching* (McGee, Menolascino, Hobbs and Menousek 1987) for a thorough discussion of this kind of equitable philosophical stance.

CHAPTER 2

The Theoretical Background to Intensive Interaction

Introduction

In this chapter we take the reader through a review of much of the relevant literature. This includes psychological and developmental studies of the interactions between caregivers and their infants. These are the studies which formed a crucial basis for the development of Intensive Interaction teaching by the staff at Harperbury Hospital School. We include in this literature review a discussion of how sociability and communication can be seen to develop through the interactive process in the natural model of infancy.

We will go on to review and discuss some of the literature concerned with the application of interventions with infants with disabilities which are based on a model of optimal social interaction, that is the kind of social interaction thought to be most favourable for the developing infant. Finally, we will address the work of those who have attempted to draw out from the natural model of early social development, an approach for working with people with severe learning difficulties. Throughout the chapter the fundamental principles concerning how communication and sociability are taught and learned in the earliest stages will be gathered from the literature and we will reflect on their relevance to our work with people with severe and complex learning difficulties.

18

The theoretical background

As we have explained in outlining the history of the development of Intensive Interaction as an approach, this way of working evolved from a group of teachers, of which we were members, seeking to address the fundamental communication and social development needs of our students with severe and complex learning difficulties. In trying to work out how to address these needs, the literature on how communication and sociability develop in infancy in the natural model of child development was an inspiration.

The surge of research into interactions between infants and caregivers that came with improved video technology has meant that there is much literature available in this field. We draw your attention to three themes crucial to our quest which can be seen to emerge from the research. First, there is increasing recognition that early learning takes place in a dynamic, social context (see Schaffer 1977a; Newson 1979a). Second, there is increasing awareness of the infant as an active and competent participant in the learning process (see Brazelton, Koslowski and Main 1974; Trevarthen 1974; Bruner 1975; Schaffer 1977b; Brinker and Lewis 1982; Carlson and Bricker 1972). Third, evidence can be cited of the differences in the social learning environment of infants with and without developmental disabilities (see Jones 1977; Bromwich 1981; Walker 1982; Eheart 1982; Warren and Rogers-Warren 1984; Hanzlik and Stevenson 1985; Langley and Lombardino 1987). This chapter will explore each of these themes in detail.

In looking to the literature for guidance on how to facilitate social and communication development, we were also interested in the research from the United States on infant-focussed and relationship-focussed intervention programmes (Affleck, McGrade, McQueen and Allen 1982; Odem, Yoder and Hill 1988). These programmes recognised the value of certain styles of parenting, and recognised the educational and developmental significance of a responsive, child-oriented style of interacting (see Brinker and Lewis 1982; Kysela and Marfo 1983; Mahoney and Powell 1988). We shared this recognition from our practical work in the classrooms and became excited by the potential.

We did not begin from the assumption that direct parallels could be drawn between early infant development and the developmental levels of people with severe learning difficulties, nor that our students could be 're-parented'. We did feel, however, that the processes fundamental to the interactions which promote sociability and learning in early development, could offer the basis for a powerful teaching model to be built. We were guided towards this by the work of Gary Ephraim (1979), a psychologist working in a nearby similar institution, who was already exploring the potential of using interactive processes or 'mothering' in working with adults with profound and complex learning difficulties.

The dynamic, social context of early learning

Research into the learning which takes place in the first few months of life has clearly highlighted that the context for this is interactive and that with this come the central features of interdependence and reciprocity. To explain further, the interactions involve a mutual exchange, the giving and receiving of feelings and actions. Bell (1968) recognised quite early on that the interactions between infants and caregivers have two-way effects and Lewis and Golberg (1977) showed that both mother and infant have control of the interaction. The dynamics of the interactions are seen by Newson (1979b) to be sophisticated and complex with the format of a 'two-way alternating dialogue'.

Also fundamental to this social context is enjoyment which is shared by both infant and caregiver (mutual enjoyment – Bromwich, 1981) and mutual involvement, which is seen by Hodapp and Goldfield (1983) to be 'the necessary condition for further interactions to proceed'.

The changing view of infant development

Early ideas on child development, including some of Piaget's (1953) earlier writings, view the infant in terms of her/his limitations; as naive, passive and incompetent. These ideas are challenged by the interactive theories of Brazelton and Trevarthen who document social interaction as occurring from birth (see Frye 1989; Price and Bochner 1991).

Implicit in all this is the recognition that the infant is not just influenced by, but also influences, the social and physical environment. This complex process of two-way influences is seen by Sameroff (1975) in terms of a 'transactional model', that is, the infant has an effect on the environment, and the altered environment in turn has an effect on the infant, and so on. As Hogg and Sebba (1986) conclude, the infant emerges from this literature 'not as a passive recipient of maternal stimulation, but as an equal and influential partner in the relationship', giving as much as receiving. We are reminded by McConkey (1989) that the interactive games we play with infants are often child-initiated and child-maintained, which is what, he argues, makes them at once both safe and exciting as learning environments.

Summary of the literature reviewed and discussion of its relevance

- Early learning takes place in the context of a dynamic, social environment.
- Interactions between caregivers and infants are two-way and each person continuously affects and is affected by the other.
- The social context of the learning is characterised by mutual enjoyment and mutual involvement.
- Infants are not passive in the interactions, they take an active part.
- Infants can initiate and maintain interactive games.

This leads us to question just how dynamic and social are the learning environments we provide. Often classrooms, especially those where behavioural programmes and high levels of structure are utilised, are stark and stilted environments. Sometimes our efforts to behave in keeping with notions of age-appropriateness can mean that interactions in day centres and residential settings can be more forced than playful. This literature raises the issue of the extent to which we have mutual involvement and fun in our daily interactions with the students/clients with whom we work. We may need to question the extent to which we allow them to take an active part, to take the lead or to initiate. Certainly the learning environment of the old curriculum at Harperbury School could not be described as dynamic and social.

Interpersonal behaviours in caregiver-infant interaction

It is clear from the literature that caregiver-infant interactions are initiated and maintained by a range of mutual or reciprocal responses including 'mutual visual regard, mutual vocalisation and reciprocated touching or embracing' (Ferguson 1971). It is also clear that these interpersonal behaviours, which are effective in the interactions, are elicited or evoked by both caregiver and infant.

We can see that infant gaze in particular acts as a 'releaser' or trigger for social behaviours in the adult carer, causing her/him to offer modified, 'maternal' facial and vocal behaviours (Stern 1974). Gaze has also been identified as having the functions of sustaining and controlling the interactions (Field 1977) and of providing the infant with experience of a form of exchange like a dialogue (Stern 1974).

This whole concept of the infant eliciting altered interpersonal behaviours from the adult is an important one. These dynamic facial, vocal and gaze behaviours make up much of the social stimulation that the infant receives. The infant elicits behaviours such as vocalising and touching (Calhoun and Rose 1988), smiling, head-bobbing and using exaggerated facial expressions (Kaye and Foegal 1980).

On first reading about these aspects of everyday interactions with infants we became acutely aware of how we naturally alter our behaviours when we meet an infant, how successful this is in establishing some mutual pleasure, and how this can be complex and vital in our interactions with our students.

'Motherese' and the verbal environment

Following on from this, we can see from the literature specific to the language environment of the infant, that infants are active in eliciting the responses which work for them. In response to their infants, caregivers alter their language when relating to them. Their language includes structural changes, the speech rate is slower, there are more frequent questions, sentences are put together more simply, the intonation is different, and the talk is related to the infant's experience. Caregivers are said to speak the same language and about the same subjects as their infants (Clark and Seifer 1983). This register or style of verbal input has become known as 'motherese' (see Weistuch and Byers-Brown 1987).

The research also shows other elements of the verbal environment of the infant. Included here is a structure of brief adult sentences with gaps which are filled by the infant cooing and murmuring in a kind of 'proto-conversation' (Bateson 1979). There is evidence that adults monitor the degree of attention and understanding of the infant, and adjust their language accordingly (Snow 1977). It is also apparent, however, that adults make the kinds of alterations described here, long before this could facilitate the infant's understanding, or before the infant could be expected to reply. This, it is argued, is part of believing that infants are capable of reciprocal communication (Snow 1977) and part of intentionality (detailed below).

Intentionality

As Schaffer stresses (1977b) 'early interactions are sustained only through the mother's initiative in replying to the infant's responses as if they had communicative significance'. This is an important intuitive

22

strategy called intentionality. The literature shows that it is through caregivers assuming that infants are communicative, that shared meaning and true communication emerge (Newson 1979a), and through adult treatment of infants as social that they become so (Lock 1978). It is argued that intentionality helps infants to learn that dialogues are two-sided and that they themselves have a role to play.

Summary of the literature reviewed and discussion of its relevance

- Caregivers (and others) alter their looking, vocalising and touching behaviours in response to the infant and particularly the infant's gaze. The resulting modified behaviours provide the infant with valuable social stimuli at the right level.
- The infant's gaze serves to control and sustain the interactions.
- Caregivers similarly alter their language in response to the infant and the infant's levels of attention and understanding.
- The altered language, sometimes called 'motherese', has been seen to form an ideal style for developing infants.
- Caregivers talk to infants as if they understand long before this is likely. They respond to infant behaviours and sounds as if they have meaning. This is called intentionality.
- Intentionality helps infants to learn that communications involve them and help them to become communicative.

Infants obviously do something, probably not intentionally, which triggers adults to behave in a way which is interesting and easily understood. It is our experience that this is not generally the case with people with learning difficulties. Often our responses are controlling and do not encourage interaction; we want to change behaviours rather than respond to them as communicative. Our experience of the practical exploration of using interactive approaches, however, has shown us that we can reverse this, and that we can successfully apply the kinds of interpersonal behaviours which have been described as 'maternal'. Looking at these aspects of the literature draws attention also to the type of language we use and how we can make this more effective. In developing Intensive Interaction we became acutely aware of the importance of intentionality and both intuitively and purposefully made good use of this strategy. We had often lost the sense of our students as social and communicative beings and had to reclaim this.

Mutual pleasure

Intrinsic and crucial to caregiver-infant interactions is the element of mutual pleasure. This is effectively what the interactions are all about; the primary motivation is for the two participants to 'interest and delight one another' (Stern, Beebe, Jaffe and Bennett 1977). Some of this pleasure evolves around the well-documented interpersonal games (Trevarthen 1979) and playful ritualised routines (Bruner 1983). These infant games, such as 'pat-a-cake' and 'peek-a-boo', occur frequently and are said to provide the infant with a pleasurable way of learning about the conversational rules of the two parties referring to the same topic of conversation (joint reference) and taking turns (turn-taking) (Field 1979). The games are sensitively adjusted as the child develops (Field 1979; Bruner 1983) and they help to build up positive emotions and ways of relating.

How interactions flow

We can see in reviewing the literature that there is a recurring theme of the timing within interactions being of much importance. The activity of the caregiver and infant is often synchronised, sharing a common rhythm. Arco and McClusky's (1981) study of maternal timing (or 'temporal pattern') highlighted the importance of this synchrony. Schaffer (1977b) talks about this in terms of the mother elaborately interweaving her behavioural flow with that of her infant, allowing herself to be paced by the infant, watching and waiting and holding herself ready in an 'exquisite sense of timing'.

Many of the writers concern themselves with analysing how the interactions flow. Stern et al (1977) found there to be three chunks of maternal behaviour; the 'phrase' – a burst of communication behaviour, the 'run' – consisting of a string of repeated phrases, and the 'episode of maintained engagement' – a series of phrases. They also stress that there are pauses of 'cooling down' time. The chunks of behaviour interspersed with pauses serve to regulate the timing of the interactions and allow for maternal adjustment and evaluation.

Brazelton, Koslowski and Main (1974) similarly describe the need for the caregiver to adjust her rhythm to that of the infant and to be sensitive to the infant's capacity for attention. They divide the inter-active sequence into temporal segments of 'initiation', 'orientation', 'state of attention', 'acceleration', 'peak', 'deceleration' and 'withdrawal'. Tronick, Als and Adamson (1979) also described phases of initiation and withdrawal or 'disengagement'. They refer to the phases in between as 'mutual orientation', 'greeting' and 'play-dialogue'. They stress that the phases work together to keep the infant's levels of involvement within certain optimal limits. Sensitive timing is used to maintain and refocus infant attention to a harmonious end (Beebe 1985).

Contingent responding

Inherent in the interactive experience of sensitively timed sequences is the displaying and reading of signals (Carlson and Bricker 1982). Good interaction is said to depend on sensitive signalling and on the caregiver balancing her/his agenda with that of the infant (Clark and Seifer 1983). This partly comes about by a process of contingent responding (Watson 1985) which is equally crucial for the feelings of effectiveness it generates (Lewis and Goldberg 1969; Goldberg 1977). Contingent responding is when the caregiver's behaviours or responses are caused by, or related to, a behaviour or change of state in the infant; there is very little time delay.

By responding contingently to the behaviour of the infant, the caregiver allows her/him to take control and to learn that she/he can influence the environment; this in turn encourages exploration and facilitates infant development (Goldberg 1977; Lewis and Coates 1980; Carlson and Bricker 1982). The infant's contingent responses to the caregiver give rise to feelings of effectiveness in the adult also, and motivate her/him to interact in the above, important ways (Goldberg 1977).

Smith (1989) sums up what caregivers/parents do in this supremely responsive interactive process:

> They arrange, manipulate and structure the environment in order to facilitate and maximise children's interactions. They do this by making use of the children's interests and inclinations, and most importantly by being very sensitive to feedback from the children in determining what to select as the focus of joint attention. (p.113)

Summary of the literature reviewed and discussion of its relevance

- Interactions between infants and caregivers are essentially about them sharing an enjoyable time together (mutual pleasure).
- Some of their pleasure comes from playing games like 'peek-a-boo'.
- The pleasure means that the infants and caregivers will want to

share interactions over and over again. The infant will know that she/he is good to be with.

- The games provide a kind of practice for some of the abilities the infant will need later in using language and having conversations.
- Many of the researchers have been concerned with the timing and flow of the interactions.
- Important in this timing is that the caregiver often synchronises her rhythyms with the infant, follows the infant's pace, and waits for the best moments for some of her contributions.
- Interactive sequences have been divided into chunks showing that they warm up, peak and cool down.
- Caregivers respond contingently to the behaviour of the infant. This gives the infant an important feeling of being effective and in control.

In our experience it was initially difficult to share pleasure with our students because many of their behaviours meant that they were not good to be with. One of the lessons from the model of caregiver-infant interaction must surely be that such pleasure is a basic essential. We must find a way of having fun with our learners and of communicating to them that they are good to be with. An important part of Intensive Interaction is the establishment of mutual pleasure and mutual games and we found that this could be done with the most 'anti-social' of students. As with the natural model an outcome of this was that both we and the students were keen to repeat the experience.

Many people with learning difficulties are very active or very passive. It has been more usual for practitioners to try to impose a different pace on them rather than to share their tempo. The caregiver-infant interaction literature shows us the potential for positive interactions when the more sophisticated partner takes on responsibility for altering her/his tempo to suit the less sophisticated one. We found that it was possible to establish good interactive games 'on the move'! We also became aware that with some people we can fail to leave a long enough thinking and action gap. We can instead press on and fill the gap which in effect denies them their turn. This, we think, must give the learner a very negative message indeed.

In using an interactive game for the purpose of facilitating a positive way of relating and progressing we must also attend to the issue of how the interaction flows. When we become analytical about why our learners have become too excited or alternatively why they have stopped being involved in a session, we can remind ourselves of the role of timing in creating peaks and troughs and in making these harmonious.

A common theme in provision for people with severe learning difficulties is their powerlessness. Nevertheless, we are becoming much more aware of the importance of choice and of ways in which people who are pre-verbal can express choices. The literature reviewed above is interesting in its illustration of the power infants gain from adults responding contingently to them. This is another way in which we can give people control over their own learning.

Imitation

One way in which caregivers respond to infants and make their worlds predictable is by imitating elements of their behaviour (Field 1977). The research shows that smiles, tongue-pokes, mouth and head movements, frowns, waves, claps, laughs, yawns, whimpers, and most frequently, speech sounds, are all imitated (Pawlby 1977). The nature of this imitation is not cold, direct, and limited to single exchanges, however, it actually forms part of a communication sequence, with actions selected for imitation which can be endowed with communicative significance (Pawlby 1977). Schaffer (1977a) emphasises the dialogue-like nature of imitative interactions:

> early interaction sequences generally begin with the infant's own spontaneous behaviour . . . the mother then chimes in to support, repeat, comment upon and elaborate his response (p.12)

Again this process is two-way, with imitations of the caregiver by the infant helping to sustain interactions and facilitate shared meaning.

Turn-taking

The literature shows that in these interactions the timing, the contingent responding, and the exchange of signals between caregiver and infant all come together to form turn-taking. Again reciprocity is fundamental and as Mayer and Tronick (1985) contend, this turn-taking structure 'is neither solely the product of maternal skill, nor the product of the infant engaging in regulating his own arousal level'.

Kaye (1977) looking at the burst-pause patterns of sucking in early feeding, regards this as the basis of later turn-taking in language. Indeed rehearsal for more sophisticated communication can be seen throughout the turn-taking and other structures of early interaction.

Progression in interactions

The issue of progression is recurrent throughout the literature. Making adaptations over time is another way in which the caregiver/adult has been shown to be contingent and responsive (Green, Gustafson and West 1980; Holmberg 1980; Fogel 1982). Pawlby (1977) found that over time, mothers and infants became 'progressively more skilful in their exchanges'. Bruner (1983) offers the metaphor of the caregiver providing and then gradually removing 'scaffolding' to describe the way in which the infant becomes more competent, gradually requiring less and less support from the adult.

Harding (1983) similarly focusses on the gradual progression in the development of communication, stressing the stages preceding the infant's achievement of intentional communication. Initially, the mother or infant are said to simply have an effect on each other, the mother then deduces intent from the infant's actions, and then either party starts to interpret that a communication has taken place.

The literature shows the ways in which the caregiver constantly intervenes to make the environment enjoyable and possible to understand. We see that the kinds of behaviours selected by caregivers for contingent responding are sensitively adjusted according to the infant's growing repertoire of skills and knowledge.

The role of touch

Perhaps least well-documented in the literature is the role of touch in caregiver-infant interaction. This may be because of a perceived link with attachment and bonding rather than with other areas of development (Ferguson 1971). It has long been assumed, however, that physical contact with the caregiver is vitally important for normal development (Schaffer and Emerson 1964). Warmth and affection are seen to be part of an effective, child-oriented style of 'maternal interaction' (Mahoney, Finger and Powell 1985).

What is apparent from the research is that the stimulation of holding and rocking plays a part in affecting the infant's physiological and emotional well-being (Ferguson 1971), and that tactile experience in the earliest stages is critical for continued growth and development (Montagu 1971). Montagu (1971) postulates that as the infant matures, the importance of skin contact gives way to the importance of looking and listening about which we understand much more.

Summary of the literature reviewed and discussion of its relevance

- One way in which the caregiver responds contingently to the infant is by imitation. This is not an isolated strategy, but one of many complementary features of an interactive sequence.
- Throughout interactions infants practice turn-taking which they will need later when using language.
- As infants develop so do their interactive games. Caregivers respond to their infants' increasing skill by taking less responsibility for the interactions and by adjusting their expectations and input.
- The role of physical contact in early interactions is understood to be vital for the infant's well-being and development.

Imitation is one element of caregiver behaviour which has been teased out and sometimes used separately as a teaching tool (see below), perhaps because it is something tangible to ask practitioners to do. From our experience, however, this is not effective and we should perhaps recognise that in the literature this element is significantly placed within the context of all the other elements which contribute to communicative interactions.

The whole issue of progression in interactions is very relevant when we are concerned with promoting the development of people with learning difficulties. In applying the natural model to facilitate social and communication development we are not just concerned with establishing some rapport and isolated pleasurable interactions. We are concerned with promoting interactions which become more complex and in which the learner begins to take turns, to anticipate, to be more active, and to rehearse ever more complex communication behaviours. It can be seen that the interactive game is not just a stepping stone to other, more formal, teaching and learning, there are instead enormous possibilities for progression within it.

We do not want to become involved with a full discussion about physical contact here, this can be found in chapter five. We would, however, note that physical contact is part of the complex whole of caregiver-infant interaction. This means that it cannot be ignored when we come to apply this model of interaction to our work.

The importance of interactive style

The more striking features of caregiver-infant interaction which have been described above form part of an interactive style. We have examined, up to a point, their role and importance in infant development, but we can go further with this. An overview tells us that whatever the theoretical standpoint, the importance and impact of caregiver-infant interaction on social development will be recognised (Hanzlik 1989). Much of the research has focussed on distinguishing an interactive style which is optimal in terms of the developmental and learning outcomes for the child.

The literature shows that early interactive play functions as a crucial precursor to language development in particular (Bruner 1975, 1983), but also that this provides a crucial context for the development of social and cognitive abilities (Bruner 1975; Schaffer 1977; Lewis and Coates 1980; McConachie 1986; Klein and Briggs 1987) and even motor abilities (Hanzlik 1989). Indeed it is difficult to see the different areas of development as separate from one another at this early stage (Hess and Shipman 1968; Schaffer 1971; Bullowa 1979; Hoffman 1981; Lewis 1986). The link between sociability and cognitive development (Stevenson and Lamb 1979) and the intertwined, interdependent nature of all development at this stage must have particular pertinence to us in our task of facilitating development in people with more severe learning difficulties.

It is clear from reviewing the literature that the caregiver role is a dual one, both offering direct social stimulus, and acting as a mediator of the physical environment (Bromwich 1981). It is also clear that the interactive processes within the infant's social world are sources of intense pleasure and powerful influences in terms of teaching and learning. These points again must be directly relevant to us in our work.

Studies of the links between later competence in the child and the nature of earlier interactions also have important findings for us. It has been argued, for example, that the antecedents of infant competence could be defined in terms of a 'competent mother-infant pair' (Olson, Bates and Bayles 1984) or of 'reciprocal social interactions' (Beckwith, Cohen, Kopp, Parmalee and Marcy 1976). Good foundations for later language development are said to contain interactive patterns which are mutual and synchronous (Guralnick and Bricker 1987; Vitagliano and Purdy 1987).

There is growing evidence to suggest that optimal social interactions also have ongoing, less direct consequences for development (Dunham and Dunham 1990). It would seem that mutually satisfying and reciprocal interactions play a role in developing intimacy and trust and that this trust plays a motivational and general role in language (and other) development (Clark and Seifer 1983).

Similarly, such interactions lead to the emergence of a 'sense of self' and the ability to establish relationships which provide a secure basis for exploration of the environment (Lewis 1986).

There are clearly aspects of interactive style which facilitate development, but as Schaffer (1984) argues, this 'intricate process' is carried out 'so smoothly' that one is generally unaware of the diverse skills employed. Carlson and Bricker (1982) talk about this as an 'implicit pedagogy' referring to the subtle and yet highly technical and complex teaching techniques which are used and taken for granted. It must be in our interests when working with people at early stages of development to try to describe, understand and utilise what has been a hidden teaching approach.

Summary of the features of caregiver interactive style

- The caregiver shares control of the activity with the infant.
- She allows herself to be controlled by the infant.
- She enjoys the interactions.
- Her style of interpersonal behaviours is modified; elicited by the infant.
- She employs visual regard, mutual gaze, mutual vocalisations, head-bobbing, touching and embracing.
- She exaggerates her facial expressions.
- She uses motherese: slower, simpler speech to talk about the infant's experience.
- Her verbalisations are in short bursts, allowing gaps for the infant's coos and murmurs.
- She believes that the infant is capable of reciprocal communication and acts accordingly (using intentionality).
- She uses games and playful ritualised routines.
- Her tempo is synchronised with the infant's.
- She watches and waits and holds herself ready to act at the best times.
- She keeps the infant's levels of arousal and involvement within certain optimal limits.
- She balances her agenda with that of the infant.
- She responds contingently to the behaviour of the infant.
- She is very sensitive to the infant's signals and feedback.
- She uses imitation especially of actions she regards as communicative.
- She lets the infant take a turn.

- She adjusts her input as the infant progresses.
- She provides social stimuli.
- She mediates the physical environment.
- She is warm and affectionate.
- She touches, rocks and holds the infant.

The processes of interaction between caregivers and infants with disabilities

At the beginning of this chapter we made reference to a theme in the literature concerning the finding that the social learning environment for infants with disabilities was different from that for infants without disabilities. Early comparative studies tended to focus on a breakdown in the interactive process between the caregiver and the infant with disabilities as inevitable. Overview of the range of literature in this field, however, indicates that the reality is somewhat more complex (see for example, Mahoney 1988).

How interactions differ when the infant has a disability or learning difficulties

We will initially address the literature which has focussed on the themes of interactive breakdown and difference when the infant has disabilities. An important issue here refers to a lack of mutual pleasure in the interactions. McCollum's (1984) literature review emphasises that the establishment of mutually enjoyable interactions may be less automatic in caregiver-infant pairs in which the infant is developmentally delayed.

Clark and Seifer (1983) relate the lack of pleasure in the interactions to an adverse effect of the disability on the signalling system. They attempt to determine the path of the breakdown in the interactive process and cite Field's (1979) suggestion that this begins with the mother working harder. This, it is said, ultimately means that she is overstimulating and intrusive in her attempts to promote a response in the child. A more controlling style of interaction (Goldberg and Brachfield 1979; Bakeman and Brown 1980; Kogan 1980) and the mother's feeling of helplessness, which leads her to respond in ways which are not contingent (Goldberg 1977), are also seen as contributing to this breakdown in the natural process.

The issue of problems with the caregiver and infant giving and receiving signals is a concern in much of the literature. Klein and

Briggs (1987) looked at infants with immature central nervous systems who were, as a consequence, hyper-irritable and unpredictable. The parents of these infants were devastated when they found them difficult to arouse and their signals difficult to read. Thoman (1975) similarly highlights the frustration and exhaustion which can result when an infant gives ambiguous cues. Kogan, Tyler and Turner (1974) investigated the warmth factor in caregiver-infant interactions. They found that positive feelings and expression of warmth by the mothers of infants with cerebral palsy diminished over time, and they suggested that this was related to the problems they had in receiving encouraging feedback. This lack of positive reinforcement in the infant's behaviours is also a recurrent theme in the literature (see Rogers-Warren and Warren 1984).

What will be readily apparent to the reader here, as it was to us, is that there is a 'chicken and egg' situation, with both infant and caregiver behaving atypically, each affecting the other, and some ambiguity around which comes first. While some of the studies emphasise the role of the atypical infant, many acknowledge that infants with disabilities have a counterproductive effect on the behaviour of their caregivers (Cunningham, Reuler, Blackwell and Deck 1981; Brinker and Lewis 1982).

Analysis of the effects of the infant characteristics on the caregiver's interactive style leads us into the realm of interactive 'fit'. Walker (1982) argues that the infant who is handicapped may be less responsive, less ready for engagement in social interaction, less readable, and less fun as a social partner, and acknowledges that the infant's qualities 'affect his or her abilities as initiator, responder and maintainer of synchrony in the interactive bout'. Bakeman and Brown (1980) argue that in response to the characteristics of atypical infants their mothers carry more of the 'interactive burden'.

Studies of infants with Down's syndrome illustrate some of these problems with interactive fit. They are said to be more difficult to arouse intellectually and affectively (Guralnick and Bricker 1987), to engage in less eye contact, to initiate less, and to vocalise with fewer pauses (Jones 1977). Their mothers are said to overstimulate and to fail to expand on their vocalisations and intent (Berger and Cunningham 1987; Guralnick and Bricker 1987).

Carlson and Bricker (1982) look at the interactions between caregivers and infants who are developmentally delayed in terms of caregiver 'errors'; the caregiver they say responds at the wrong time in the infant's behavioural cycle, responds too rapidly, and provides stimulation which is developmentally mismatched with the infant's level. Again we come back to the issue of this 'critical communicative match' to what the child is attending to and able to understand, and that this will be difficult to establish and maintain when the child's signals are inconsistent and difficult to read (Warren and Rogers-Warren 1984).

Earlier in the chapter we saw that successful interactions are related to sensitivity to the infant's readiness, allowing the infant to take a turn, maintaining an optimum arousal level, and establishing a balance between the caregiver's agenda and that of the infant. The research of Clark and Seifer (1983) among others, however, shows that mothers of infants with disabilities frequently show 'overriding behaviours' and have difficulty in allowing the child not to respond. The more controlling and directive interactive style has been shown to be apparent even in the physical contact of mothers of infants with cerebral palsy.

The more complex picture

We have made some reference to the complex 'chicken and egg' situation that pertains to the interactions between an atypical infant and the caregiver. To explore this further we must look at what the caregiver brings to the situation. As Clark and Seifer (1983) point out, 'playfulness and taking delight in one's child is not compatible with depression, hopelessness, anxiety or low-esteem'. The state of emotional well-being of the caregiver may be related to adjusting to having an infant with a disability, but it will also be affected by the levels of support received. Yoder's (1990) discussion of the wider issues includes evidence from Dunst et al (1986) that there is a mutual relationship between a facilitative maternal interaction style and families who have social support. We are reminded in all this that the factors influencing interactive style extend beyond the individual characteristics of the parent and child.

Much of the literature we have referred to above, regarding the adjustments made in interactive style when the infant has a disability, focuses on the adjustments interfering with, rather than promoting, infant development. While this is the dominant view amongst the researchers, it is not always clear cut. Beveridge (1989) notes that the employment of higher levels of stimulation and directiveness on the part of mothers of infants who are developmentally delayed, is a reasonable and responsive adaptation to the children's difficulties. The problem may be that the directive style continues despite the child's growing competence.

Another complexity in all this is that which is contended by McConachie (1986) that 'directiveness and sensitivity can be shown to be quite separate dimensions integrated by different mothers into their style in different ways'. Thus, some of the apparent contradictions of different writers may not actually be so (Terdal, Jackson and Garner 1976; Rondal 1977; Mogford 1979, all have evidence of mothers of infants with disabilities who are not directive). It is feasible that the same caregivers may be overstimulating and directive, but still, as Burford (1988) found, share with their children a common timing in interactive movements. There are also, of course, variations in interactive style amongst caregivers of infants with disabilities as with any other group.

We understand from this that not all aspects of the interactive style of caregivers of infants with disabilities interfere with rather than promote development. Not all caregivers with infants with disabilities interact in the same way and the causes for the different interactive styles are complex. It would seem, however, that whether or not an infant has disabilities, a responsive, child-oriented style of interaction is most likely to facilitate cognitive, social and communication development.

Summary of the literature reviewed and discussion of its relevance

- Many studies have shown that the interactions between caregivers and infants with disabilities are different from when the infant does not have a disability.
- Other studies have shown a more complex picture.
- There can be a lack of mutual pleasure in the interactions.
- The caregiver can experience difficulty in reading the infant's signals.
- The caregiver can respond by working harder, overstimulating the infant and becoming directive.
- There can be poor interactive 'fit' regarding timing and content of the interactions.
- The infant affects how the caregiver behaves and vice versa. Both are also affected by other, outside factors.
- Not all of the caregiver's adaptations to the infant with disabilities interfere with development.
- Not all caregivers of infants with disabilities have the same interactive style.

When we look at the relevance of this literature we can compare the styles of interaction described above with the styles of interaction found in classrooms, day centres and residential settings and find similarities (Beveridge and Berry 1977; Evans and Ware 1987; Gleason 1989). We can probably all relate to times when we are intrusive, when we push and direct rather than encourage and interpret. Teachers especially, can lose spontaneous contingent responding when working within the constraints of pre-planned programmes.

We can also relate this more controlling style of interaction to factors other than just our own characteristics and those of our clients. With increasing pressures of accountability we can feel pressured by our managers to always be doing and getting results, never just enjoying getting to know our clients. It is difficult to be sensitive and responsive as a practitioner when feeling stressed and undervalued, just as it is difficult as a parent feeling depressed and confused.

The lack of encouraging feedback can also be a problem for both caregivers and practitioners. This can lead us to behave differently, to work harder perhaps, but also to feel more coldly towards the client and to be less tolerant of their other behaviours. This in turn can decrease the likelihood of receiving positive signals from the client. When we relate the chicken and egg dilemma to our work with people with learning difficulties it poses the question of who is behaving oddly and why – it rightly makes us look at our own responses.

Interventions with infants with disabilities based on a model of optimum social interaction

The growing awareness emerging from the research reviewed here, that there is a relationship between a certain style of interacting and child development, has obviously been of great interest to those concerned with early intervention. Field (1978), having looked at the elements of successful caregiver-infant interaction, suggested that despite not fully understanding harmonious and disturbed interactions, 'interaction coaching' could be employed to enable adults and infants to interact in different ways.

Training parents to adopt responsive interactive styles was shown experimentally to be associated with general sensorimotor and language development (see Yoder 1990) and the United States saw an emergence of these 'relationship-focussed' or 'social reciprocity' interventions (for example, Guralnick and Bennett 1987; Calhoun and Rose 1988). These interventions are characterised by the style of interaction forming the focus for the intervention goal or procedure

(Mahoney and Powell 1988); the emphasis is on developing the quality of the interactions to be mutually satisfying (Calhoun and Rose 1988).

Central to these interventions is the recognition that the influences in the parent-infant pair are two-way, and that child development is enhanced through involvement in progressively more complex patterns of reciprocal, contingent interaction with someone close such as the caregiver (Affleck, McGrade, McQueeney and Allen 1982). They apply a concept of an 'ideal' parenting style or cluster of behaviours which includes emotional involvement, high vocal and visual contact (Stern 1974), responsiveness, and playfulness (Bruner 1975; Fogel and Thelen 1987).

For a more detailed study of these interventions the reader is referred to some specific examples: the Family Consultation Program (Affleck et al 1982); the Charlotte Circle Project (Calhoun and Rose 1988); and the Transactional Intervention Program (T.R.I.P. – Mahoney and Powell 1988). The interventions can be seen to be environmental, based on a recognition that problems with the interaction are less a function of the child's inability to respond, than a continuous malfunction of the organism-environment transaction across time (Kysela and Marfo 1983). This transactional interpretation (Sameroff 1975) highlights the relevance for us – the interaction between the learner and the caregiver/teacher is both crucial and open to change.

The way in which change is brought about in the interactive styles varies with different interventions. Clark and Seifer (1983) effectively used evaluation of videos, together with guidance towards using imitation, to modify mothers' interactive styles to become increasingly involved and engaging. Indeed, coaching in imitation has frequently been seen to be a successful intervention of this kind (Field 1978; Odem, Yoder and Hill 1988). In the T.R.I.P. program (Mahoney and Powell 1988) the strategies taught to the parents centred around turn-taking and interactive match.

Rosenberg and Robinson (1983) influenced the quality of mother-infant interactions using modelling, encouragement and feedback, and identified areas to be worked on using an inventory of skills. Similarly, the U.C.L.A. intervention program (Bromwich 1981) included an assessment stage using a 'Progression of Parent Behaviour'. This illustrates that the concern of the programme begins with the essential precursor of mutual enjoyment and works towards the caregiver becoming a sensitive observer and responder to cues.

The literature concerned with interventions of this type includes some evaluation of their success. It would seem that parental interaction styles can be altered in line with the optimum and that these alterations have been related to enhanced child development. While we are yet to see more thorough and long-term evaluation of this type of approach, the potential is evident.

Summary of the literature reviewed and discussion of its relevance

- The relationship between a responsive, child-centred style of interacting and child development has been recognised.
- Interaction coaching has been used to help parents to use this optimum style.
- Interaction coaching has formed the basis of what has been termed 'relationship-focussed' or 'social reciprocity interventions'.
- There is documentation of these interventions being successful, but long-term evaluation is still needed.
- Those readers who are working with (or who actually are) parents of young children with learning difficulties may quite rightly be encouraged by these interventions in the United States. We would emphasise that maximising the educational potential of interactive style is not about blaming parents, but about celebrating their intuitive abilities.

Interventions beyond infancy and the family

Approaches for people with profound learning difficulties

Wang (1990) notes that an emerging theme in special education literature concerns the changing perception of the learner such that 'students are seen as active processors, interpreters and synthesisers of information'. From our experience of work in this country, however, people with profound learning difficulties continue to be viewed as passive respondents. Indeed, McCormick and Noonan (1984) liken the disturbed caregiver-infant interactions which foster helplessness and dependency with the overly structured and controlled interactions which prevail in special school classrooms.

A general overview of educational provision for pupils described as having profound and multiple learning difficulties, or as in need of 'special care', gives rise to a picture of uncertain curricular approaches and aims, but frequent behavioural objectives (Evans and Ware 1987). Often 'operant instructional procedures' are used with this student group (Sailor, Gee, Goetz and Graham 1988) and they have 'programmes' as opposed to 'education' (Bray, MacArthur and Ballard 1988).

Commonly, then, a behavioural (or skills analysis) approach is in evidence. It is not our intention here to criticise such an approach outright, but to look at the contrasts between this and an 'ideal' style of interacting. Bray, MacArthur and Ballard (1988) question the lack of reciprocal interchanges (or mutual interactions) allowed for in behavioural methods and the impact this may have on pupil initiations, teaching and learning. Smith, Moore and Phillips (1983) challenge the 'product-centred teaching' for not encouraging children to direct their own activity and therefore develop understanding. In contrast to the scenario of caregiver-infant interactions, behavioural curricula are seen to give the teacher all the power and place great limitations on the pupil (Wood and Shears 1986; Billinge 1988).

Research has shown that pupils with profound learning difficulties demonstrate a relatively low level of spontaneous social behaviour (Beveridge and Berry 1977; Beveridge and Hurrell 1980) and that teachers play a part in perpetuating this by doing little by way of responding to and maintaining pupil-initiated interactions (Beveridge and Hurrell 1980; Ware 1989). In an institutional setting, Gleason (1989) found that interactions with people with profound learning difficulties were always initiated and terminated by staff, again reflecting staff assumptions about their clients' passivity. Interestingly, Gleason documents evidence that this assumption is wrong. We have seen that young infants play a very active role in interactions with their caregivers and people with profound learning difficulties can be active in this way also.

Despite the lack of research into the education of people with the most severe learning difficulties (Hogg and Sebba 1986; Sailor et al 1988; Hart 1990) some more interactive approaches have developed. McCormick and Noonan (1984) went some way towards this in their proposal of a responsive curriculum which draws from both developmental and behavioural theoretical sources. Sternberg and Owens (1985) similarly combined behavioural and social elements in their work on establishing pre-language signalling abilities. Some of the advances in technology-assisted teaching, such as the Contingency Intervention Project (advocated by Brinker and Lewis 1982) and the work of Schweigert (1989) have also incorporated interactive elements and social contingency.

Approaches to teaching communication have most frequently reflected the caregiver-infant interaction literature. White and East's (1986) look at the Wessex Revised Portage Language Checklist fully acknowledges the interactive context of language development and specifically Schaffer's point that while the parent teaches the child a desired communicative response, the child in turn teaches the adult how to obtain the response. Ouvry (1987) includes interactive approaches within the pre-verbal communication curriculum for people with profound handicaps, maintaining that one of the main aims will be 'to encourage responsiveness to the presence of others and establish reciprocal interaction patterns'. The role of interaction as an 'essential pre-requisite for teaching' is acknowledged, but little guidance is offered as to how to establish it. Similarly, the need to apply the accumulating body of knowledge on the pre-verbal development of the normally developing child, to those with mental handicaps (sic) at pre-verbal stages, is acknowledged by Jones (1981). He also sees a paradox, in that while for these children more structured teaching is a generally accepted need, a successful communication programme would need to be structured by the child.

Summary of the literature reviewed and discussion of its relevance

- People with profound learning difficulties are still often seen as passive rather than active participants in their learning.
- Use of behavioural approaches is common and control of the learning is unlikely to be shared.
- There have been some moves towards more interactive approaches with this client group.

Although people with profound learning difficulties may be at a level of social, cognitive and communication development comparable with early infancy, their learning environment is likely to be very different. We, as practitioners, have tended to use high levels of structure in programmes which allow the learner little control. Familiarity with the literature on the importance of the unstructured, intuitive and child-centred teaching which takes place in caregiver- infant interactions must lead us to question the wisdom of this.

Approaches for people who demonstrate challenging behaviour and for people with autism

In our schools, residential settings and day centres we often work with a mixture of clients, where there is great cross-over between learning difficulty, ritualistic and challenging behaviour and autism. In theory, however, there is often less cross-over with separate research, theories and interventions, particularly with regard to those with autism. We could not hope to give an extensive review of the literature on autism here, but we will look at that which is most pertinent – the research and interventions which are responses to the characteristic social and communication 'deficits'.

Before looking at autism, it is worth noting that, as with profound learning difficulty, many of the approaches to working with people with stereotyped and challenging behaviour are behavioural. As Koegel and Koegel (1990) sum up, the variety of approaches which have been used to reduce stereotypic behaviours includes shock treatment, overcorrection, physical exercise, time-out, delayed reinforcement and differential reinforcement of other behaviour. There has also been some evidence that environmental changes such as deinstitutionalisation (Molony and Taplin 1988) and increased provision of occupational materials and greater classroom structure (Ware 1989) can reduce sterotyped behaviour.

There has been some acceptance that 'aberrant' or deviant behaviour has some function and that teaching appropriate alternatives, notably symbolic communication, would be effective as an intervention (Donellan, Mirenda, Mesaros and Fassbender 1984). Often, when teaching communication to people with these behaviours is considered, it is assumed that the behaviours have to be improved before the communication work can begin to be embarked upon. It is also assumed that the person will be developmentally capable of producing a symbolic or verbal alternative to the behaviour (see Donellan et al 1984; Durand and Carr 1985). McGee, Menolascino, Hobbs and Menousek (1987) have given a radical reappraisal of our approaches to people who demonstrate challenging behaviour (see below).

With regard to people with autism, Olley (1985) notes that often the area of social/affective communication is regarded as too difficult and therefore omitted from programmes altogether; the communication that is taught takes place in sterile settings with tangible reinforcers. Olley recognises that, in teaching communication, the reciprocity of interactive games must be considered as a potentially useful approach. Tiegerman and Primavera (1984) similarly see the potential of adult-child interaction approaches (particularly imitation which gives the child control over others) for facilitating gaze interaction in children with autism.

The literature shows that interventions with people with autism have lead to improvements in social competence and isolated social skills, but that true social interaction and initiation of social contact remain elusive goals (Howlin 1986). Garfin and Lord (1986) accept the need for mutuality in communication, but still propose educational approaches which emphasise structure and skills training. While a partial move towards interactive approaches is common, most interventions with people with autism continue to remain within the realm of either intrusion approaches or sensory training (Knoblock 1983) and to focus on overt behaviours and skills training (Clare and Clements 1990).

Duchan (1983) proposes that in our interactions with children who have autism we should strive to creatively combine a 'nurturing' interactive style (characterised by semantic contingency, motherese and orientation to the child) with a 'teaching' style (characterised by adult-initiated activities and adult demands). Christie and Wimpory (1986) use a musical approach based on the dialogue of caregiver-infant interactions, but continue to combine this with using behavioural approaches to teaching gesture.

Summary of the literature reviewed and discussion of its relevance

- Many of the approaches to working with people with ritualistic, challenging or autistic behaviour are based on behavioural psychology.
- Social and communicative abilities are seen to be lacking in people with autism and are seldom successfully taught.
- There have been some partial moves towards interactive approaches with this client group, but formal structure and skills training are usually retained.

The more complex and reciprocal social and communication abilities, which the literature has described as developing in the social context of caregiver-infant interactions, are a difficulty for people with autism. It is hard to imagine how such abilities might successfully be formally trained. Our exploratory work using Intensive Interaction, however, has included successful work with people with autism (see Nind 1993 and the case studies in chapter six). We have experience of autistic students learning to take part in and even initiate mutually enjoyable reciprocal interactions. This leads us to suggest, therefore, that it might be more beneficial to exchange the rigid structure of many of the programmes for the alternative analysis and sensitivity of Intensive Interaction.

Approaches based on caregiver-infant interaction

Vitagliano and Purdy's (1987) approach with children who are deaf-blind moves further along the interactive continuum than most of the approaches described above. Here, movement activities are combined with 'mother-infant nurturant activities' to establish a basis for interaction and communication. This means that students are given opportunities to take an active role and to control their classroom environment.

In Harrison, Lombardino and Stapell's (1987) early communication curriculum, interactive elements are applied as goals and treatment principles. Aspects of caregiver-infant interaction are incorporated, including: recognising and responding to the child's signals of desire to initiate, maintain or terminate an interaction, developing mutually satisfying interactions, following the child's line of regard, and engaging in reciprocal actions and turn-taking.

Also similar to an application of the processes of caregiver-infant interaction are the approaches advocated by McGee et al (1987) and by Seigal-Causey and Guess (1989). McGee et al's 'gentle teaching' focuses on 'human participation and interactions . . . rather than skill acquisition'. The approach is based on emotional bonding and teaching 'mutual affection to those who do not yet know its meaning'. Seigal-Causey and Guess (1989) offer more practical guidelines and curriculum content as well as a philosophy. They emphasise teaching interactive abilities as non-symbolic pre-verbal communication, but although they try to avoid rigid structure they do become quite prescriptive.

Perhaps closest to a social reciprocity intervention for older people with more severe learning difficulties is Burford's (1986) 'communication through movement'. Here the goal of interpersonal communication is reached by the adult taking the 'perceptive, flexible and adaptable approach used by caregivers with their babies'. Enjoyment, synchronicity, sensitivity, intentionality and working in partnership are all elements of caregiver-infant interaction employed in Burford's movement therapy.

Summary of the literature reviewed and discussion of its relevance

- There are some approaches with people with learning difficulties and disabilities that link more closely with the natural model of caregiver-infant interaction.
- They incorporate such elements as sharing control, responding to

signals, establishing bonding, mutual enjoyment and reciprocity, synchronising movements and applying intentionality.

More direct applications of the processes of teaching and learning inherent in the model of caregiver-infant interaction are largely limited to the exploratory work of Ephraim (1979), Fyfe (1980), Davis (1985) and Hewett (1985, 1986) and based on this, our work (Nind and Hewett 1988; Hewett and Nind 1989; Nind 1992) and the work of Miller and Ephraim (1988) and Knight and Watson (1990). Olson, Bates and Bayles (1984) among others recognised that understanding how the interaction process relates to the development of competence is of much practical importance. In developing and researching the efficacy of Intensive Interaction Teaching we have begun to explore this practical importance in the field of profound learning difficulty.

CHAPTER 3

How Knowledge of Infant Learning Helped the Development of Intensive Interaction

How knowledge of infant learning can help us in our work

We commence the 'how to do it' part of this book with a further, practical appraisal of the way that infants seem to conduct much of their learning, particularly those things we are mostly concerned with here – the ability to be social, to understand and use the fundamentals of communication. As we have seen, this learning mostly takes place in social situations with parents or other available people – the 'apprenticeship'.

Interactions between people are best seen in real life or on videotape. When we watch other people interact in all sorts of situations, many things take place between them which we understand in wordless ways based on our own ability to relate emotionally and with empathy to the experiences of the people we are observing. It is difficult, if not impossible to describe the richness and dynamism of even the simplest human interaction in words alone.

Nonetheless, and taking what we have just written into account, we have decided that we must attempt to illustrate this chapter with descriptions of a variety of interaction sequences. We have attempted to write the descriptions as vividly as possible, and for that reason they are presented in a style which may be seen to be more lively than the rest of the text – the more liberal use of adjectives will be particularly noticeable. We recognise that because the reader does not have access to the videotaped sequences which we are describing, the interaction will be experienced through our interpretation alone.

Since we first started reading about early interactions, we have become more and more intrigued by thoughts about the learning which takes place during the first two years of a person's life. Actually, if we give consideration only to the first year even, the learning which

44

is usually achieved is considerable, if not amazing, both in quantity and intensity. It seemed to us (as teachers) that all teachers (though nowadays we include everyone involved in helping people with severe learning difficulties) should be very interested in the achievements of infancy. Clearly, if there is wonderful learning taking place, so considerable in quantity and intensity, then there must be some very powerful and effective teaching causing it. Surely this should be a topic of the utmost interest to teachers; if teachers and other practitioners could start to understand the structure and principles of how this highly effective natural teaching takes place, there may be all sorts of benefits in our everyday work.

There are further interesting speculations connected with this line of thought which would seem to have a direct practical bearing on any technique of teaching which arises out of understandings we might have about infant learning. When parents and other available people are assisting or facilitating the early development of infants, they do not necessarily give conscious thought to the fact that they are teachers. We have sat in discussion with parents who, on reflection, can relate the continuing rapid development of their infant to various things that they do, to their own parental behaviour. Parents don't on the whole, however, display a detailed technical understanding of what it is they do on a day by day or an hour by hour basis which is so crucial to continuing progress. They would be unlikely to describe or define a play activity with their child as 'learning and rehearsing the fundamentals of communication'. Parents usually do not write programmes of work for the achievements they nonetheless wholeheartedly aspire to for their child. Unless they are driven parents looking to 'hothouse' another Mozart, they do not compose timetables of differentiated activities. They do not have tick-lists or wallcharts or a file to record the administration of the programme of development, though these days periodic video recordings are common for enjoyably recording that person growing up.

In fact, by comparison to the way that learning is presented in schools and most other places where learning and development is in any way formalised, the learning of early infancy is chaotic and seems incoherent in its organisation. It is highly informal and relaxed. It is not divided into separate topics or skills or subject areas. It can potentially take place at any time in any place. Indeed, we can speculate that the only time that the learning stops taking place is when the infant sleeps. The 'teachers' do not need to have undertaken any rigorously assessed course and examination before being let loose with a vulnerable human being in order to carry out this most crucial of undertakings.

As has already been related in this book, we started to read the available knowledge on infant learning because much of the learning which takes place in the first year was the same learning we wished to teach many of our students. What we found helped us to start developing an approach to helping our students, and as in the natural model of infancy, we found it to be powerful and productive.

Illustration: Thomas and Sue

Thomas is nine months old. He is sitting on the carpet of their living room, with his back against the sofa. Sue, his mum, is sitting directly in front of him. She is partly kneeling, but sitting back to place her bottom on the floor between her heels. She is close to Thomas, her knees touching his feet, her face thus hovering two feet or so from his and slightly above.

They have been playing together for a few minutes and the atmosphere they have created and which seems to enfold them, is quietly compelling. The room is strewn with colourful toys, but as we start observing them, their attention is on plastic stacking bricks; they each hold one. The room is quiet except for the noise of Sue tapping her brick against his. Thomas withdraws his brick, waves it, sucks it, bangs it back against Sue's once more, but in the process drops it.

Sue has been watching his performance avidly, and now comments 'ooooh', her voice light, humorous, rising toward the end of the statement, as if dropping the brick was the most important thing he could have done with it. Simultaneously, Sue picks up his brick and taps it against hers, holding them forward, offering. Thomas takes them, but raises them silently into the air to hold them triumphantly above his head. His raised face now beams open-mouthed at Sue's between his upraised arms. Sue has not been passive during this episode, but has intently followed his activity, literally by raising her head in unison with the movement of his arms and allowing her face immediately to reflect the expression he wears. The effect she creates is that as he makes eye contact with her, they are simultaneously and joyfully beaming at each other, holding the moment for two or three seconds. Once more she affirms the importance of what they have done: 'Aheerrr', (as if all his recent activity is a statement with which she is in complete agreement).

Thomas drops his arms, his gaze, then one of the bricks, scrabbles a bit, clatters his brick against Sue's – 'clippotty-clop' she comments descriptively. He then spends a few quiet seconds manipulating the bricks between his hands and Sue's, trying to give them to her. Sue has been quiet and still during this episode, but is still scanning him intently, 'tuned in'. 'Shall we build something?' she asks in whispered excitement. 'Shall we put them together?' 'Ehoogh' from Thomas, (as if 'no'). 'Ooogh' from

Sue, voice lowering (as if 'no' in agreement). He continues his manipulation of the bricks, drops them, picks up two others stacked together. Sue pounces. 'Shall we make three?' grabs another brick and clips it on his. Everything then seems to happen at once. Thomas grabs the three-stack, again in triumph. Sue withdraws her hand quickly in dramatic mock deference uttering a dramatically whispered: 'oh!'. Thomas puts the stack to his mouth and raises his head to gaze at Sue's face, beaming. Sue's face still wears the 'oh' shape held still, her eyes wide in mock surprise, but warm, smiling.

Her little drama seems to hold him and they sustain mutual gaze for five or six seconds, seemingly gently transfixed on each other. 'That's a good one,' she whispers conspiratorially, leaning a little closer.

Discussion and commentary: Sue's style

We can start to look at what is happening between Sue and Thomas in an analytical way, examining their play to see if we can identify the principles and the structure in Sue's style of behaving which support Thomas' learning. Later we can also consider the sorts of things which Thomas might be learning by taking part in such an experience.

Quality one-to-one time

Sue freely indulges the luxury of having no-one else around who is likely to cause a disturbance. Thomas is her only child and she organises her day so that she can have a number of such play experiences and she is able to devote full, powerful attention to Thomas in short, intense bursts. One of the effects for Thomas must be to make him feel very good. We all enjoy the undivided attention of another person from time to time, indeed we would argue that such an experience is among the more important of human activities. We can speculate that Thomas feels a deep sense of emotional reward by having a skilled and experienced person demonstrating such interest. It must be one of the factors which makes him feel good to be with, and helps him to be in possession of a healthy sense of self-esteem. He needs to have some optimum sense of self-esteem if he is successfully to conduct the crucial and rapid learning that is the task of this stage of his life.

Sue signals her availability

Sue's attitude to this activity is that she is there for Thomas, available to him to a great extent, on his terms. Her posture, her body language, vocalisations and general concentration on him give continuous graphic signals of her attitude and intentions. Thomas must feel pretty good about this.

Sue has her face available
Sue has positioned herself for this activity so that her face is readily available to Thomas. Thomas is potentially learning all sorts of things during this activity, not just about communication, but Sue's intuitions have dictated that her face should be in a position where he will be able to look at it at any time.

She goes to him
Sue has made a subconscious acknowledgement that the activity will be enhanced if it is carried out in a location where Thomas is comfortable and feeling secure. She goes and gets down on the floor with him where he feels secure and at ease. Adults usually do not have a problem with respecting infants' needs here. Most of us get straight down on the floor and indulge our own enjoyment of infant play.

Another way we may usefully portray this aspect of adult technique, is that we go and join an infant in her/his little world of more limited understandings – psychologically, intellectually and emotionally. We would not expect someone like Thomas to do the reverse, to conduct his learning in an adult style in a formalised setting, we naturally assume the responsibility for being the sophisticated partner who can do the necessary adjusting to accommodate the infant's needs.

Sue is in close proximity
In the act of going to him, Sue has also placed herself in close proximity, literally within Thomas' personal space, close enough to make frequent, if not sustained physical contact (e.g. her knee against his foot). They know and trust each other well enough for this proximity to be comfortable for both of them. Such closeness may particularly facilitate their ability to pick up on each other's signals.

Sue promotes an atmosphere which is relaxed and informal
This is one of those aspects of Sue's style which it is almost not worth mentioning. With nine-month-old people we all tend to be relaxed and informal if we want to be with them at all. Nine-month old people do not find formality very interesting and engaging. However, since we are examining Sue's style with a view to enhancing our practice, it does seem worth stressing this point. One colleague, having watched this video of Sue in action, commented that it was almost as though Thomas and Sue are equals. They are not, of course; Sue is more knowledgeable, sophisticated and experienced, but the way she behaves does not seem to burden him with that realisation, and make

him feel in any way inferior. To put it another way, she doesn't pull rank on him, she is participative, consultative. She is available as a gentle, and reassuring interpreter of the world, not an instructor.

Sue is attentive, focussed, scanning him constantly for signals and feedback

If the interaction between Sue and Thomas is to be effective, one of the components of that effectiveness is the degree to which Sue picks up Thomas' signals and feedback and then accordingly makes a response of her own. In the sequence described, Sue virtually never takes her eyes off him, she scans him constantly for the minutest nuances of his behaviour. In fact, most adults are good at this sort of 'tuning in'. Of course, in turn, Thomas will gradually become more and more expert at this himself, learning to scan for, and respond to, the signals of another person. We never stop doing this. Adult soph-isticated language users nonetheless continue to scan for the non-ver-bal signals which accompany speech. There is one aspect of this, however, which must be mentioned as a caution, particularly in the way that this aspect of activity relates to work with older learners with disabilities. Although Sue's eyes constantly scan Thomas, she does not stare, her eye contact is not fierce or intense, unless she means it to be in mock and humorous drama. Thomas would not flourish so well under visibly stern scrutiny.

Sue celebrates Thomas' behaviour

One of Sue's methods of giving regular, almost systematic feedback to Thomas, is that she clearly signals her enjoyment of his behaviour. One of Thomas' needs at present is to have the realisation that the things which he does are basically okay. He needs to feel free and confident about continuing to produce more behaviours and Sue does not hesitate to support him in this in a variety of ways. She smiles, she laughs, her comments are full of fun, she interprets what he does or utters as meaningful or even profound; he must realise the extent to which she is attentive and tuned in to him, and the extent to which she accepts his behaviour as good, worthwhile, legitimate.

Sue has her *fun*

One of Sue's most fundamental signals, and the basis of her style of celebrating his behaviour, is that she really is having a good time. She is not pretending to have fun for his sake, she isn't shaping and styling her behaviour purely for his benefit, she is literally, unequivocally, unashamedly having a great time and indulging her own needs for enjoyment. When adults are with infants, we do actually enjoy ourselves at our own intellectual and emotional level. It is essential that we do; our signalling of celebration, of 'you are good to be with', of necessity should be sincere. When it isn't, interaction is difficult, and that too is true of interactions between sophisticated language users.

Sue uses imitation
Imitation is a commonly observed aspect of adult behaviour with infants, and is of course a really good method of celebrating the other person's behaviour. In this book we suggest a slight adjustment to use of the word 'imitation', since we have observed many response signals which are like an imitation, but not quite, or at least not seeming to be a precise enough representation of what the other person did to rate as an imitation. For this reason we offer also 'modified reflecting'.

Sue allows pauses in their activity
In the short illustration offered so far, we have seen Sue calmly and confidently pausing in her contribution. She does not seem to have a need to dominate the activity or drive it along particularly, she is happy to respond to what Thomas is doing. If nothing is particularly presenting itself to be celebrated, Sue simply pauses. She continues scanning, she is still very much available, but her own activity and input is reduced. Perhaps her intuitions tell her that too much activity from her would be stressful for Thomas, that a major purpose of the activity for him is to be an explorer, both in the physical and the social world. The role for Sue is that of the intuitive facilitator and respondent. Perhaps also, part of Sue's role is to offer the right stimuli at the right moment, and that means not at every moment.

Sue has the ability to 'hold' some pauses
This aspect of Sue's behaviour became particularly apparent toward the end of the illustration which has been offered so far. She has the ability to use herself to 'hold' Thomas' attention for some seconds, and she does this particularly to sustain eye contact and mutual gaze. 'Oh!' she whispers dramatically. Her face is dramatic too as she holds her face in the 'oh' shape as he looks at her. Her facial expression is big, surprised, humorous, still, and with it she holds his gaze for some seconds. This part of their activity together is hugely enjoyable to watch, especially after you have the intellectual realisation that this

aspect of the adult style is so skilful. Those held moments must be important for the part of Thomas' learning to do with eye contact and the use and meaning of the vast and subtle array of facial expressions which he must master in order to become a sophisticated communicator.

Sue's style includes a variety of gently dramatised behaviours

There is gentle, humorous dramatisation in much of Sue's behaviour. The way that she raises her head in unison with him holding aloft the bricks, her instant readiness to use imitation or modified reflecting, the dramatic contrast between the pauses and the activity, her utterances, frequently with just an edge in her voice, of surprise, of joy, of query. The sensation that what she says, though gentle, carefully paced, free of stress, is nonetheless important. Similarly, she uses face and eyes in a slightly exaggerated way, emphasising something pleasurable or surprising or remarkable.

Illustration: Thomas and Sue (continued)

'That's a good one,' Sue whispers and Thomas holds her gaze for a few more moments, the bricks still to his mouth. He lowers the bricks and his gaze, fiddles intently with the bricks for a few seconds, brings them down and clashes them with other bricks on the floor. Sue has lost him briefly. During this last episode she has paused throughout. She has kept up her scanning, and she clearly continues to signal availability, but she has been exhibiting a disciplined stillness.

Then, she acts and picks up a squeaky toy. She squeaks it five times rapidly, in front of Thomas' line of vision. He does not respond and is now stirring and clashing the loose bricks between his legs. Sue puts down the squeaky toy and pauses once again.

Thomas lifts his hands from the bricks and does the characteristically babyish rhythmic hands and arms outstretched waving movement in the direction of the bricks. 'Ur-ur-ur-um,' Sue comments, picking up the rhythm of this movement before Thomas has finished it, and immediately taking up two of the bricks Thomas had just put down. As Thomas completes his rhythmic arm waving, Sue continues the rhythm, but by banging the two bricks together three times. Laughingly she comments: 'That's a good noise, isn't it?' Thomas reaches out again to take them from her, and he has now started a rhythmic utterance, 'awawaw,' as if picking up from the bricks and from Sue's verbal cueing. Sue has immediately grabbed two more bricks: 'You do it and mummy will do it as well.' She bangs the bricks together, this time picking up on the rhythm of his babble, then adding herself to the harmony, 'mememememem'. As the rhythm progresses she raises her two bricks to just below her face. Thomas' gaze follows, and for a few seconds he now pauses, looking up at his mother's face, beholding her simultaneously banging the bricks, and beaming back at him saying, 'mumememem,' then gently moving her face toward his in emphasis.

Discussion and commentary: Sue's style (continued)

Sue mostly takes her cues from what Thomas does – she follows him
Perhaps the most striking aspect of Sue's style, perhaps the most crucial principle which she uses, is that she basically follows and picks up on what Thomas does. Certainly from the point of view of considering Sue's behaviour as a teaching style, it is significant that she does not seem to have a plan or an agenda for what should be taking place.

In a sense, there is no particular task for this activity, it is exploratory, with Sue as a kind of experienced mediator and facilitator. She exercises a degree of practical control and organisation – she may have chosen the toys, the setting, the right moment, all based on her knowledge of Thomas, her understanding of his abilities and her judgements as to appropriate materials for these activities. But once the activity is under way, we see her using this particular and interesting style. She simply holds herself ready to select and then celebrate items or episodes of Thomas' behaviour. In so doing, she signals her approval of whatever it was that Thomas did at that moment; she signals also that his behaviour is important and has the potential to interest and involve her.

Furthermore, simply celebrating a particular episode may not be sufficient. Sue will often start a run of her own activity based on an item of his, then continue her celebration, extend and develop it, at the same time fully involving him in this process. The episode we have just offered presents a good example. Sue picks up Thomas' rhythmic hand waving by falling in to his rhythm with a little sound, 'ur-ur-um,' then bringing the sound made by two bricks meeting into the rhythm as well. Thomas, now stimulated and attracted, takes the bricks and starts a verbal rhythm of his own. Sue again falls in with this, using bricks and voice, and then says something seemingly quite directive: 'You do it and mummy will do it.' In fact, what she said was not really directive at all. Rather, she was literally telling him that she is prepared to follow his behaviour, that he is basically the leader at this time, acknowledging also however, that part of her role is to offer stimuli.

It is worth dwelling on and emphasising this aspect of adult behaviour with infants. It is, in our view, one of the more important elements of these interactions, and one which is readily and generally seen in the adult style. Operation of this principle would seem to have the power to convey to infants that their behaviour and activity is important and interesting, exciting even. It also means that there must be a very reassuring process for the infant learner of having the learning activity, or the various learning components of an activity, continually starting with and being based upon things with which s/he is familiar and about which s/he is already knowledgeable. The experience might be extended and developed by adult contributions – moved on from there into new experiences, but the starting point offers comfort and familiarity. It also means that an infant's behaviour and activity is the dynamic centrepiece of interactions with others.

Moreover, when adults start in this way from infants' behaviour, we are unlikely to be considering these technical matters; we are primarily interested in enjoyment, but this brings with it a degree of sensitivity which means that infants are not overburdened with too many new experiences all at once. We are mostly able to exercise intuitions about an infant's present state of awareness, and of how much more can be added to it in one go.

From the adult perspective, use of this principle of taking the lead from the child must have many advantages. One practical consideration in teaching and learning terms concerns what we need Thomas to be doing at the present time. At nine months of age, he is involved in a terrific burst of energy directed at rapid learning in many domains, particularly communication and the ability to be social. It is difficult for us, with our present state of knowledge, to draw up daily plans or formalised teaching programmes for his learning and development. What he is presently undertaking is a bit too complex for us to be able to divide it into daily stages or increments. Rather, we rely on the natural teaching and learning processes which stand most people in good stead.

A way of looking at what Thomas is absorbed in, is that to a great extent he has to continue to feel comfortable and secure with a process of experimenting with his own behaviour. He probably feels comfortable and secure with this procedure because most of the people he knows, Sue particularly of course, think that what he does is absolutely brilliant and let him know this. They celebrate what he does in many different ways, often joining in with his activity then proceeding to add something of their own if it feels right to do this. Being reassured that something he did was quite alright and worthwhile means that there is a greater likelihood that it will get added to his expanding repertoire of knowledge and ability.

Sue offers stimuli or options to Thomas – but she does not insist that he takes them up

This aspect of Sue's style might be assumed to be in contradiction to that of following and picking up on what Thomas does. In a sense, there may be a sort of dynamic tension between these two principles. However, we can see that with, for example, the squeaky toy, there is a preparedness from Sue to put aside what she is offering if it is not taken up. She seems content to allow the main motivating force to be his own, and that whilst she may promote or tune in to his motivation, part of the process they are involved in is the development of his own decision-making capacity and his ability to make choices. When Thomas takes the bricks she has offered, she looks upon what he then does with them as an opportunity – he is providing further examples of his activity for her to celebrate and go along with.

Sue has no particular agenda or task for their activity together

Since Sue's style is mainly reliant on the principle of using his behaviour as the starting point for her activity, there is not a pressing need for her to do too much planning for what might take place. She may have organised the room and the toys which are available and with the flexibility of her behaviour she is able to exercise some control over what is taking place. She always has the option of promoting a game or episode already known to them both, and already shown to be successful.

Beyond that however, Sue does not seem to have a precise vision of what Thomas should do, what will be achieved during the activity, or what the outcome will be. This does not mean that she does not have expectations and aspirations; she expects that what they do together will be purposeful, valuable, enjoyable, but she is relaxed about precisely in which way. Neither does Sue's style mean that their play, and by implication Thomas' learning, is unstructured. We are in the process here of identifying the elements and principles of her activity which help form a structure which is supportive and effective for Thomas.

The overall effect of this taskless aspect of Sue's style must be to make Thomas feel pretty good. One benefit for him is that he is not having what he does on a minute by minute basis compared by Sue to her vision of what he should or could be doing or achieving. He is therefore not receiving messages of rightness or wrongness, unless we construe Sue's general celebratory behaviour as a general signal of rightness. Thus, he is operating during this activity within an atmosphere which is very supportive and he is not confronted moment by moment with failure or with criticism of his performance. The nearest that Sue gets to doing something which might be seen as a criticism during this sequence, is to refrain from celebrating something which he does – an example is the frequency with which he puts objects to and in his mouth. At this stage, with this sort of activity, Sue seems to have confidence that the process of learning that Thomas is undergoing has a momentum of its own which drives continuing development.

The tempo of the session is relaxed – Sue does not 'drive on'
The activity between Sue and Thomas has a lovely tempo which seems to suit him very well. Of course, if Sue is using the principle of basically working from his behaviour, then the tempo of the activities will be, to a great extent, governed by him. Her respect for pauses is linked to this aspect of style. There must be temptations to drive on with the activity, to give plenty of further stimulation to Thomas when there is a pause, to keep things going. Something in Sue's intuitive style helps her to resist these temptations, in fact it may be that because her style is so deeply intuitive and natural, they are not temptations at all.

Sue responds to Thomas' behaviours, particularly his sounds, as if they are meaningful
In the previous chapter this element of the interactive style that adults use with infants has been described by use of a technical term – intentionality. Basically adults continuously respond to infant behaviour as if it is meaningful even when it isn't. This can be part of a precise process of gradually shaping sounds into meaningful words, adults responding to 'da' in such a way that it becomes 'dad' for instance. Intentionality is also a broader concept than this however. In the earlier stages, it is more important that adults consistently respond than that all adults give the same precise response to the same behaviour. In other words, it is vital for adult response to give powerfully to Thomas the concept that his behaviour can be meaningful before it moves into areas of exact meaning.

Sue uses intentionality in various ways. In their activity together, she does not allow any sounds from his voice to go unremarked upon. Her verbal response to an utterance from him is frequently confirmatory, as if she completely understood and agreed with him. Also, she almost always adds more meaning, if only in the way that she uses tone and pitch. His 'no'-like cry was immediately confirmed by her with a similar, but more developed one.

Sue uses Thomas' sense of rhythm
Thomas indulges in various episodes of rhythmic activity – his noises, the arm and hand waving. Sue seems sensitive to it and uses it, continually incorporating his use of rhythm into her own behaviour, as when she picks up his hand-waving with the noise of bricks banging together.

Sue sometimes holds objects near to her face
Toward the end of the second illustration, Sue is banging two bricks together, verbalising rhythmically, smiling, beaming at Thomas, and holding the bricks just below her face so that he looks up and takes in the whole lot simultaneously in one glance. If we identify the bricks as the main stimulus at that moment, then her intuitions have caused her to use them to draw his attention to her face as well – a social learning achievement. If we identify her face and voice as the main stimulus at that moment, then she is cleverly helping Thomas to relate to the bricks by using her face and voice to make them safe, reassuring and interesting. Sue uses this type of tactic often.

Illustration: Thomas and Sue (continued)
'Mumememem,' Sue is saying to Thomas with her wide, beaming facial expression holding his regard. She is tapping her bricks together in emphasis, holding them just below her face. She pauses. Thomas has paused too, still looking upward to her face and the bricks.

'Mumememem.' Once more Sue does her little burst of behaviour. She still has Thomas' attention keenly held.

'Ahaaa . . . ' from Thomas, and he reaches out to take Sue's bricks from her. Sue has paused for this. Thomas, bricks now in each hand, gives a delighted squeal and holds his stacks aloft, shaking and waving them as if they were maraccas. Sue has been studying him whilst she quickly selected more bricks for herself. She immediately responds with face, eyes and voice: 'Aaaaaaa' as if to say that she really enjoyed that bit too. Her vocalisation is accompanied by a rhythmic side to side movement of her head. Sue straightaway follows this with a pause as Thomas once again tries to take the fresh bricks from her hands in order to supplement the considerable handfuls he already possesses.

For a while Thomas' concentration is fully committed to the difficulty of managing all those bricks. Sue remains still and quiet, merely opening her hands fully to make things easier for him. She murmurs, 'oh, ooop' in commentary to his difficulties, and at last the physical world has got the better of him and his bricks are on the floor. He scans around him as if to assess the extent of the problem, and momentarily his attention has completely left Sue.

Sue picks up two more stacks of bricks and starts banging them together again, but this time with a faster, more urgent rhythm. She brings her bricks up to just below her face again, and it is clear that she is trying to win Thomas back with the stimulus that has been successful so far. Thomas simultaneously brings a brick to his mouth and raises his eyes to the bricks in Sue's hands. As soon as he does this, Sue stops banging the bricks and scrapes them together instead, as if to hold his attention, right there. This lasts perhaps five seconds, an intense, quiet five seconds. Sue then significantly stops scraping and simply holds the bricks, still and silent. Thomas observes the stillness for a long moment, then reaches out to take one of her bricks. 'Ooooh,' consents Sue softly, following with a quiet, warm chuckle as he once more waves his bricks like maraccas, but now looking gleefully up into Sue's face. Her chuckle has been enough, somehow, to crease his face and start him laughing. Sue has picked up more bricks and fallen in with his movements again, and he is laughing, exclaiming, 'aha' in agreement. Sue laughingly celebrates immediately with a louder, longer, confirmatory 'ahaaaaaaa'.

Discussion and commentary: Sue's style (continued)

Sue uses burst-pause
Sue clearly employs the 'burst-pause' technique identified as general to adult style with infants. Sue offers a little burst of behaviour, then pauses expectantly, the message being, 'Your turn Thomas'. In fact of course, burst-pause is general to human communication at all levels. We would all be experiencing the utmost difficulties if we did not employ burst-pause. In sophisticated speech interactions the bursts may be longer and more complex, the pause sometimes grudgingly observed, but if we did not employ this principle, we would all be blasting speech at each other without assessing the effect of what we just said on the other person (yes, we all do know people who communicate in that style). That is one of the purposes of the pause. It allows Sue to observe the effects on Thomas of her burst of behaviour, before persevering with it for too long.

One result of her observation may be that his signals tell her to do something different from what she did during the last burst. Perhaps more importantly, the expectancy which Sue loads into the pause using her voice and face, gives a cue to Thomas that perhaps he could do something, since it is now his turn. Once more, the theme is that the expectancy that is transmitted to Thomas is very powerful, but congenial, supportive, optional. It would not be Sue's intention to place stress on Thomas to take his turn, indeed, putting too much stress on Thomas to reciprocate may have the opposite effect to that desired. He may then look upon taking his turn as a task, something he must do in order to please or fulfil Sue. This would miss the point that we want him to learn to take his turn for his own reasons, because it pleases him, and because he is starting to find this process of communicating an extremely interesting thing to do. We must all have examples from our own experience of infants of the maddening refusal to reproduce something wonderful they have learnt to do, when you ask them to produce it to order, for the benefit of onlookers.

Sue uses modified language

This is a complex aspect of Sue's style. She does not use many sentences. When she does they are simple and short. Her voice is light and warm. Even with her use of syntax simplified from that which she would use with other adults, it is nonetheless questionable whether Thomas understands every word. This does not seem to deter her from using the phrasing that she does, but she does add to the words a modified voice, facial expression and use of body language, helping to make it meaningful to him. It is difficult to be precise about the 'rules' Sue is using to govern her use of words.

One consideration is that of course, she and Thomas have spent nine months getting to know each other and gradually generating their communication routines together. She has deep, subjective knowledge about how to use her voice most effectively for him. Interpreting that knowledge as a set of 'rules', may not be the best way to portray it.

There is probably some kind of optimum route for her to take with her use of language at this stage of Thomas' development. If the language directed at him is too complex, it will probably discourage him from attending to it. If it is too simple or insufficient in quantity, he will not be receiving enough language concerning his life to assist him with his own ability to start to use words. As stated, how to judge this optimum is the problem. Perhaps we generally get the language level right for infants quickly and with ease, because we so successfully use our ability to scan for signals and feedback which guide our activity carefully to the optimum for that person.

Sue allows Thomas to lose interest in the activity, but does try to win his attention back if possible

In the last part of the illustration, upon dropping all of his bricks,

Thomas stopped paying attention to Sue altogether. Sue was not unduly worried by this, it did not stress her or make her anxious. She seemed extremely respectful of his need to pay attention to something else. Eventually however, she did offer a stimulus to regain him, tapping the bricks together again, something which had already worked for them. Her use of herself in this episode can be regarded as particularly skilful. She held the bricks near her face again, and the tapping she set up was quite urgent. At the same time however, she was respectful, not bombarding, not metaphorically grabbing him again as soon as he started to show renewed interest in her. Rather, as his gaze came back to the bricks, she modified slightly, scraping them, then she paused again, creating a quiet moment with time and space for him to produce something if he wished. Sue's behaviour seems to indicate a real, positive desire for him to interact with her and remain engaged, but not at any cost. Part of the learning for him here is finding and identifying his own motivation to take part in such activities and find them interesting.

Illustration: Thomas and Sue (continued)
Sue has changed her position slightly, moving one leg out from underneath her to bring it alongside, almost around Thomas. She continues now to bang and scrape her bricks as Thomas, joyfully and with upturned gaze, is using his bricks like maraccas again. His mouth is very wide, partly in laughter, partly in seeming wonderment at the pleasure of it all. He puts one of the bricks to his wide open mouth and in semi-pause moves his eyes to watch Sue's hands again. He drops one of his bricks, looks directly into Sue's eyes. 'Ooops. Dropped it. We've dropped it,' she says in a voice of mock sorrow and disappointment, at the same time freezing her physical activity and allowing her own bricks to trickle from her hands.

For a few seconds Sue is still, frozen in that position of mock grief, her now empty hands held open in front of her. Thomas looks at her face briefly, mouthing. 'Ahoo . . . ,' she comments with a laugh in her voice, confirming how good it was.

For fifteen seconds Thomas returns to scrabbling with the bricks between his thighs. Sue is attentive, but seems to be resting briefly also. She tosses a couple of bricks into his lap. Thomas starts to mouth a brick again, really sucking this time. 'Does it taste nice?' Sue asks, but her voice is more adult-like. It lacks the usual obvious celebration.

Another period where Thomas' attention is more on the bricks. At one point he mutters 'aher'. 'Ahummmm,' from Sue, very thoughtful and confirmatory as if yes, that was very interesting.

Thomas has dropped a brick to his right and is leaning over Sue's left leg to retrieve it. She uses the opportunity slowly and smoothly to extend and relax her other leg. He now has his own secure workspace between her legs. Because of the change of position, they now make continuous physical contact. As Sue moved, she dislodged a rattley toy and is in the act of putting it to one side when Thomas, attracted by the noise, turns to look at it. Sue did not miss the look, and immediately brings the toy back into their little space, shaking it. She offers it to Thomas, he holds it, pats it, but Sue does not release it. There is a lull while Sue sits still and attentive and Thomas continues to explore the toy in her hand.

Discussion and commentary: Sue's Style (continued)

Sue uses her body language to create the environment where they play together
We hope that the written illustrations have done something to convey a sense of Sue's use of her physical presence and her body language. Throughout the sequence, we can look at her and relate to the messages relayed by her posture and positioning, and by her movements. Her posture is so attentive, so fixed on Thomas. She is opposite, but close – there is a minimum of space between them.

Her body language, particularly when she moves her legs around him, is effective in creating a special place for them and communicating that to Thomas. Her movements are mostly minimal, simple. She does not do anything too 'big' or jerky or startling. When she moved her legs to more comfortable positions, she visibly did it slowly and smoothly, taking care not to make her movement into a stimulus or distraction of any kind for Thomas.

Sue's behaviour is completely positive – she does not employ use of negatives during this activity
Throughout the whole sequence, there is not one occasion when Sue utters a negative word, or uses noises, body language or facial expression which could be construed as communicating a negative message of any form. This is a very interesting aspect of her style. Why is it that something in her instincts prevents her, during this session, from saying 'no', or 'not like that', 'stop that and do this', 'come back here not over there'?

One answer probably relates to a principle we have already identified, that of celebrating what Thomas does, of encouraging him to continue to produce new behaviour. She needs to keep Thomas in good shape emotionally and intellectually so that he can forge ahead with this important learning. One of the pictures that emerges from studying infant learning at this level, is the extent to which, even during the first year, the infant is active, often in control, leading the activity, exercising choice and power. These issues of activity and control are elements of the process which drive and structure the learning, but Thomas' ability to exercise them is also essential learning as a result of the process.

If these things are to happen for Thomas in the most effective way then we are forced to consider the emotional atmosphere in which this optimum, or something like it, will be achieved. For infants in the first year that atmosphere seems to be to do with the available adults providing the most supportive and encouraging atmosphere possible, not giving emphasis to tasks, but responding highly positively to their infants' experimentations.

We can see from Sue in this one sequence, a seemingly effortless but nonetheless powerful dedication to keeping Thomas' self-esteem well up. The degree to which he feels O.K. about himself is fundamentally connected with how well he learns. We can surely all relate to the extent to which self-doubt affects our ability or desire to take on new things. Even if Thomas makes mistakes or does completely stupid things in this type of session, that's perfectly acceptable, because he is supposed to. Making mistakes and being free to, is part of the process. Correcting those mistakes or signalling wrongness is not as important for Sue as maintaining a highly positive, purposeful atmosphere in which he forges ahead under his own motivation. If Sue were continually seizing upon and criticising things which he does that she does not like, if she did that powerfully and consistently enough, then it might make him reluctant to try out new behaviours, and prefer instead to stick to the things of which Sue clearly approves.

There is one more very subtle consideration on this topic. There may be a sense in which Sue does do something negative. Throughout the session, one of the behaviours which Thomas most frequently produces is putting objects to, or in his mouth. This is a natural aspect of his behaviour at this stage of his development, but not something that Sue feels a need to focus on or develop, in fact adults often cannot help themselves feeling a concern about this infant behaviour. However, it is something from which he will, again naturally, move on. Accordingly, Sue does not celebrate this aspect of Thomas' behaviour and this is the extent of her negativity.

Illustration: Thomas and Sue (continued)
Sue maintains her stillness for twenty seconds or so while Thomas continues to explore the toy which fixes his attention. Then, for no visible reason, but almost as though she has been plotting it, Sue extends a

finger. The toy has a button which causes a squeak. She presses it ten times in a rapid burst.

Sue pauses for five seconds while Thomas still just looks at the toy. Sue repeats, a shorter phrase, this time with voice in unison: 'Squiddy, squiddy, squiddy, quiddy'. Thomas' attention is still held. She repeats again, this time shaking and weaving her head in punctuation, sliding her face close in to his. He starts to smile. His face opens. Sue leans back taking a dramatic, preparatory breath, 'aaaaah . . . ,' and repeats her performance again. This time she leans in so close their cheeks meet and her hair falls across his face. Thomas starts to laugh. Sue immediately chimes in with a louder, delighted laugh of her own. Thomas now looks up into her face. Sue straightaway performs her run again, the squeak, the 'squiddy, squiddy,' and the lean forwards towards him, but this time holding his intent, delighted gaze as she performs. Again she repeats this.

The atmosphere is really heightened now. Thomas looks back to the toy and Sue repeats once more, this time staccato, more dramatic even. Thomas is back to her face again, laughing, beaming, delighted. Sue's face reflects his. For a few moments they are held, each beaming and gushing into the other's face. 'Can you make it squeak? Can you make it squeak?' Sue asks squeakily. Thomas presses the button, looking laughingly into Sue's face. The toy squeaks and Sue squeaks. Again Thomas presses the button, laughing, expectant.

We can now realise that Sue is literally offering Thomas a button which he can use to control her. When he presses the button she produces the funny behaviour. 'Oooh, very good,' Sue says, warmly, congratulating. Thomas laughs. Thomas looks down to the toy again. 'Oooow' he says happily, immediately repeated and affirmed by Sue.

However, their last mutual burst seems to have been enough; Thomas' attention is down from Sue's face again, and she seems to have lost momentum. Perhaps she too has had as much stimulation as she can manage in one session. Thomas fiddles for a while with the toy and the bricks, burbling softly, then makes to stand up and climb onto the sofa behind him. Their play is finished. 'What are you going for eh?' Sue asks, moving her leg out of his way and helping him up onto the sofa.

Discussion and commentary: Sue's style (continued)

Sue blends objects and their properties into her behaviour
Here is an issue we have already examined – Sue using herself to demystify objects and make them safe and interesting – but taken one stage further. The properties of the object are blended into her own behaviour with it, in an amusing and attractive way for Thomas. Sue does this especially of course in the last part of the illustration, blending her movements and vocalisations with the noise she produces from the squeaky toy. It may be that this is a particular routine for them with that particular toy.

She offers Thomas control
In the next section we will give some consideration to the things which
Thomas is learning or potentially learning through taking part in this
activity. One thing which we can be fairly certain about is that it is one
of the situations where he learns about social cause and effect, literally:
'I do something, and it makes Sue do something.' It is important that
he finds this an interesting area of endeavour. He needs to get a good
working knowledge of that concept if he is to become a sophisticated
communicator. Again, we can see the role here of Sue basing her
behaviour primarily on what Thomas does, it assists him to get the
notion. With the squeaky toy, Sue literally gives him a button to press
which will have an effect on her.

Sue makes sure they have episodes of face-to-face
Thomas does not have to look at Sue's face all or even most of the
time, but she does seem to have an expectation that there will be
regular episodes where this takes place. However, this expectation
does not cause her to insist to him that he pay attention to her face,
her technique is more about seizing upon and intensifying significant
moments which his behaviour makes available to her.

During the last part of the illustration, there occurred the most
emotionally heightened moment of all when they held each others'
gaze for some moments, both with great transmission of joy and
enjoyment of the other. In learning terms, the reasons for having good
face-to-face episodes seem clear enough – he still needs to do more
practice on eye contact and use of facial expression. A month or two
earlier, their interactions would have consisted of a great deal more
direct, intense face-to-face; now the episodes we have noted seem
sufficient during this session.

One reason for this development may be that Thomas, as here with
Sue's assistance and mediation, is becoming a little more involved in
learning about objects. He cannot do this properly if he is completely
fixed on her, though he undoubtedly finds reassurance in the presence
and availability of her face. To refer to the literature of the last chapter,
Sue is still supporting Thomas mightily and interpreting the world for
him, but she has also removed some of the scaffolding.

Sue does not use dominance or compulsion
Sue doesn't use dominance or compulsion here with Thomas, he's only
nine months old and it doesn't enter her head to do that with him. She
is not stern with him in order to promote his learning. If she had forced

him to pick up the bricks again after he had discarded them, or pulled him back after he started to move away, he would probably have become distressed and there would certainly then be little possibility of further constructive progress. Adults use effective instincts on these matters. At the heart of Thomas' learning is the development of his self-worth, his ability to be self-motivated, to be interested in things around him, to exercise choice and power, particularly cause and effect. Use of dominance and compulsion do not serve these ends well.

Thus, when he has had enough, he gets up and crawls away and that is fine with Sue, she does not compel him to continue. In fact, he probably finds it easier to take part in activities such as these because he doesn't have to. The knowledge that he can end it when he feels like it is probably very reassuring. Actually, in the first place, Sue would not have attempted to start the activity if, in her judgement, he was not in the mood for it.

Of course, there are plenty of other occasions during Thomas' day when Sue will use negatives or correction, particularly if he is on the brink of doing something hazardous. But, our estimation of Sue's style toward Thomas is that any negatives she employs have their place within this general trend to the positive. Positivity is the theme, but there are negative incidents. Within this general trend to the positive, Sue's style of saying 'no' is likely to be effective, without being too negative.

Summary of Sue's style

- She follows him – picks up on what he does – then celebrates and extends
- Sue offers stimuli or options – but does not insist that he takes them up
- She makes possible a session of quality one-to-one time
- She signals her availability to Thomas
- She has her face available
- Sue goes to Thomas – joins him in his little world
- She is in close proximity
- She is relaxed, informal – there is an atmosphere of equality
- She is attentive, focussed on him – 'tuned in'
- She scans constantly for signals and feedback from Thomas to guide her activity
- Sue has her fun

- Sue uses imitation and modified reflecting of items and episodes of Thomas' behaviour
- She allows and respects pauses in the activity
- She has the ability to 'hold' pauses
- She uses gently dramatised behaviour
- She has no particular agenda for the activity, no real vision of task or outcome
- Sue does not 'drive on' with activities – the tempo is relaxed
- She uses intentionality – responding to his behaviours as though they are meaningful
- She picks up on and employs Thomas' use of rhythm
- She holds objects near her face
- She uses burst-pause
- She uses modified language and verbalisations
- She allows Thomas to lose interest in her, but sensitively attempts to win him back
- She uses her body language to create their special place
- She uses a general trend to the positive – no negatives
- She blends objects and their properties into her behaviour
- She offers Thomas control of her
- She particularly facilitates enjoyable episodes of face-to-face
- She does not use dominance or compulsion or force

What is it that Thomas is learning during, or as a result of, this experience?

During the commentary and discussion we have made some reference to those things which Thomas presumably has an opportunity to learn during such experiences, but we now turn to look in more detail at the learning which may result from such an activity. There are some things which Thomas is learning during the session which are quite tangible. Some of this learning is evident in the exchanges between Sue and Thomas, but there is more about which we may make interpretations, based on knowledge of infant learning processes.

In this book we are particularly concerned with how communication and the ability to be social are learnt, and when we consider Thomas and Sue, those are the areas we most focus upon. We also make efforts, however, to identify those many other things which Thomas has opportunity to learn about during this session with Sue.

Less analytical observation might bring about the conclusion that the whole session was dedicated to learning how to put bricks together and make squeaky toys squeak. However, one of the aspects of Thomas' learning which we have already highlighted, is that there are not boundaries or distinctions between the subject areas. In the session we have described, his learning about the social world and his learning about the world of objects are intertwined. It is difficult to say where one stops and the other starts.

Eye contact and use and understanding of facial expression
Perhaps most tangible in the activity is that Thomas is learning and rehearsing these communication abilities, confirming the need for Sue to keep her face available to him. Throughout the session Thomas and Sue are paying particular regard to each other's face, and they make direct eye contact frequently and sustain it on a number of significant-seeming occasions. Thomas is learning about those things literally by doing them with an experienced communicator, particularly during those sustained moments of intense, joyful scrutiny of each other. From Sue it's almost as if she is affirming and matching his feelings, and showing him the facial expression that goes with them. Thomas knows so much more about use of facial expression than he did nine months or so ago, but he also has so much more to learn about this complex and subtle aspect of being with other people.

Let us just think for a moment about an alternative technique for helping Thomas to learn about the variety and uses of facial expression. Think about whether it is possible to organise daily sessions for him where you plan in advance what the content of the session will be, and which aspect of use of facial expression he will learn during each session. It would of course, be difficult if not impossible to do it that way. We do not have enough conscious, rational knowledge about the tremendous subtlety of our use of face in communication, to break it up into daily teaching steps. Sue's seemingly chaotic, but highly sensitive approach seems to be the one which works for people.

We do rely, though, on Thomas continuing to be active, interested and motivated to take part in these activities, particularly to be motivated to keep on paying attention to other people's faces. We suggest that for people with severe learning difficulties whose learning needs are still concerned with these fundamentals, one of their difficulties is often the loss of such motivation.

We know of practitioners in our work who advocate use of rewards, such as sweets, to help people with learning difficulties learn, for instance, to start using eye contact – even to the extent of sticking the sweet between one's eyes with Blu-Tack. We suggest that of all human activities, communicating is one for which we do not need extrinsic rewards, such as sweets, which have no connection to the activity; indeed, such an approach to motivating the learner may also be a positive hindrance. The reward for communicating is communicating. Human beings communicate because communication with another person stimulates and fulfils us. The very act of doing it is interesting and intriguing. So many of our daily communications have no tangible or practical outcome apart from their effect on each other. This must be the way in which it is learnt. If we offer extrinsic rewards, we are not asking the learner to find her/his own motivation for taking part and finding the activity itself worthwhile – one of the essential learning components.

Before leaving this topic, we must acknowledge that Thomas doubtless also learns about eye contact and facial expression by means other than direct face-to-face interaction, by observing other people communicating who are not communicating with him, for example. However, those other contexts and experiences must support and help him generalise from direct first-hand experience. It must be that first-hand experience is an irreplaceable learning experience.

'What I do is important and worthwhile'
Thomas is getting lovely, sustained encouragement, if not confirmation that what he does is important, worthwhile, valued by another. Hopefully, the effect for him will be that he will continue to be motivated to do things, especially new things. He needs to have this sensation about life if he is to continue to learn and become a sophisticated communicator.

'My noises have meaning'
Sue's consistent use of intentionality – responding to what Thomas does as if it was meaningful, and conveying or reflecting that meaning to him – is particularly apparent with regard to the verbalisations he produces. Again, we would very much like Thomas to come to know that he can produce meaningful sounds with his voice. In fact, in the near future, Sue and others who know him will be using techniques such as intentionality to help him shape noises into proper words.

Perhaps more crucially at the moment, Sue's continued devotion to celebrating Thomas' sounds is continuing to help him have the necessary motivation to produce sounds. He needs to know that making noises is a very good and worthwhile thing to do.

68

To understand words

Sue's carefully modified use of language must be helpful to Thomas. She does not say too much in words, and what she does say is in that light and playful manner we have highlighted. In addition, her syntax, the way she puts her phrases together is simplified, though not so simplified as to be meaningless. Her utterances are mostly about what is going on at that moment, so that any words she uses are in context with what he is doing, the objects, noises he generates, how he seems to be feeling. In this way, Thomas has the opportunity to match simple use of words and phrases to what is going on in the here and now and how that is affecting him.

Cause and effect – 'I have power'

If Thomas does not come to understand the simple proposition that he can do something which causes another person to do something, then he is always going to have difficulty with communication. He will have been experimenting with this notion from the earliest days, but the positive responsiveness of Sue and others will have a bearing on the extent to which he learns to use this ability constructively. Yes, he will probably also develop some ways too of using this power negatively. One of the features of what we often term 'brattish' behaviour among children, is the inclination to use the power of cause and effect negatively and manipulatively. Many of the students/clients we have worked with seem to have learnt only this aspect of social cause and effect, being most able to produce responses from other people by use of what we identify as 'challenging behaviour'.

During their play, Sue exemplifies what it is that adults do to help infants learn positive cause and effect in social interaction. Firstly, her continued and detailed responsiveness to his behaviours gets that message across loud and clear in general terms. Secondly, there is the particular example already mentioned, of Sue blending her behaviour with that of the squeaky toy, so that Thomas could press the button on the toy, and Sue would produce her squeaky behaviour in response to it.

Taking turns

Taking turns in exchanges of behaviour (or as it is sometimes known, 'turn-taking'), is an essential ability for a communicator. As already mentioned, just think how difficult life would be for all of us if most people did not have this ability. We would all be blasting speech at each other without pausing for another person's input. In fact there are people one meets in everyday life who seem to lack sophistication with this ability. It is usually a trying experience to communicate with them.

Some such people we have met have learning difficulties, and do have considerable mastery of speech production, yet may not have some other valuable skills which would make them a sophisticated communicator, such as taking turns and reading another person's non-verbal signals. Some of those students/clients seem to project speech in an almost obsessive way, and staff working with them may make major efforts to change this way of behaving, often because they judge that it is detrimental to the quality of life of the person or those around them. Again, observing the complex and subtle manner in which Thomas is learning this ability may make us despair of helping our students and clients with this skill, but maybe we can think of Sue's natural, relaxed abilities and find hope.

To interpret another person's non-verbal signals
Taking turns is only one of the areas in which Thomas must become masterful at reading another person's signals. Once more, we need only to make the briefest objective observation of human beings communicating with one another to acknowledge that speech production is only one part of their communication. Thomas can only learn the enormous complexity of this endeavour by doing it with other more experienced communicators in this relaxed and supportive apprenticeship. Once again, consider the difficulties of attempting to draw up daily task sheets for Thomas in order to teach him about non-verbal signalling.

Many different situations will enable the learning of non-verbal communication, but this is an example of one of them, and a very intense one too. Here is another area in which Sue's playful dramatisation of their joint behaviour is likely to assist Thomas greatly. Sue highlights much of what they are experiencing together and 'holds it up' in a larger-than-life way for him to examine and experience. This very 'largeness' of episodes of her behaviour gives him opportunity to consider the significance of what is portrayed in her face and body.

Attending to another person – concentrating
The sequence we have used as an illustration lasts for three and a half minutes. Thomas is attending to Sue or to the objects for all of that time. He already has a considerable concentration span and is learning to commit himself to activities almost without effort. Sue does not

have to use any form of compulsion or insistance to gain his attention, he gives it of his own free will, partly because her mediation and interpretation of the activity in which they are involved is so sensitively gauged to his enjoyment and to what he likes doing. The activity, and Sue's part in it, is just right for what he is as a person – intellectually and emotionally.

'Being with other people is good'
Informal observation of adults with infants usually show that infants are learning that life and the people in it, are enjoyable. That must be one of the implicit messages in the extent to which we use pleasure as an attracter and as a motivator with infants. Thinking of Thomas' motivation, we want him to continue to desire to take part in social activities, so he needs to think that people are basically fun and good to be with. At some later stage, when he is more sophisticated, Thomas must deal with the knowledge that actually, not all people are good to be with, but for the moment he needs life to be more simple than that.

'I am good to be with'
Thomas must be getting tremendously reassuring messages about his self-worth from Sue. One of the important products of Sue having a good time, sincerely, for herself, at her own intellectual and emotional level, is that this message is transmitted powerfully. Thinking again about the rapid and complicated learning that he is undertaking, we can all relate to the necessity for Thomas' self-esteem to be kept at some kind of optimum level.

Thomas needs to be in good shape to be motivated, particularly to be motivated to take part in social experiences. Who has not had experience of the difficulties in learning or doing anything new, if at that time we are having a bad time in our lives and are not feeling good about ourselves? Of course sophisticated adults may have the ability to overcome these difficulties and persevere regardless, but Thomas is not yet sophisticated in that sense.

We are again in tricky and sensitive territory here, because much of this is speculation based on our individual knowledge of our own emotional states and how that affects our view of the world. For instance, we can probably all think of examples of infants not nurtured with anything like the care being given to Thomas, yet who still seem to turn out well. At the least there seems to be a broad spectrum to what we consider to be 'O.K.', and presumably therefore a broad spectrum to what we consider to be an emotional optimum.

However, there is increasing inquiry taking place into the relationship between emotional experience in infancy and achievements and outcomes in adulthood. Some texts on this subject are referred to elsewhere in this book. For the sake of this section on Thomas and its importance for what we are conveying in this book, we will make do with this crude but important generalisation, that Thomas' emotional state, his sense of well-being are central to his progress. This is a theme to which we will return.

About objects and the properties of objects
As we have stressed, in practice – and this is clear in Thomas and Sue's session – learning about objects is indivisible from the social and communicative learning on which this book concentrates. During their activity, Thomas has opportunity to learn about the noises which plastic bricks can make, how to stack them together, how to make a squeaky toy squeak, and skills which we like to label in such ways as: hand-eye co-ordination, stacking, fine-motor manipulation, tracking, sequencing, shaking, scraping and so on. Additionally there are broader horizons; Thomas is developing confidence in exploring the physical world, curiosity about new objects he encounters and a growing set of schema – his mental plans about how the world works – which allow him to make an analysis about the potential of a new object.

We reiterate that we are not intending to devalue or set aside the learning concerned with the physical world by concentrating on the social and communicative. Rather, we are trying to point to the priorities in Thomas' learning and by inference how that might assist us in our work with people with learning difficulties. We can clearly see that important understandings and abilities connected with the world of objects are being learnt and rehearsed by Thomas. However, the basic tool by which this is being achieved is the guided participation being so sensitively offered by Sue's use of her ability to communicate with Thomas at his intellectual and emotional level. This basic tool, effective communication, needs to be established first, before other complex understandings can come about.

Summary: what is Thomas learning?

- Eye contact and use and understanding of facial expression.
- 'What I do is important and worthwhile.'
- 'My noises have meaning.'
- To understand words.

72

- Cause and effect – 'I have power.'
- Taking turns
- To interpret another person's non-verbal signals.
- To attend to another person – to concentrate.
- 'Being with other people is good.'
- 'Communicating is fun and interesting.'
- 'I am good to be with.'
- About objects and the properties of objects

General discussion of Sue and Thomas' play and how it relates to work with people with learning difficulties

Thomas' communication abilities and understandings are greater than those of many of our students/clients

Thomas' needs and abilities, what he is learning, are in certain areas, similar to those of the people for whom we are concerned in writing this book. In fact, when we consider Thomas' achievements, particularly his ability to give sustained attention, to concentrate, to stay put in one place, to participate, to give enjoyment and reward to another person, to interpret signals and to use face and eyes, his abilities and understandings are far in excess of many of our former students. Once more let us stress that there is no value judgement here, certainly no attempt to devalue people with learning difficulties by making a comparison to infant development, simply a necessary recognition that some people's learning difficulties mean that what they need to learn is still the stuff of infancy.

Sue's style is so practical and straightforward – if not easy

We have analysed Sue's style with Thomas in detail, technically, to show the technique, but we hope this serves to emphasise that Sue's way of helping Thomas is downright practical. If you are working with students/clients who are pre-verbal, do you not recognise that there is much in this way of behaving which you use quite unconsciously and without thinking? It may be on the fringe of everything else, during relaxed moments in between formal programmes and other activities, perhaps even when the boss is not around, but isn't it so natural to be at the least relaxed, playful, focussed, to celebrate bits and pieces of your students' or clients' behaviour joyfully? When you do that, do they light up, smile, give you better quality attention than at any other time?

Elsewhere in this book we expand on thoughts concerning attitudes to children and to people with learning difficulties and our general philosophical orientation to our work. But let's be clear that Sue is an example to us not simply because she is so nice and respectful and warm and so on, but because the way that she behaves naturally seems to have the power to assist Thomas to learn the things in which we are interested in our work.

If having made access to the recommendations of this book, you would like to take this further, then one of the reassuring thoughts must be that the basis for the approach we call 'Intensive Interaction' is this practical and relaxed repertoire of behaviours which most of us possess naturally. In this book we of course complicate matters quite a bit more with other considerations which our working situation brings with it, but the basis is practical.

Not using something like Sue's style may be a further disabling factor for students/clients

For many people with learning difficulties who have not achieved use of language, their original disability will have been a powerful block to them being able fully to take part in, and learn from, interactive experiences in infancy. If the fundamentals of communication and being social are not learnt to a considerable extent, it then becomes difficult for that person to learn anything subsequently. We know many people with learning difficulties who give the impression that this is the case; not everyone – some individuals also seem to have an initial disability which is great, if not overwhelming in its effects.

In the learning of even the earliest stages, the infant is active, participating. Sue needs signals, feedback and reassurance from Thomas that she is doing well, just as much as he needs them from her. Disabilities – brain damage, sensory impairments, can be blocks to this signalling. If the adult is not getting the sort of feedback needed, this starts to affect what the adult does. This, in turn, affects the infant even more and so on.

We suggest that if you observe what is going on around older people with learning needs which are still concerned with these fundamentals, you may see some key things happening in the behaviour of adults or members of staff, which can be compared with the example we have from Sue.

We may give up using intentionality
It is possible that we simply lose the ability to respond to the student/

client's behaviour powerfully, to assume that this person produces meaningful behaviour and show it in our behaviour. An effect of this will surely be that less behaviour, particularly less new behaviour, is produced. Our lack of ability to use intentionality may in part be because the person has got bigger, and we inevitably start to have expectations about what the person should be doing at this age, which may not be related to what the person is realistically capable of doing. It may also be because we are programmed to use intentionality with children, and if we are to use it sensitively with adults, we may have to do a bit of re-programming of ourselves – use our natural behaviours, but think about it a bit more.

We stop doing burst-pause sensitively enough
We hope that we have successfully got across the importance of burst-pause. In our work with many students and clients, sensitive use of burst-pause has proved to be powerful. One of the simple things that we may get wrong, is to leave a pause, but one which is not long enough. We may say: 'Hello?' in a voice quietly and effectively suggesting an expected response. We may pause with some expectancy, but after five seconds or so, become anxious about the silence and do something else, something more. The unintentional, though implicit message to the student/client, is that we did not want that person to respond. S/he may still have been thinking about the response when we went ahead and took her/his turn.

Alternatively, the expectancy needed from us during the pause may not be present, or not powerful enough, or not fun enough, or too powerful and dominant, or we may be getting signals back, but have not tuned in to the person sensitively enough to pick them up.

We may stop celebrating behaviours
There may be many reasons why we may simply, generally, give up celebrating the behaviours that a person with a limited repertoire may produce. It may be that we become completely de-motivated ourselves, give up any expectation that the person will become a communicator. We may have become disinterested in that person's limited and repetitive range of behaviours. We may have got to the unfortunate stage in our work where we literally view that person's behaviours as being meaningless and not worthwhile. The person's way of behaving seems to be entirely negative or horrible or challenging in various ways and we prefer to keep away as much as possible. We may wish to use enjoyable celebrations of that person's behaviours, but have

been forbidden to do so by the boss on the grounds that it is not age-appropriate to be in any way enjoyably dramatic with a person of that age. Alternatively, it may simply never occur to us.

We may lose the ability to use detailed scanning for signals and feedback from the learner

We hope we have made clear to the reader the extent to which part of Sue's 'tuning in' to Thomas, is the simple, practical skill of detailed scanning of him for signals and feedback. However, it should be clear too that this scanning is not in any way intimidating, or challenging. During their play, Sue hardly removes her eyes from him, but her gaze is at all times gentle, amused, supportive and encouraging. We know too well from our own experience, the way in which we may lose or overlook the necessity to do this in our work. Again, it may be the result of our loss of the expectation that our students/clients are going to become communicators. On the other hand, we may simply become jaded and de-motivated by our very difficult work. The result for our students and clients may be a corresponding lack of motivation, since they may have been giving us all sorts of signals in their view, but we have not been watching sensitively enough to pick them up.

We don't do enough adjusting to our students/clients – joining them in 'their little world'

Sue is so sensitive about the extent to which she recognises what are, in effect, Thomas' frailties. He is not experienced and sophisticated in the sense that she is. If asked to do anything too much removed from that with which he is familiar and comfortable, he becomes distressed, and this will affect his ability to learn. She has no hesitation about doing things on his terms. She carries out this activity with him when he is clearly feeling good, and in a place where he feels comfortable. She also joins him emotionally and intellectually, adjusts herself to be someone who is meaningful and attractive to him. Everything she does with him is referenced to a minute by minute assessment of how he is feeling.

Do we do this for our students and clients whose understandings of what is going on around them are limited, maybe even more limited than Thomas'? So frequently, we suggest, our workplaces do not enable staff to do this. Someone who prefers to be head down, rocking in the corner, may do so because what is happening in the rest of the room is too complex and anxiety-provoking. Forcing that person, for instance, to sit with the group at a table produces distress which we may then describe as challenging behaviour, which in turn has to be dealt with. We find this notion of going and joining them in their little world, geographically, intellectually and emotionally to be an appropriate attitude for work with people who have limited understandings. It must be common sense that the ones who do the adjusting should be the ones who are more experienced and confident. Once security and relationship are established in this way, we may, as Sue does, suggest further, new experiences based on that security and relationship.

Our styles of teaching and management often rely on too much use of dominance and compulsion
Once again let's be clear that in putting this argument, we are not advocating in any sense complete laissez-faire, letting our students/clients do whatever they wish, not having controls, checks, boundaries and so on. Our point is that, often quite understandably, we may resort to methods which strive to achieve control. In doing this, they may have the effect of suppressing production of new behaviours and of de-motivating the student/client from participating. Lack of initiative on the part of the learner is always a potential side effect of teaching and developmental approaches which are too rigidly planned and delivered, with what is to be learnt precisely prescribed and targeted.

We come here also to a discussion concerning the difference between participation and compliance. Participation is different from, and better than compliance. Many practitioners in our work obtain compliance and call it participation. It isn't. Participation is an active, voluntary, constructive step on the part of the learner, compliance is doing what you are told to do. There are enough occasions in our work when getting compliance is all that can be done in order to manage situations, but we should be aware of the difference between that and proper participation. Let's make available a similar, or preferably greater number of potential situations for true participation. A simple way of thinking about and planning activities, which we have used, is to consider whether the activity is something that you are going to do with the student/client, or do *to* or *at* the student/client.

Consider the extent to which Sue is getting participation from Thomas, the amount of time and space she makes available with flexible use of her behaviour, for his contributions and explorations. He is active, mostly leading, powerful even. All of the activity is taking place within a situation which is controlled and structured, but controlled and structured to provide security and encouragement. Isn't this what we desire for our students/clients?

Unfortunately, we meet practitioners in our work, and they are a powerful minority everywhere, who do not have the ability to do things for, or with the students/clients on their terms. In fact, these practitioners may even have the attitude to life that it is wrong for the students/clients to have things on their terms, and that they will learn and progress better by being treated very forcefully and told what to do at all times. Naturally, we hope that those practitioners will be reading this book too.

In our work it is so difficult to obtain quality one-to-one time
We will discuss approaches to facilitating good quality one-to-one time by use of room management systems in more detail in chapter four. For the moment we must acknowledge that in the hurly burly of, for instance, a day centre, it can be so difficult to get the sort of peace and quiet that Sue has created in order to give Thomas this experience. We cannot suggest strategies to the reader which will fully overcome this apparent difficulty, though it does not have to be an absolute block to making progress with a student/client. Special schools tend to be better equipped with human resources than facilities for adults, but we have nonetheless had teachers complain that it is not possible to engineer good quality one-to-one time in their classroom. We suggest that it almost always is possible, but that achieving it may be through taking some pragmatic, even tough-seeming decisions about how you organise your use of time. A key issue here is that yes, we advocate strongly that this type of learning and progress can only happen through finely tuned attention from the staff member, but that as with Thomas, these bursts of intense interaction are mostly quite brief, a matter of minutes.

Sue has an intense emotional relationship with Thomas which we cannot emulate with students/clients
There is no doubt that the profound bond between Sue and Thomas is a contributory factor in his learning. This is a kind of 'tuning in' which we cannot hope to acquire in our work; we rightly should not try to replace parents, nor have anything like the emotional bonds which exist between Sue and Thomas. It is surely the case however, that in order to help students/clients with limited understandings, we have to work through relationship, and that relationship brings with

it some emotional bonding. It is undesirable that this bonding should be anywhere near as intense as that of Sue and Thomas, but nonetheless it is present in effective work between students/clients and carers/teachers. Furthermore, despite what we now consider somewhat old-fashioned definitions of professionalism and objectivity, it is actually desirable, we suggest, for both staff member and student/client, that we should work with a degree of emotionality.

There are two further issues here. Despite this bond between Sue and Thomas, it is the structure and principles of Sue's behaviour as a 'teacher' which are of interest to us and this style will be effective for Thomas no matter who employs it. Most of the adults he meets behave in this way, or something like it, with him, but he is not bonded to all of them. Secondly, it is probably the unavoidable truth that because we do not have deep emotional bonds with our students/clients, there are aspects of this early learning which they will miss out on. It is difficult to be precise about what these aspects are, but we must suspect that this will be a result.

The topic of emotional bonding will be discussed further in chapter five, as an important ethical issue.

Thomas is learning most effectively in a light-hearted and playful atmosphere

In the workshops which we give, we usually stress that we are not devotees of some sort of Victorian work ethic, and that such a notion is not helpful to the learning which we are seeking to promote. However, we recognise and acknowledge that there are forces acting upon most of us in our field of work which seem to impose on us something which feels like a work ethic. Which of us has not felt the need to keep everyone in a group looking as if they are fully involved and on task, long after the learners have lost the ability to continue concentrating?

So frequently also, you hear about the attitude which says that if people are having a good time then they cannot be engaged in effective learning. Our society often seems to espouse a concept of work and learning which is serious, dour, formal. Yet, here we are clearly recommending enjoyment, fun, playfulness as powerful motivators in learning, and in order to use them, we in our work somehow have to deal with the forces which seem to prevent this. We must also become familiar and confident with our ability to be adult, but nonetheless be lighthearted and playful – and this is something more that our culture often seems to frown upon. We will be referring to this issue, in various ways, throughout the rest of the book, but it is not one for which we have all the answers. Rather, we put it to the reader that we must all accept some degree of individual responsibility for arguing a case here.

Conclusion

As far as our knowledge and experience allows, we have tried to make clear the ways in which normally developing infants conduct the learning with which we are concerned – communication and sociability. We hope that as you have been reading this chapter, it has been provoking thoughts about your work, and individual students/clients and their needs.

We hope too that those practitioners reading this, whose dedication to a notion of 'age appropriateness' will usually cause them to dismiss any associations with infancy, will nonetheless have paused for thought.

We recommend consideration of Sue's style for its sheer practicality. In the next chapter we will theorise further about techniques for interacting, but in doing that, we would not wish the reader to lose sight of the fact that this approach is practical. We are not advocating a complex technology for our work; the basis of Intensive Interaction is a set of natural behaviours which most adults share.

CHAPTER 4

How to do Intensive Interaction

Introduction

We hope that the previous chapters have now made clear how knowledge about the development of the fundamentals of communication in infancy has intrigued and influenced us. To us it seemed logical that the power and potency with which adults help infants to develop, and the teaching style used, can be harnessed in the classroom. The style being used by Sue forms the basis for effective interaction sequences. There will be variations, modifications and exceptions to this style for individuals depending on their circumstances, but the principles which make up her style form the basis.

We can move on to consider work with people with learning difficulties in more detail – how to use the knowledge of the principles and structures which are involved in learning the fundamentals of communication. We are attempting to describe 'how to do it'. We hope that after reading this part of the book, practitioners from all disciplines will feel more confident and capable about setting up meaningful and progressive interaction sequences with even the most socially remote and challenging person.

The early part of this chapter has sections on observing and preparing, then getting started. There will be short written illustrations during these sections, occurring throughout the text. The rest of the chapter will use the same device as in chapter three with Thomas and Sue – a descriptive illustration of an interaction sequence will occur in episodes. After each episode we explore interaction principles, techniques and related issues in some detail. In doing this we will also offer further, shorter illustrative descriptions of work with a range of students/clients.

We commence by returning to a basic statement, or re-statement of what we are trying to do – the aims of Intensive Interaction.

Aims of using Intensive Interaction

We admit to a degree of imprecision in the way in which we have categorised the items in the lists below. There is also room for continued discussion concerning definitions of categories. For instance, we experience unease when trying to make definable distinctions between some attainments listed under 'sociability' and some listed under 'fundamental communication abilities'. There is clearly a great deal of necessary overlap between these two categories. Additionally, we cannot claim that this list is exhaustive, but we have attempted to set out the main achievements we are working towards with individuals.

To develop sociability

- To increase desire and ability to be with another person.
- To increase desire and ability to be with a group of people.
- To understand various ways in which social contact can be enjoyable.
- To tolerate and be at ease with other people's proximity.
- To develop understanding of how to use proximity.
- To take part in social interaction.
- To initiate social interaction.
- To develop sensations of emotional empathy.
- To develop understandings concerning relationships.

To develop fundamental communication abilities

- To use and understand eye contact meaningfully.
- To use and interpret facial expression.
- To use and understand body language.
- To intellectually and emotionally engage with another person.
- To take turns in exchanges of behaviour with another person.
- To exchange meaningful signals with another person.
- To develop extended communicative engagements with another person.
- To develop production of sounds.

To develop cognitive abilities

- To make distinctions between the social and the physical environment.
- To use and understand social cause and effect (the ability to affect the behaviour of others).

- To predict the behaviour of others.
- To be interested in communication.
- To explore and experiment with the social world.
- To understand social rules and principles.
- To start to explore and understand the physical world through social relationships.

To develop emotional well-being

- To diminish fear and anxiety.
- To build self-esteem.
- To know sensations of 'I am good to be with'.
- To have good feelings arising from relationships.
- To have the good feelings arising from intellectual stimulation.
- To know the joy and satisfaction arising from communicating effectively with other human beings.

To promote constructive interaction with the immediate environment

- Communicative social behaviours will become more significant and rewarding to the individual than previously more challenging ones.

To promote and teach ways of spending time, other than in organised self-involvement

- New stimulations and new abilities in relating to and understanding other people should also offer alternatives to stereotyped, ritualistic and self-stimulatory behaviours or organised self-involvement (Nind 1993).

Getting started – 'observing'

In our work there is an established tradition of observation, frequently as part of an assessment process, and it is usual to undertake an assessment before commencing a new programme of work, so that as the work develops, the progress of the student or client can be checked. We heartily advocate dedication to observation before starting work using Intensive Interaction with a person. Essential in our view, however, is that you undertake observations in two dimensions, objective and subjective. The objective, or we should say, more objective, observations are ones where you attempt to collect information, but make conscious efforts not to allow your emotions, intuitions or instincts to affect what you observe. Observations and assessments which are quantifiable, where you count behaviours, might be examples. This type of observation might also include use of published assessment regimes using a ticklist format or something similar. In the section on 'Organisational Issues' we offer advice on some of these formats. Meanwhile, in this section we will provide as much advice as we can on what we term subjective observation, where you deliberately start to observe your student/client with all of your feelings, intuitions and emotions engaged.

Get a 'feel' for the person and their behaviours

We do not recommend any particular length to an observation period. This will be influenced by factors such as the experience and ability of the member of staff, particularly in using Intensive Interaction, whether the staff team and the student/client are completely new to each other, the existing abilities of the student/client in communication and sociability. We do recommend however, that members of staff, even at this stage, adopt that posture we have discussed elsewhere – relaxed purposefulness. We strongly recommend giving yourself time; stress and urgency are the enemies of good communication. We do appreciate the sorts of pressures originating from all around us which come to bear on staff. However, there is no substitute for giving yourself time to move forward slowly, as you feel comfortable and confident with what you are doing.

This aspect of observation is about allowing yourself this time and space to observe the person with a view to getting to know, and to know about, the student/client. We think of this as developing an emotional and intuitive 'feel'. This period includes adjusting to and familiarising yourself with who that person is and what s/he likes doing. We have already set out our view that one of the first basic steps in Intensive Interaction is to have the attitude that you will accept a student/client for what s/he is at this moment in time. You may not like everything that a person does, some of it may be annoying or repelling, but the reality is that the behaviours are not likely to stop because you find them annoying or repelling. Alternatively, much of what a person does may seem bizarre or meaningless, repetitive and obsessive. Again, most of us may agree with that assessment, but those are the things which this person does, and probably likes doing and finds meaningful.

We now take the view that whatever a person does is likely to be meaningful to that person; it may simply be the case that sometimes we are not able to share that meaning and understand it. Often these feelings we have are more about our own irrational expectations that people with limited understandings will behave rationally, than about realistic expectations of what they might achieve. We should remember here too, the general principle that working with Intensive Interaction is about focussing on the promotion of positive behaviours and a positive outlook, rather than stopping negative ones.

These points are worth dwelling on as part of this observation process. The attitude that you bring to these early sessions has a direct bearing on the success of later ones. Since part of the process of Intensive Interaction is to involve yourself with the person by celebrating episodes of her/his behaviour, it is as well to pay attention here to identifying which aspects of the person you do find enjoyable. This has got to be one of the main purposes of the observation, since a primary principle of operating the approach is that of establishing mutual enjoyment. Be good to yourself here, don't wade in and force yourself to be with a person if you are still not sure that you can cope in close proximity with what the person is or does. Don't forget that how you are feeling is central to whether the activities will be effective; these interactions need both parties to be in reasonable condition emotionally. The 'professional' thing to do here is not to be tough on yourself and drive yourself to overcome what seems like your own shortcomings, but to acknowledge them and pay sensitive attention to your needs too. It is you – face, voice and body – which is the piece of equipment for the interaction sessions you are aspiring to promote.

Difficulties with accepting odd behaviour are often not so acute if the student/client is a child, particularly an infant. Adults are naturally more tolerant of strange or difficult behaviour from infants, and we tend also to find it easier to enjoy and be attracted by children generally. The other extreme is that this process of subjectively enjoying the other person can be more difficult and complex if the student/client is an adult, possibly large, hairy, smelly and equipped with habits that in the normal run of things we would find obnoxious. Even experienced staff may find that making the leap into subjective work with such a person, with its emphasis on relationship and accepting that person for what s/he is, can be daunting.

Give yourself time to start becoming familiar with signals from the student/client

Thus, give yourself time at this stage. Actually, don't rush even if you are planning work with a very cute four-year-old. Take time to situate yourself near the person for frequent observations of a few minutes duration. If the person is someone who is particularly withdrawn, or made fearful and anxious by the proximity of another person, then take this into account. Even at this stage you are starting to create the necessary trust, so your body language and use of your face should carry with it appropriate signals of reassurance and respect. Don't get too close, sit, even on the floor (it is always a good idea to have your eye line below that of a person who may be nervous or anxious). Don't stare fiercely, do relax and especially, respect and obey signals of negativity from the person. If you suddenly receive signals that you are too close, or that having you sitting there is causing anxiety, then move away, immediately. It is essential to respect the other person's feelings here, if trust and true participation are to be established.

This all makes it sound as if, for people who are truly socially withdrawn, even the early stages can be a very long drawn-out process; realistically, this is so, it just has to be accepted. Any rushing of things, imposing yourself, failing to respect the other person's feelings and preferences, merely compounds her/his difficulties. Probably, in the past, virtually all of the staff who have worked with that student/client have imposed on that sensitivity in one way or another. It is an inevitable consequence of our understandable drive to 'get this person doing things'. If you and your colleagues are now to succeed in helping this person enjoy social contact, you must be positive and sensitive in a way that previous staff may not have been. The first and foremost necessity is to recognise and respect the fact that progress may occur only with time and sensitivity.

On the other hand, the student/client may be young, little and instantly appealing, though not able to speak, make eye contact or use much facial expression. Despite limited communication ability, s/he may nonetheless be active and friendly, and come and start climbing all over you because you look safe and interesting. In this case your observation phase, despite the fact that you are deliberately taking your time, has taken on a new dimension at an early stage and there may now be a blurring of observation and getting started.

We have found that the people we have worked with vary between the two extremes we have offered as examples here. This obviously makes demands upon your ability to be flexible, and truly to meet each individual person's needs, abilities and preferences. It also means that there is no one way of getting started that we can recommend to you.

Illustration: Helga and Melanie

Helga is 26 years old. She is sitting cross-legged on a chair, rocking. She holds a pencil which she is flicking in rhythm to her rock. Her gaze is mostly fixed on the pencil, and her facial expression is grim, intense. Occasionally she glances up if a movement or minor disturbance attracts her attention. On these occasions her expression is wide-eyed, clearly anxious, ready. This is how she mostly likes to spend her day, and she likes to do it undisturbed. The space within a two-metre semi-circle of her remains startlingly clear of people, even though there are another twelve people in the large room, and eight of those are people with very active, if not challenging behaviour. However, everyone who knows Helga understands clearly that she has an 'exclusion zone' around her, of two metres. Enter it and she will become quickly fearful and aroused, with the likely result that she will spring up and hit you, open-handed, very hard, probably in the face or head. Everyone respects Helga's wishes. Caring for her is of course, anxiety-provoking for the carers because on numerous occasions, they must go near her and may suffer the consequences.

Melanie and her colleagues wish to change this. Melanie is involved in the observation period leading to full-blown attempts to help Helga with her fear and anxiety about other people and her general lack of understanding about communication. Melanie is still only observing her, not doing anything active yet, but Helga is sensitive and observant enough herself to know that this is taking place – that some new and special interest is being centred on her. Consequently part of Melanie's observation at the moment is to acknowledge with her face that she is indeed thinking about Helga and looking at her, but at the same time be reassuring – she does not stare fixedly at her, nor offer her eye contact that is intimidating, and especially, does not enter her exclusion zone yet.

Melanie crosses the room picking up a cushion along the way and walks to within ten feet of Helga, but off to her left. Her movements are smooth and slow, predictable. She murmers a warm 'Hello Helga,' as Helga looks up and checks her, before placing her cushion on the floor and smoothly letting herself down onto it.

Helga's anxiety level goes up a bit – her rate of rock increases and she checks her every few seconds – so Melanie bum-slides herself a few feet further away. Melanie remains in her position for ten minutes. She makes no secret of the fact that she is interested in Helga, but she keeps her gaze, her facial expression warm and mild. If she makes eye contact during one of Helga's checks, she widens her eyes and smiles reassuringly, may even murmur something comforting. If Helga starts to look more uncomfortable because they are meeting eyes, she removes direct eye contact, but keeps her face turned in her general direction.

Throughout, even whilst she changes position to keep herself comfortable, Melanie's body language signals relaxation and confidence. She knows how to use her body language. She is practised at it, and she and her colleagues discuss this aspect of their work and observe each other. Melanie's posture is turned toward Helga, open, available and reassuring.

Melanie and her colleagues have already been doing this observation several times daily for six weeks, and are prepared to carry on doing it for some time yet, until they feel confident that they can move on.

You may already know your student/client quite well

Many staff reading this, may find our suggestions helpful and be thinking particularly about students/clients they are already working with. They may be working with people with whom they have already established a good relationship, but wish to assist them to move further on with their ability to relate and communicate. In such circumstances, a period of observation may be shorter, perhaps even not necessary; the foundations for working through Intensive Inter-action may already exist. These are matters of judgement for individual staff and staff teams. On the whole, however, we would still advocate a period of relaxed preparation, together with all of our recommendations about taking your time, rather than wading in enthusiastically tomorrow because you have read this and it feels like a good idea.

Additionally, even if you have established a relationship with the person you have in mind, which feels good and effective, it may still happen that working in this way will cause changes and adjustments to that relationship. The degree to which you are intending to share power and control with the student/client during activities is an example of a principle of the approach which may well affect your existing working relationship. With all the best intentions and sensi-tivity in the world, staff in schools, day centres and residential settings tend to be more dominating and driving during activities than is required in Intensive Interaction. This point was demonstrated over and over at Harperbury School, where many of the students were known to one of us for years before working through Intensive Interaction was introduced. Former knowledge of individual students turned out, in reality, to be skimpy and superficial, and there was a salutary realisation that with many students we had simply not made a relationship of any quality or meaning.

The student/client may already have some confidence in encountering people

We have already stated that our use of the crude generalisation 'pre-verbal' covers a multitude of abilities and orientations to the world. The example we have given of Helga, is of a person who is withdrawn from other people in the extreme. We have known many students/clients who have plenty of confidence about you being near them, sharing space and physical contact, but perhaps little actual idea what to do with you. Some may even demand social contact from you, but still clearly need to find out more about it and practise the abilities that go with it. This may make for a blurring of the observation period and the stage of making 'access' which we will come to next. Thus, you may be in the position of trying to give yourself your time and space to observe and know the person in a relaxed way, and every time you are in that person's vicinity, she/he comes over and flops on you, or takes you by the hand to the cupboard, or bombards you with seemingly meaningless repetitive utterances from six inches away. There are two possible ways of handling this; one is to somehow contrive circumstances which truly enable you to be anonymous and out of contact, though your ability to find out about a person is reduced the further away you are; the other is to accept that your observation and accessing periods have truly blurred together and your observations have become not just subjective, but quite active as well.

Illustration: Diana, Barbara and Pete

Diana is five years old. As far as can be assessed, she cannot see anything but bright light. She is very active and exploratory, though with the caution of much experience of hard surfaces and sharp edges. She uses speech, not to the level of ability of an average five year old, but in short, staccato phrases, and the occasional short sentence. This use of speech is also repetitive, sometimes rhythmic and mostly does not have anything to do with what is happening to her at that moment.

Barbara and Diana are on a crash-mat in their classroom. Pete enters, exchanging hellos, and immediately gets down on the floor next to the crash-mat. He watches Barbara and Diana for some time. They are slowly and gently romping and there is lots of physical contact – Diana crawls and rolls freely on Barbara – but also lots of face-to-face contact. Barbara and Diana press faces together often, and they frequently exchange utterances and laughter in this position. Pete watches Barbara carefully. She is extremely responsive to Diana, no utterance is left without a behaviour from Barbara in return, and Barbara frequently repeats these responses in varying tones and with laughter and rhythm. She also uses pats, shakes and jiggles on Diana's shoulders and back, simultaneously as she speaks, in a sort of rhythmic emphasis. Even if Diana's utterance is completely without relevance to what they are doing, Barbara goes with it and comments. There are also pauses, some of them long, particularly when it is Diana's turn in an exchange. Again, Pete notes that Barbara is very good at holding herself back in order to allow this pause.

Pete watches Diana's body and face intently. He suspects that he might soon have an opportunity to play with Diana if he is lucky, and he wants to be as tuned-in as possible. He reminds himself, trains himself for a few seconds, not to rely on eye contact or facial expression. Instead, he notes the way that Diana holds her head, particularly an inclination she uses when she is thinking during burst-pause.

Gradually, Barbara draws Pete in, mentioning the visitor, asking him to throw in short contributions to the game. Again, Pete reminds himself to make himself relevant to what Diana says. Diana's face is turned toward Pete now, and she is quiet, listening for his occasional words. She crawls a short distance and reaches out to Pete, though she has maintained contact with Barbara with the other hand. Barbara is providing further security with soothing voice. After a few minutes, Diana abruptly decides that Pete is okay, that the situation is secure with Barbara nearby, releases Barbara completely and takes hold of Pete's head with both hands. 'My ears,' she says four times, twisting Pete's ears and pressing her nose against his.

Observing: Summary

- Subjective and more objective observations are both recommended.
- Subjective observations should allow you to get an intuitive 'feel' for the student/client and the way they behave.
- Give time to the observation period – there is no rush.
- Look for things about the student/client which you enjoy.
- Don't drive yourself to work intensively with the student/client in ways with which you are not comfortable.
- Even during observation, pay special attention to reassuring the student/client with your presence – your face, body language, voice.
- Some students/clients are at ease with social contact straightaway and blur the observation and access periods.
- Look carefully for signalling behaviours which the student/client uses.
- Train yourself not to be put off by, for instance, a lack of facial expressions.

Getting started – 'Accessing'

What do we mean by 'accessing'?

As we were developing and thinking about the approach, we sometimes found ourselves searching for language to describe what we were doing or what was happening to us. We cannot remember exactly when, early in our work, we began to use this term 'accessing'. Presumably someone borrowed it from computer terminology in order to describe the sensation of getting through to a student/client, establishing mutuality with a person who was formerly remote from social contact. At first we thought about the concept in a rather one-sided fashion. It was as though we had made a breakthrough, at last got to the person, connected with them in a more profound way. As we have worked and thought more, however, we have realised that it is not sufficient to think in terms of accessing merely as we, the staff, doing things to get through to the learner. The concept is equally as much about doing sensitive things to make ourselves available to access from the student/client – enabling a two-way process.

With this increasingly clear way of thinking about the first stages of starting to interact successfully, we became more effective at doing it. Thinking about access as a one-way thing which we do *to* the learner, disguises the reality that much of the responsibility for a person being socially remote lies with the rest of us, particularly those of us who are near the person every day. It may be our failure to be sensitive enough to that person's needs and understandings, to picture the world from her/his point of view, and particularly our failure to allow ourselves gradually to learn how to interact effectively with that individual, which is the most powerful factor in the withdrawal. In other words, some of the person's learning difficulties are not only within the student/client, but are also within us, the staff. Our behaviour has not become tuned in to the communicative ability of that person. Thinking of access as a two-way process helps us to accept fully our responsibility to modify our own communicative behaviour to the individual's ability to comprehend. It also helps us to recognise the degree to which we must make ourselves available – face, voice, body and personality. Implied, too, is a change in our use of language; making access *to* the student/client should be replaced by making access *with*.

Furthermore, accessing is a loosely definable term to cover that period when it is felt that mutuality, making contact, establishing games and routines, sharing behaviour and joint focus, all these events or sensations, are being established. All of the individuals we work with are just that, individual. Making access feels different with all of those individuals and their differing abilities, likes and dislikes. We have emphasised the extent to which use of the term pre-verbal in actuality describes people within a very wide spectrum of ability. The degree to which access is readily available will depend in part on the degree to which the student/client is already able to use basic social abilities, and in part on the ability of the member of staff to be sensitive, to look for and read signals, to make her/himself available and to signal in return, to be lighthearted, encouraging, participative.

Sometimes making access can be rapid, sometimes it may mean a year or more of painstaking work with a particularly withdrawn person. There was one student with whom we attempted to make access over a period of four years without apparent success. We held numerous discussions to evaluate our efforts and to re-think what we were doing. We constantly asked ourselves whether the reality was that the degree of the young man's organic damage was such that he simply would not be able to relate in the way we desired for him. Always we came to the conclusion that the problem was probably with us – we simply still had not got it right for him, had not yet sensitively tuned in to him – and continued our work on that assumption. We did not succeed, but we have subsequently learnt that staff who came after us, still using Intensive Interaction, have gone some way to achieving what we could not.

Illustration: Richard and Dave

Richard is five years old. He does not speak. He has use of a range of noises, but they do not seem to have communicative functions, and they do not sound like words. He does not walk, but in recent months he has developed into a competent bum-shuffler. Richard does not seem to use a wide variety of facial expression; above his mouth his face remains strangely static, his eyes do not quite point in the same direction, and he does not blink as often as most of the rest of us. This immediately means that attempting to interact with him can be a difficult experience for a sophisticated communicator. The sort of visual feedback we rely on from face and eyes is not given by Richard, or to be more accurate, is subtle and different. Richard needs to learn more about being with other people. He likes people, but he often seems more interested in things and will play with and manipulate toys and other objects for long periods, becoming deeply absorbed.

Dave is trying to get to know Richard. He wants to help him to learn more about communication. This is one of their first sessions together, still very early stages. Dave is a tall man, and has sensitively got himself down on the floor resting on one elbow, near where Richard sits rotating a toy truck, rocking his body slowly. The effect is that Dave's eye-line is actually below Richard's. Dave has composed his body language and posture to be simultaneously relaxed, attentive and available. He has learnt this piece of body language from many such experiences, and from watching colleagues' skilful use of body language. In his school the staff talk about it as the 'available' look.

Dave is two or three feet away from Richard, which seems fine for him, though at times he gives the impression of having forgotten about Dave altogether. Now and again though, Dave identifies a minimal sideways glance from Richard – as if he is just checking.

For some minutes nothing much more happens. Richard continues to play – to manipulate, shake and bang the various toys and objects strewn around him. Dave remains relaxed and available, not motionless, not silent either – he occasionally laughs gently, makes a murmured comment, or lets out an 'oh!' of surprise drama if, for instance, Richard drops something loudly. On one of these occasions, Richard is momentarily captivated by Dave's behaviour and turns his face fully toward Dave, a clear smile forming. Dave seizes the moment and slowly leans his face closer to Richard's at the same level, full eye contact, beaming pleasure, laughing gently. Richard enjoys this situation for a few moments, his enjoyment turning into an infant-like hand-flapping motion which moves to a rhythmic slap on Dave's forearm. Richard is now watching his hand rather than Dave's face. 'Oh-oh-oh-oh' says Dave in play-pain, but in synchronised rhythm with Richard's movements.

Thinking about and preparing for accessing

Once again we return to one of the messages of this book: take your time. Always give your student/client time, but be good to yourself, give yourself time too, don't rush anything, particularly at this stage, this is the difficult bit. You need to be as relaxed and at ease as possible at all times in order to do Intensive Interaction, but especially now, crucially if you are having a go for the first time. We do appreciate the pressures that may be associated with managers, headteachers, parents, National Curriculum, I.P.P.s, other students/clients, the inadequacy of your workspace and so on, but there is no substitute for doing everything at the right tempo. If you succeed in achieving access with the person you wish to help, one of the things you will not be doing is driving everything along at your preferred tempo. Instead, things will start happening because you have sensitised to the preferred tempo of life of your student/client. For some people that is a very slow and tentative pace; appreciate it and even enjoy it.

Take care not to do too much in interactions

Remember also, that when staff are starting to use Intensive Interaction for the first time, the most frequently-seen mistake is that they do too much in an interaction. We definitely include ourselves in this comment. It is understandable that in our enthusiasm to use our behaviour naturally, to have mutual pleasure and give fun, we end up bombarding the student/client with our own behaviour. The main point of the interaction is to give the student/client space, time and opportunity to develop their own behaviour. For us, even when we were aware of this problem and were purposely attempting to relax more and bring down the quantity of the behaviours we used, it was still problematic. One effect is that you may succeed in controlling yourself, but still have tense, alert body language, responding urgently to the student/clients' behaviours – giving the impression that you are hovering and waiting to pounce.

It can take time to get this right. A good working principle is to simply relax yourself as much as possible before starting, though we know how difficult this can be. If you can bear to watch yourself on video, this helps enormously in understanding the messages that your posture, body language and behaviour are transmitting to the other person. At any stage during the work with an individual, if things are not going well, it is worth asking whether the student/client is being overwhelmed by the behaviour of interactive partners. Doing a bit less in an interaction is always an available option.

Don't expect rapid developments
It is worth emphasising to yourself and remembering at all times, that even once you have established access, it is extremely unlikely that any developments will occur at the speed which they do for Thomas and other infants; far from it, in fact. You may be surprised at the speed with which things may develop with a particular student/client, but that tremendous burst of energy and enthusiasm which Thomas shows in his development is unlikely to be present. We need to remember and understand this at all times, because there may be many occasions, especially in the early stages, when we have to do some compensating for the fact that we are not getting the feedback from the other person which we may need or desire. We have to be ultra-sensitive to minimal signals, to signals which may be atypical. We need also to find ways to be relaxed during long periods when, even though some sort of progress may be evident, the student/client is still not rewarding us emotionally for the effort we put in. Even when staff become experienced, it can still be the case that our own desires for progress to be quicker or different, will lead us into periods of despondency.

Other examples of making access with students/clients

Robert
This young man in his mid-twenties spent much of his time seemingly self-absorbed – rocking, scratching and rubbing himself rhythmically,

mostly whilst staring into space. Sometimes he seemed to enter a happier mood where laughs, smiles and hand-clapping were present, sometimes seemingly in response to something happening nearby, often for no identifiable reason.

Access with Robert was achieved after a long period of preparation and indeed, trial and error with him. In the end success was brought about by two members of staff using a very literal interpretation of the principle of joining him in his own world. Over a long period of time, Robert became comfortable with the regular proximity of staff who were just near him, not imposing or expecting anything particularly. Gradually, mildly, the staff imitated, reflected and joined in with his rocking and other behaviours, using gentle running commentary, clear signals of enjoyment, and responding especially as Robert signalled awareness or pleasure at what the member of staff was doing. After a few weeks of this part of the process, the regularity of moments of full eye contact, the increase in rate of rock and smiling in response to something the member of staff did, and a particular inclination of head and shoulders taken as a 'more' signal, indicated that the basis for progress was established.

Julia

Julia was 24. She had lived in a long-stay hospital for many years and seemingly, could see or hear little or nothing. She spent much of her time involved in her own rhythms: knuckles jammed into her eyeballs, half-bent posture, bobbing her head up and down between her knees whilst grunting in time; sometimes sitting on a chair, rocking, hand over mouth, whilst making a repetitive 'ha' sound into the palm of her hand; sometimes upright, silent, fist clenched so that her thumb tapped endlessly into the crevice between nose and eyeball. She never smiled or changed facial expression, she did not seek other people and her body felt hard and resistant to a touch.

Establishing use of touch was the priority for staff. A long period followed where staff made it an ongoing effort to give Julia many brief, but warm and meaningful daily touches. Gradually it became apparent that Julia was softer and more welcoming to these touches, until gradually it was possible to get her to sustain physical contact and even 'snuggle in'. From there romping games evolved. Two particular games developed where Julia needed to give 'more' signals to keep the game going. In one, staff would join in with Julia's rhythmic grunting, making their noises into her hand or on her cheek. This would transform into turn-taking and tension/expectancy, where the member of staff would pause teasingly, with Julia's role quickly becoming to provide the prod or squeeze as a signal for more. A similar burst-pause game was established involving a full scale romp, with Julia quickly getting the hang of the squeeze signal which would bring her a warm, laughing cuddle.

Stephen

A person who was quite resistant to eye contact, Stephen liked his own space with no-one else too near. His response to proximity, however, was usually anguished cries and flight, rather than violence. The new and careful period of observation by staff had established the frequency with which, even though he rejected facial regard from others, Stephen none-theless looked at other people's faces when they were not looking at him, a sort of 'just checking'.

One of the staff team created an activity to make use of this. Penny would sit within range of Stephen, give lots of full, friendly face, with body language directed toward him, signalling friendly availability. Stephen kept his face averted to the wall, fiddling endlessly with small objects. Penny simply maintained her position quietly, holding her friendly look toward Stephen. Every now and then, Stephen flicked a quick look in her direction, just checking of course, but Penny would seize and celebrate the moment: 'Hi!' she would say laughingly, leaning forward slightly. Even during the early stages of this, Penny noticed that Stephen was starting to check her more often, and then to hold her eyes for just a little longer. It then became apparent that Stephen was starting to become interested in the possi-bilities of this game. There seemed to be a realisation that he could exert some amusing control over another person, and smiles became apparent as he engineered the look and the 'Hi!' from Penny. This smile in turn became a further behaviour for Penny to celebrate and join in with, so that within a couple of weeks of introducing the game, they were holding mutual gaze and experiencing mutual pleasure.

Accessing: summary

- Accessing is a term used to describe the process of staff and stu-dent/client creating the first mutual experiences.
- A person may be remote from social contact partly because other people do not tune in to her/his behaviour.
- The length of the accessing period varies with individual abilities and preferences.
- Making access can take time, and a relaxed approach is necessary.
- Many staff make the mistake in the early stages of doing too much in interactions.
- Don't expect rapid developments or progress at first.
- You can tune in to any aspect of a student/client's behaviour to start interactions.

Accessing and then establishing sequences – some general staff abilities and attitudes

In this section we offer some important general abilities and attitudes that we have identified amongst staff, together with advice and detail as to how these abilities and attitudes affect Intensive Interaction.

Much that we offer here leads on from the practical abilities which Sue demonstrated for us in the previous chapter, and we do suggest that referring back to Sue and Thomas at various times will be helpful to the reader. Further illustrations of interactions will be provided as we proceed.

We find it difficult truly to distinguish between staff abilities and attitudes. For instance, the ability to be playful could probably be described as a set of separate skills which we could identify and list. More important, however, in this example, is the possession of the attitude that you are prepared to be playful. Without this attitude, there is not much possibility that the skills will develop. In our minds therefore, there are frequently areas where attitudes and abilities overlap, or even where a particular attitude is crucially a part of the ability to do something.

As may be seen in the title of this section, we introduce the notion of 'establishing' – the sensation that activities with an individual have moved on from being in the access stage and are now established, with the way ahead to continuing developments available.

The inner switch

The inner switch is a working concept which we developed at Harperbury School to describe an important aspect of activity for the staff member. This concept relates to the extent to which, when interacting, we are using either natural, intuitive behaviours, or a rational and intellectual deployment of the principles of Intensive Interaction as we offer them in this book. This has been the topic of much discussion and debate for us, and the inquiries we have carried out with other staff indicate, not unnaturally, that the best work has a judicious blend of natural responding and intellectual judgement. However, all staff consulted have indicated that the best way to work is to tune in and let yourself go; thinking too hard minute by minute tends to diminish your spontaneity and ability to use intuition, and interfere with your signals of enjoyment to the student/client. With infants this is rarely a problem. It is well established that the very physical characteristics of infants make most of us extremely responsive to them. We can't help ourselves from producing the natural behaviour style which is right for them – they 'trigger' adults with the way they look.

However, many of our students/clients will not have these physical characteristics, in fact the reality is that many of them may not appeal to us in this way at all. This is where the inner switch comes in.

Somehow or other, we have to work on ourselves to help us to enjoy the presence and behaviour of even the lest appealing of our students/clients. The ability to achieve this feat depends, of course, on all sorts of things. In part, it is to do with the basic attitudes of the individual member of staff; we make no attempt in this book to offer a method for changing these basic attitudes. It depends also on the degree to which the type of subjective observation we have recommended is carried out, and the extent to which this assists a member of staff to find attributes of an individual particularly appealing and enjoyable. Ultimately also, it will depend on experience; once you have experienced the use of this 'inner switch' with a number of different individual students/clients, it simply becomes easier to put yourself into this natural, relaxed mode of thought and behaviour.

Good teamwork assists with this issue. We have found that staff always find it helpful if they are able to freely and honestly discuss matters such as the way that they find some of the behaviours of a particular student/client to be repellent.

The body language which signals you are 'available'

We have referred many times to this notion of being 'available' to your student/client, and somehow signalling it, making it clear. It will re-occur as an issue throughout the rest of this chapter.

This ability is first and forcmost about having the attitude that you are prepared to do this, to make yourself available on their terms. It is then a matter of posture, use of space and proximity, together with those magic ingredients, body language and facial expression.

Our knowledge of human experience has not yet reached a stage where we can precisely and scientifically choreograph people's use of body language. We all have a great deal of use and understanding of body language – much more than any of us can express in words. Such knowledge is sometimes referred to as 'tacit' – unspoken or silent, inferred, unconscious. There are some broad general 'rules' which have been identified – the use of aggression signals among humans and other animals is understood to some extent. There is also, for instance, scientific work now being done on the tell-tale body language people adopt when they are not telling the truth. But all of this is still fairly crude compared to the immense subtlety with which we actually communicate non-verbally. If readers are interested in pursuing these topics further then there are good standard works by Argyle (1975) and Bull (1983) and popularised work by Marsh (1988).

The problem we have here is that despite this lack of conscious knowledge about body language, we wish to use it in highly skilled ways in our work, and to communicate some of that ability in the written and spoken word. Skilful, even knowing use of body language is central to effective Intensive Interaction. It is frustrating that some people are obviously so much more naturally good at body language than others. Even when you know it and observe them, it can still be difficult to put into words what it is that they are doing which is so different and so magical and effective.

Adopting the 'available' look is a case in point. Here is our attempt to describe some gross rules for the 'look'. The body is turned toward the other person, the shoulders are down and relaxed; body slightly turned rather than directly face-to-face and chest-to-chest. Legs are positioned in a relaxed way whether standing, sitting or lying; the head is tilted slightly to one side or slightly back or both. There is frequently a gentle, subtle imitation of the other person's posture, for instance leg or arm positioning; face inclined toward the other person; facial expression open, no frown, eyes wide but mild, slightly questioning and waiting. With this description however, is the constant knowledge that there are other things happening and being communicated, which are not describable.

A further problem is that though we can describe what this body language looks like on the outside, offering this description may not be the best way to teach it to people who do not have it. It may be more effective to help people to have the appropriate thoughts and attitudes on the inside, the mental processes which will have the effect of generating this body language on the outside.

It may be asked why we do not have better solutions to this question after the years of work in our school. One answer is that when it came to selecting new staff, their effective use of non-verbal communication was one of the prime attributes for which we looked and selected. In this way we ended up with a group of people working together who were good, natural users of body language. Another is that though we did indeed tussle with this question for some years, we did not come up with solutions any more scientific than that which we have already related.

Nonetheless, by one means or another, we have found that staff can develop their skills in this area. One of the main methods of staff development is a 'gentle apprenticeship' – working alongside and carefully observing members of staff who already have the ability to use body language knowingly. We recommend too that you can develop these abilities by keeping use of body language and associated issues in the forefront of your daily routine. Think about these issues often and discuss them regularly amongst your team.

Observing each other carefully as much as possible is very helpful. Discuss specific moments when body language was clearly significant. Try to analyse what was effective and why, however difficult it might be to find the right words. It might be helpful also to develop some language by which you and your team can describe specific uses of body language, for example, our term, the 'available' look.

Watching yourselves on video is a powerful and helpful medium in this area. One thing to remember is that you know less about how you look, than you do about anyone else. Use of body language is a prime working ability for staff in our work, whether or not they use Intensive Interaction. We should pay maximum attention to it as a topic at all times, despite the difficulties of doing this.

Join the student/client in their little world – especially their favoured place

We have seen, in the previous chapter, the extent to which this concept was an important one for Sue with Thomas. The illustrative descriptions of staff making access with Robert, Julia and Stephen also show staff operating this simple, basic principle, and at risk of labouring this point, we feel that it cannot be emphasised enough. Our way of describing it, 'join them in their little world' is intentionally simple. We mean do that – empathise as much as you can emotionally, psychologically, intellectually. We mean also that you literally join them geographically in their favoured place where they feel most comfortable and at ease. In the early stages, the comfort and sense of security of the student/client is crucial. We need to do as much as is possible to make sure that they are in an agreeable mood before interacting.

In geographical terms therefore, this means resisting the urge to compel the person to come to the table or a seemingly better part of the room, but instead recognising that you must fit in with that person. In our work we have experience of establishing access with people in a variety of different ways in different locations. Here are some further examples:

Adrian
Adrian is a young man with a diagnosis of autism. He is rarely motivated

to do anything, preferring to remain in a corner of the room or out in the corridor, massively involved in his own stereotyped behaviours. The staff working with him spent months going to his corner to be there with him and establish interacting routines and relationship there. The interactions with him were primarily based on staff pleasurably joining in with his hand-flapping and flicking. At an early stage Adrian signalled enjoyment of this and responded to the game potential offered by the staff attention. As the repertoire of interactions was established, and trust formed, Adrian was able to feel more secure about moving and working in other contexts away from his corner.

Ben

Eight years old, very handsome and charming, Ben's appearance is beguiling. Prolonged sensitive observation revealed little true social contact, though plenty of smiles and laughs as he rushed endlessly round the room, over and under furniture. Lesley is one of the care staff at the respite care hostel. She recognised that for Ben, joining him in his little world meant joining in with what he did nearly all of the time. Luckily, Lesley is in her early twenties and fit. Access and establishment of interaction was achieved through Lesley joyfully joining in with Ben's activity, giving running commentary, using lots of touch – hugs and pats, picking him up, but especially finding pauses and moments of eye contact and facial regard to celebrate and hold.

Bernard

More than all other places, Bernard would rush to be in the sand-pit. There he would sit for hours if allowed, totally self absorbed, allowing sand to trickle endlessly from one hand through the fingers of the other. He might become distressed when taken from the sand-pit. However, this became one of the places where staff started to make themselves available to Bernard. They would take it in turns to spend short sessions sitting there with him (if he allowed it that day). They would simply join in with him, putting their hands into his focus and trickling sand too, laughing gently, giving running commentary.

The ability to be a playful adult

In our experience, adults vary enormously in their individual abilities to be playful, and in their attitudes toward play amongst adults. We have never had difficulty in indulging the playful side of our natures, and see no problem in all adults indulging a need to play and to derive benefit and fulfilment from doing so. However, many people do not share this view, and may maintain that play is something that should be left behind with childhood. It may also be asserted that encouraging adults with learning difficulties to play or be playful is disrespectful - it is perhaps, not age-appropriate. Naturally, we do not agree with these views. In the next chapter we offer an extended review of notions of age-appropriateness, but in any event, we cannot accept that play is left behind with childhood. Robin Skynner once wrote: 'It is never to late to have a happy childhood' (Skynner 1990) and he included in this statement the inference that it is perfectly acceptable for adults to indulge their child-like instincts and qualities.

Our work has shown us emphatically that playfulness, lighthear-tedness, and the relaxed responsiveness that goes with these postures, is so effective for reaching those people who are difficult to reach. We do urge all staff to find the playfulness within themselves and use it carefully and thoughtfully in their work. Once again we reiterate that this does not mean having a lack of direction, failing to describe boundaries, nor allowing our students/clients to do what they like. Nor does it imply not having programmes, structures, assessments and so on; you can have all of these things and still be playful and lighthearted with a purpose.

Any behaviour has potential as a focus for interaction

When observing someone for the first time, with a view to attempting to make access, it is often encouraging if that person indulges in a great deal of stereotyped behaviour. Our sensation is that the person at least has some well-established behaviours which are significant to her/him and which we can celebrate. In contrast there may be a need for finely detailed sensitivity with a person who has such physical disabilities that there are few visible behaviours on the outside.

So frequently we have found that the way to become mutual with a person is to involve yourself warmly in the repetitive activities or behaviours which are clearly important to that person. This view is at odds with some past 'wisdoms', that things like stereotyped behaviours are 'unnatural', or 'inappropriate' and should, above all else, be stopped or discouraged. We would agree that in the long run we desire that a person interacts with the immediate environment more purposefully than by, for instance, constant rocking or hand-flapping. For the moment, however, the best way to achieve this aim is to start by accepting the person for what she/he is, in fact by enjoying this person and giving 'you are good to be with' signals. Our experience has been that as the person gains more confidence and knowledge about interac-ting with other human beings, there is actually a lessening of stereotyped behaviours. (You may like to refer to chapter five for further discussion on topics concerning Organised Self-Involvement.)

We have already mentioned this point of course, but we will do so once more and take it a little further. Some of the behaviours our students/clients develop seem extraordinary to us – purposeless, meaningless, dull, repetitive. We suggest that there are two issues here which are crucial for staff to bear in mind at all times.

First, those seemingly undesirable behaviours are unlikely to go away simply because you want them to. Stopping them – by targeting them for modification or eradication – will occur, if at all, only after lengthy and arduous work, often involving a great deal of negative interaction. In our experience also, unless you do something about the drive which causes the person to have that behaviour, there is a good likelihood that a new 'inappropriate' behaviour will replace the one you stopped.

Second, whatever else they are, those are the behaviours which are important to that person, an expression of that person's state of being – her/his understandings, communications, emotional life – that person's way of dealing with the world. If we truly are to use the concept of joining them in their little world, then the behaviours which make up part of that world should firstly be respected.

There are some cautions and exceptions to this. We have been asked things like: 'What about someone who, for instance, masturbates all the time, do you join in with that, or imitate it?' No, of course not. Remember another principle for staff is only to do those things with which you are comfortable. It is essential to safeguard your own emotional well-being, otherwise you will be merely an anxious interactor. Let's go back to one of the purposes of the early observations of a person – finding things about that person which you do like or enjoy, or at least do not find off-putting. Even people with the most distasteful of habits inevitably do something else which you may be able to enjoy and participate with.

As for stereotyped behaviour, it is far from a rule that you celebrate and join in with it. Joining in is one of the options you have open to you. Some people (Adrian, described earlier, is a good example) seem to think it is brilliant if you signal this pleasure and participation in what they do. Some other people we have met may not enjoy it at all if you do this. It is one of the things to find out – sensitively of course.

There are also some behaviours which may at first not give you time for relaxed long-term work. Very severe self-injury for instance, may cause you to make urgent, even forceful interventions. Once again though, we stress the need to give maximum regard to improvements in that person's sense of emotional well-being. Severe self-injury may be seen as a graphic outward demonstration of a person's inner state.

The attitude we recommend is that it is unlikely that a behaviour which a student/client produces is meaningless to that person, however meaningless it seems to the rest of us. Unless there are good, compelling reasons to look upon a particular behaviour as something to which we will not be responding, then all of the person's behaviour offers opportunities for us to get our responses in.

One of the important aspects of this principle which needs to be remembered, is that these celebrations of behaviours, joining in with them and achieving mutuality with your student/client, are a starting point. Interactions may be established, for instance, partly by means of joining in with a person's stereotyped behaviours. However the student/client now has at least one member of staff finely tuned in. S/he then has opportunities to learn and rehearse some more sophisticated knowledge and abilities about being with other people to which access had previously not been available. Examples of new and significant things might be using eye contact or enjoying touch. The interactions will move on to use these new patterns of behaviour for the focus of what takes place. To some extent the original celebrations of behaviour may be retained as part of the repertoire, but they will now be that – part of a wider repertoire.

Intensive Interaction sequences have no particular sensation of task

We know from personal experience that this issue is particularly testing for staff in our work. There is a long history of working through the setting of tasks, or through reaching precisely described objectives. This is an important issue which once again, we will deal with in more detail in Chapter 5. For the moment though, it is important to realise that the intention during an interaction sequence is to make yourself available to the learner so that a process of beneficial experiences can take place. The learning takes place because of this process, rather than because some goal or objective has been achieved during the session. Certainly in the early stages, it is helpful to clear your mind of any sensation that you want the learner to achieve something particular during the session. Your own needs, even your strong emotional desire that this person will make progress, can become a task to the learner. You might therefore find that this person is doing all sorts of things to perform, to please you and fulfil your needs, rather than you using your sensitive and skilled availability to explore her/his own abilities.

Knowing what are good interactive games

On hearing that we were writing this book, one or two people asked us if we would be including lists of good interactive games which they could use. The answer is no, not really. We hope that the book will make quite clear what good games are like, and how to get them, but that will not be done through offering lists.

We offer all sorts of examples of effective activities throughout the book, but if there were great lists of 'good games' one of the consequences would be that some staff will work *from* the lists *to* the student/client. That is the wrong way round. One of the main ideas is to develop activities based on what is happening during the interaction sequence, especially by following, celebrating and developing the behaviour of the learner. That is how good games arise. Working from the lists would mean the control and power in the activity residing, as usual, more with the member of staff than the student/client.

Of course, over time and with experience, all staff develop some idea of certain things which work for most people. Individual staff definitely develop a preference for certain sorts of activities at which they personally seem to be particularly effective. The overriding principle, though, is to be flexible and responsive enough to develop practically anything into games.

If the student/client is not in the mood, this should be respected

This can be hard for staff who are accustomed to organising the workplace so that students/clients get on with activities whether they like it or not. Again, in our work we all have become so accustomed to working through tasks and to having all of the power, that giving this power to the learner can seem a strange concept. We may feel this especially when working with people with very limited understandings.

However, if you bear in mind what using Intensive Interaction attempts to do, there is no point in attempting to do it if an individual is not in the mood. We wish the learners to experience and learn participation and motivation, to take part of their own free will. We are trying to develop those things as the basis for all further developments. If we insist that someone takes part in an activity when they do not wish to, at best we will have a disgruntled person who is complying. At worst you have someone who is distressed, and maybe exhibiting 'challenging behaviour'. This situation is not a good basis for promoting sensitive interactions based on mutual pleasure.

Obviously there are implications here for organising the workplace routine, as there are for the working attitudes of the staff team and their visions of the students/clients' rights. However, we have found that the more we consistently and sensitively operated the principle of respecting the varying moods of our students, then the more likely it became that we got participation.

Summary

- Spontaneous, intuitive use of the interaction principles is the best working technique during an interaction sequence.
- Some students/clients are less appealing than others, though they still need staff to tune in to them.
- Good teamwork can help staff to interact spontaneously and enjoyably with students/clients who are less appealing.
- Staff need to pay attention to the development of body language abilities – especially the signal of availability.
- The concept of joining the learners in their world is an important basic principle.
- Being lighthearted or playful is essential in setting up mutual enjoyment and attracting the attention of the student/client.
- Any behaviour which the student/client produces should be viewed as important to that person.
- Any behaviour is potentially a focus for interaction.
- The first focus provides a basis for the development of other activities in interactions.
- Interaction sequences should have no particular sensation of task or of striving to meet objectives.
- The learning in interaction sequences arises from the quality and significance of the process of doing interaction.
- Good interactive games are developed based on the behaviours and interests of the learner.
- If the student/client is not in the mood this should be accepted.
- Participation is different from, and better than, compliance.

Detailed techniques in Intensive Interaction

When Sue and Thomas were introduced, we made mention of the difficulties we experience in putting across interaction techniques in the written word, offering descriptive illustrations to help the reader understand the practical applications of aspects of technique. In this section we continue to offer a variety of illustrations from our work, together with more discussion and commentary on techniques. We feel the need to emphasise once more, that though we separately identify, detail and define components of interaction in terms of separate abilities, in the reality of an interaction there is this sensation of seamlessness, of everything that is happening blending and blurring into each other. The way we categorise everything into separately labelled packages in this book, is for the convenience of description and understanding. When actually using these abilities during inter-actions, staff should be prepared to experience and enjoy a certain amount of chaotic activity, rather than a neat and orderly progression of events.

The main illustration which we now offer in this chapter, is several episodes of work with a student/client called Marion and one of her teachers, Lin. Marion is also the subject of a full case study in chapter six.

Illustration: Marion and Lin

Before access took place with Marion, she slept much of the time and when awake, her facial expression was mostly far away, eyes focussed into the middle distance or at the ceiling. Even when her eyes met yours, her gaze seemed to be without meaning. Her most striking and visible behaviour was a rhythmic side to side movement of the head, presumably a stereotypy.

Lin is an extrovert, effervescent person who initially had to overcome some difficulties associated with this when using Intensive Interaction. In particular she had difficulty allowing pauses – Lin has more than enough behaviour of her own to fill any available pause. However, discussion with colleagues, and crucially, watching herself on video, enabled her to use this skill.

Work with Marion had progressed well for a few months, and there had emerged a sensation that accessing was done, with an increasing con-fidence and a repertoire of interactive activities established.

Marion is out of her wheelchair, sitting quite upright on a beanbag in the corner of a classroom. Her arms are in her typical fist-tight, scrunched toward her chest position, but as Lin approaches her on hands and knees, laughing softly, Marion smiles and clashes her fists enthusiastically. Lin is still laughing gently, but continues her slow and cautious approach, until she is within Marion's personal space, alongside her, one arm on her shoulders, face close and fully available to Marion's scrutiny.

'Oooh . . . ' says Lin questioningly, laughingly, as if asking what Marion is doing with her hands. Marion laughs looking into Lin's face and then away, but clashes her fists again, lifting her face to look laughingly into Lin's. Lin immediately moves her head back in mock surprise, face forming a dramatic 'oh' look – eyebrows raised, face long, mouth circular above an upright neck, holding it, offering it for Marion for a second or two. Then: 'Oh, we're clapping hands again. Can I?' Lin holds her hands up and starts to clap them gently but insistently together. Her face is two feet from Marion's, still holding the look of mock wonderment, with the tips of her fingers on a direct line between their faces. Marion can simultaneously take in both the activity of Lin's hands and the messages on Lin's face.

Marion is clearly enjoyably held by Lin's behaviour. Her face is open with a broad smile. She is gazing warmly into Lin's eyes as Lin performs her clapping. She makes an encouraging sound and starts to rock her head from side to side, still gazing and smiling into Lin's face.

As Marion's rocking starts, Lin pauses with a sudden, but gentle drama, and is still. Her facial expression transforms into a look of deep interest in the rocking that Marion is now doing. 'Shall I . . . ' says Lin laughingly, starting to rock in concert with Marion, beaming into Marion's face her enjoyment of what they are now doing.

Starting a session – the approach is part of the interaction

As comfort, security and familiarity between student/client and the usually available staff are established, this issue of starting becomes less of an issue. Increasingly, sequences may start in any fashion in all sorts of different ways in different situations and contexts. In the earlier stages, or with a student/client whose problems of withdrawal are to do with the extremes of fear and anxiety, it may be good to establish a visible and comforting routine for starting a session which ensures the security of the student/client.

The slow, low approach that Lin uses is a good example of this. Marion is always in her wheelchair or on a beanbag, so Lin always gets right down into her eye-line whilst still several yards away. At the very least this is complimentary to Marion, but it also has several practical benefits. Lin is starting to engage Marion's attention before she has made any kind of intrusion into her personal space. If Lin does this routinely, it provides Marion with time and space to decide whether she can cope with some intense attention from Lin at this moment in time. Correspondingly, if Marion decides, 'no,' she can signal this in various ways which Lin will sensitively pick up, because she has given herself time to do this by approaching slowly, already combining this method of approach with careful scrutiny of Marion for signals and feedback. It is worth noting that Marion is unlikely to give a clear, consistent 'no' signal, but her feedback is now familiar enough for the staff to accept a lack of visible enthusiasm as a 'no'. Usually though, as here, she can be quite visibly enthusiastic at the prospect of another person's attention. Here are some further examples of the ways in which care is taken with the approach to the student/client.

Mandy and Gaynor

Work has been progressing with Mandy for some time. There are a variety of game activities established with her as a repertoire, and from a starting point of fear and suspicion, she has now established trust with several members of staff. Consequently she is already laughing as Gaynor starts approaching from several yards away. Gaynor is on hands and knees, crawling forward in stop-start fashion, saying in a 'teasing' voice: 'I'm coming . . . Are you ready Mandy? . . . One . . . Two . . . Three . . . '

Mandy is laughing more, glancing from Gaynor to the hand she is waving in front of her face and back again. She knows that Gaynor is building her up, and she enjoys it. Gaynor finds this slow, silly approach effective. It gives Mandy plenty of time to get her attention 'locked in' to Gaynor's intentions. It gives Gaynor plenty of time to scan and be sure that Mandy really is in the mood and it has the added benefit of getting the sequence started before personal space is shared. One of the consequences of a mistake can be loud shouting which is likely to be repeated, non-stop, for the rest of the day.

Instant responsiveness to signals of negativity

One of the feedback signals to be looked out for as a result of sensitive scanning is any signal of negativity. Intensive Interaction sequences should be positive experiences for the learner. Therefore, we recommend that as a basic rule, any signal of negativity is respected and responded to immediately.

We define a 'signal of negativity' as any signal by the student/client during interaction, whether from face, voice or body language, that can be interpreted as something like: 'no,' 'stop,' 'enough,' 'go away,' 'I'm not sure,' etc.

The response should mainly be one of two types. First, simply stop what you are doing at that moment altogether and pause. Have a good think about what to do next whilst still scanning very carefully. Your decision may be to go away altogether, and this is a good decision sometimes.

Second, try doing something different. Introduce a new stimulus – some different behaviour or activity, a well-established game that works perhaps, or a favoured object. Alternatively, start focussing on some other aspect of what the student/client is doing at that moment, to see if that gets positive signals back.

There should be no sense of having been dominated or controlled by the learner because of this part of the process. Far from it – your sensitivity here is an encouraging signal of negotiation and preparedness to share control. The student/client will develop more trust in you because you do this consistently and the interactions will be the better for it.

Additionally, your responsiveness will be part of the process of the student/client learning cause and effect – that 'I can do something, and it causes someone else to do something'. That is one of the concepts we should be working hard to establish.

Get your face in the right place

'Get your face in the right place' is a crude motto we offer to all staff with whom we work. Its significance is simple. If you are working on activities which focus on social interaction, the tool which needs to be visible or available, more than any other, is your face. All of our work and observations, all of our research emphasises again and again the primary importance of the use of face by staff.

Getting your face in the right place is of course not necessarily an easy thing to achieve. For one thing, we cannot tell you where the right place is, you have to find out. It varies with the individuals involved and with the situations in which they find themselves. Lin is doing two main things in the early stages of this sequence with Marion, though to a lesser degree she maintains her sensitivity to this issue throughout the activity.

First, Lin has some knowledge, based on experience, of what works, of where Marion likes people to put their face in the various, but limited situations in which she works with Marion. Lin bases her approach to Marion on this knowledge and experience. Second, perhaps more importantly, Lin is constantly scanning Marion for signals and feedback about how effective she is being for her. One of the questions constantly in her mind concerns positioning. She adjusts the position of her head and face tens of times during the sequence as a result of the feedback from Marion. As long as Lin keeps doing that, she is likely to be mostly successful in keeping her face in the right place.

Lin adjusts her face position also in order to emphasise her own signalling. The mock wonderment facial expression early on, was held on an upright neck and six inches further away for Marion to inspect.

This sensitivity to signalling should be used also to make good judgements when working with people whose withdrawal from social contact concerns fear and anxiety. For them, especially in the early stages, a little facial regard from another person may be plenty. Sometimes such students/clients can take facial regard, but not full, sustained eye contact. Sometimes they maintain eye contact, but only if your face is actually turned slightly away. Once again, scan constantly, but gently, for the signals which will help you make the judgements.

If all this sounds a bit complicated and you are wondering how on earth you keep all that in your mind simultaneously, the answer actually seems to be that for most of us it is easy. It really is part of our natural interaction repertoire. You can watch sophisticated adult communicators doing adjustments of face position with each other constantly, and you can particularly see adults do it with infants, significantly so if it is the first meeting. Nonetheless, we feel it is worth remembering the motto and saying it to yourself regularly during your work.

It is worth remembering also that there are one or two techniques for our work which have been around for a while and may still be advocated, which actually ask you to remove your face from the working situation, even to the extent of operating behind the student/client. We hope that after reading this book you feel better equipped to judge the use of such techniques. Two more examples of face positioning:

Gregory
Gregory was remote from contact with other people partly because of the severity of his sensory disabilities. He did not hear much, as far as could be judged, and his detailed vision seemed limited to a zone a foot or two in front of his face. Accordingly, work by staff on use of face, and on helping him to understand facial cues needed to take place that close. It took a long time to establish the trust and security needed for Gregory to tolerate people in his personal space for any length of time. Even once direct, close face-to-face episodes were established, staff had to remain extremely sensitive to Gregory's signals that he had done enough.

Jeanie
Ten-year-old Jeanie's physical disabilities meant that she had virtually no ability to make movements. Staff had found also that she only seemed comfortable lying on her back. Thus, any face-to-face experience with her meant kneeling next to her and looming above her. Most staff felt that it was a very dominating position if held for any length of time. However, with discussion and practice they learnt to compose their body language so that they felt as though they 'loomed' over Jeanie less. They found also

that as their own sensation of relaxation improved in this way, their use of facial expression and cues also improved.

Hold objects of attention near to your face

This technique was amply demonstrated in the illustration of Sue and Thomas in chapter three. As we consider it here, we can also think ahead to later developments for the student/client, such as introducing objects into interactions.

In our example, Lin celebrated and joined in with Marion's clapping behaviour, building it up and dramatising it a little more. She wanted her clapping to be the subject of joint focus – something that they both could simultaneously share and enjoy. Her intuitions told her to place her hands in a good direct line between their two faces. The effect for Marion was that she could look at what Lin was doing with her hands, but also see Lin's face at the same moment, without changing or moving her gaze.

This technique can be helpful when using, or introducing objects to a student/client with limited understandings. By holding the object within the line of mutual gaze, it is then possible for both your face and the object to be taken in simultaneously. If the thing is new to that person, you can impart the message that this thing is safe and enjoyable and interesting. You can show your interest and enjoyment as you offer the object. Again, in the hurly burly of daily work, there is so often the temptation to work only on table tops, with the potential objects of joint focus down on the table, below everyone's eye-line. You can lift objects from table tops to your facial zone, or alternatively, and we have done this effectively, put your face down level with the table top, looking up to the student/client. Another possibility open to you is to remove the table altogether.

To put this notion another way, you are using yourself, your abilities as a social interactor, as a tool in order to introduce the learner to new concepts. As with infants, early concept formation about the physical environment occurs best with the reassurance of the new learning taking place within a familiar social context.

Using face expressively

Getting your face in the right place is one thing, using it effectively once there is the next skill. Use of relevant facial expression is one area where we all vary in ability to be expressive and communicative. This is one of those considerations where it is probably best not to be too intellectual about it on a moment-by-moment basis; you run the risk of simply being self-conscious and bashful. However, the abilities you need for use of facial expression are complex, and do improve with experience and careful consideration.

In our illustration, Lin is using her face as a monitor to what is taking place between her and Marion. She is reflecting back Marion's own emotional state, she is signalling her own sense of enjoyment, she uses little episodes of mock drama in her facial expression to mark the significance of a moment and perhaps 'hold' it briefly. The comparison in style with Sue and Thomas in chapter three is clear. Another comparison though, is that overall, Lin's use of face is less varied and less complex than Sue's. That is perhaps due to the respective abilities of the two learners – Thomas is more sophisticated in social interaction, and deals better with sustained, intense stimulation.

We return to a familiar theme: the principle is that you should be prepared to use your face freely and expressively in a variety of ways as an interaction tool. At the same time, however, what you are doing with your facial expression should be referenced to moment by moment judgements, based on your scanning and feedback, as to how the learner is coping with what you are doing.

Summary

- Though interaction sequences can be described in terms of separate principles and abilities, when they are happening they are seamless.
- Give particular consideration to the way of approaching the student/client.
- Getting down low is frequently a good technique.
- At all times scan carefully for signals and feedback from the student/client.
- Respect signals of negativity and stop or change what you are doing.
- Your face needs to be readily available to the learner at all times.
- It is usually necessary to adjust your face position during interaction sequences.
- Hold objects or another focus of attention near to your face.
- Expressive use of your face is crucial.

Illustration: Marion and Lin (contd)

As Lin claps, Marion's face opens even more in pleasure, her smile broadening to a wide open mouth-shape. Marion makes a series of short, encouraging sounds. Lin laughs in response, picking up also on Marion's facial expression and following it with her own, opening the 'oh' shape of her mouth even more, and raising her eyebrows to emphasise the change. Marion becomes still for a moment, and Lin instantly pauses, still too, but her face directing fun-filled expectancy. Marion makes a small noise again, still gazing into Lin's face, then starts her characteristic side to side rocking movement with head and shoulders. Lin takes this up immediately, rocking in unison with Marion, keeping their faces level, her face once again showing mock wonderment. 'Can I do that?' giggles Lin, rocking express-ively for a few moments, then starting to clap again, but this time in tempo with the rhythm of their rocking movement. She is providing humorous running commentary with face and voice.

Marion is still rocking, face wide in enjoyment, but now removes her gaze, looking instead past Lin's shoulder. Marion squeaks, briefly, plea-surably. Lin immediately stops clapping, holds herself still again for two seconds, studying Marion. Then: 'What?' from Lin suddenly, in a voice loaded with mock, surprised pleasure. She immediately follows this with a short, sharp clap, hands directly alongside her face. Lin pauses again, her face transmitting surprise, pleasure and expectation. Lin's little excla-mation has regained Marion's full attention, and for a moment they are frozen, gazing into each others' faces.

Lin holds herself in the pause, then clasps her hands together under her chin sharply, at the same time straightening her neck to raise her head a few inches. The effect is to increase the expectancy that is now loading the pause. Lin holds this pose for another two seconds, Marion still fully attentive. She moves her hands out again and looks down at Marion's hands with short, brisk, funny movements of her head. 'Shall we clap hands?' Lin's voice is lightly questioning, and so is her facial expression. Marion vocalises, long and low and encouraging, smiling still, inclining her head and leaning forward toward Lin. Lin accepts this as a 'more' signal and shifts position so that she can reach out for Marion's hands.

Be flexible – not fixed on any one activity or focus within the interaction

Lin was successful and effective straight away at the start of the interaction sequence. First, she enabled Marion to start to enjoy her presence simply by the way she approached. Second, falling in with Marion's clapping behaviour worked well, and raised Marion's enjoy-ment and attentiveness. However, Lin was instantly responsive to something new which Marion produced – the rocking – seizing upon it and using it to keep things going.

There is no one way to help staff make these instantaneous decisions about changes and adjustments in the interactions. Partly, it is simply to do with increasing experience of each individual student/client and what they enjoy doing. To some extent it is to do with increasing confidence on the part of each staff member as they develop knowledge about their own ability. When less experienced, there may be a tendency to be somewhat rigid; we well remember our own early tendencies to try to stick with one particular activity, the hand clapping say, because it was working really well 30 seconds ago. It is also to do with a relaxed but confident attitude which allows you, whilst interacting, to think something like: 'Well, I'll go with this bit, if it doesn't work, it doesn't matter, something else probably will.'

Part of the art with this aspect of technique is to use the information you are picking up by scanning for feedback, to guide you forward into the next enjoyable episode of the interaction sequence. It is not necessarily the actual thing that you did, like hand clapping, that was so enjoyable for the student/client. Just as likely, it was the way you did it. If you have that confidence in yourself, it is quite likely that the next episode, the rocking for instance, will be just as effective.

On the other hand, some interaction sequences do use as their focus one particular activity which will be the 'theme' of the sequence for several minutes. This is more likely to happen in the early stages of accessing and establishing. If this is what happens and it seems effective and successful, then fine, there is nothing wrong with that. It would be a mistake to try to 'push on' to introduce variety before the student/client is secure and confident enough to do so. In any event, the basic principle is to follow, pick up on, then celebrate and extend *their* behaviours. It is logical therefore that there will be something of a sensation of 'snowballing' – developments and variations in the repertoire with a person come more quickly and readily as work progresses.

Tune in to pick up on the smallest of cues

Lin's use of her own behaviour is letting Marion know loud and clear how much she values what Marion does. In order to do this she has to be prepared to pick up on the smallest of cues. Marion does not have an extensive or varied repertoire of behaviours, and her use of facial expression is still limited too. In the early stages of work with Marion the interactions were brief, simple exchanges based on Lin and others simply joining in with the rocking behaviour, making it clear that they were doing this and signalling enjoyment and participation.

Nowadays, Marion is bringing more behaviour into the interactions, she has more range of movement, and an increasing repertoire of facial expression. Lin is particularly attentive and responsive to what is happening in Marion's face, and in real life you can see micro adjustments in Lin's facial expression, in tune with the changes in Marion's. Whilst making these finely tuned adjustments to her own behaviour, based on changes in Marion's, it is necessary also that Marion is aware that Lin is doing this. It is part of the learning for Marion to start to understand how powerful she can be in affecting another person. For this reason, Lin's responses are larger than life, gently and playfully dramatised.

Responses often need to be gently and playfully dramatised

This is another area where some people will be naturally better than others. We all vary in the extent to which we can cheerfully indulge in slightly silly behaviour. It might be considered that being an extrovert, or not being self-conscious about your own behaviour, is an advantage for doing Intensive Interaction. This may be so, but only may be. We have met cheerful, confident extroverts who struggle to achieve the necessary sensitive responsiveness. This may understandably be because they are accustomed to everyone enjoying their behaviour, and they like to 'take the floor' and dominate with their sheer exuberance.

We have also met and worked with the quietest, most retiring of people who seem to have no difficulty in lighting up the most disabled and withdrawn person with the potency of their behaviour. The gentle dramatisation often needed to make responses which are significant to a person who has difficulties understanding the world, is not dependent on being extrovert. Gentle dramatisation makes behaviours a little larger than life, a little more visually significant perhaps, certainly more easily 'readable'. Sometimes indeed, it is necessary for the response to be very large, extrovert and compelling. However, the same effect is more frequently achieved without attracting the attention of everyone within ten yards.

If you are still wondering what is meant by our use of this term, 'gentle dramatisation' try reading again the section on Sue and Thomas in chapter three, or better still, find an opportunity to observe an adult saying 'hello' to an infant. Observe this aspect of the interaction, this stylised way of behaving. This would include: controlled and more slowly changing facial expressions, with those facial expressions a little 'over the top' by comparison to the way adult communicators interact facially; facial expressions which are formed and then held for a few seconds, especially expressions of pretend or mock surprise, wonderment, fear; short compelling statements providing a kind of commentary; breathy little utterances like 'oh' or 'ah', frequently combined with or preceding a held facial expression; short bursts of physical activity, especially with hands.

The purpose of these gentle dramatisations seems to be to make our otherwise too sophisticated behaviour more attractive and engaging. They also serve to simplify it and slow it down enough to make it more easily readable to a person with limited ability to comprehend and interpret another person's behaviour. As we have mentioned, some people, whether extrovert or not, seem to have considerable natural ability to do this. Most of the rest of us can learn this aspect of technique by experience, and by observing others. There are some people who unfortunately never seem to become adept at this use of their behaviour. The underpinning principle is, as always, to tune in and scan constantly for signals and feedback which let you know how effective your behaviour is for the other person.

Short pauses

Lin's use of pause during the sequence is highly skilful. We hope that this is reassuring to those of you who may not feel like natural interactors. Lin had to teach herself how to use pause, it did not come naturally to her. During these first 20 seconds or so of the sequence we have been considering, Lin is using short pauses. These pauses are carefully based on and in time with changes in Marion's behaviours. They are brief, sharp and frequently gently dramatic. They seem to fulfil several functions.

First, the pauses create clear signals from Lin that she has noticed Marion producing an item of behaviour and has paused herself to allow space for it; in this way the pauses are encouraging to Marion. This is reinforced by the way in which Lin holds direct, full, generous attention on Marion during the pause. This full, highly complimentary attention also provides a kind of warm expectancy, encouraging Marion to proceed.

Second these short pauses allow Lin to 'hold' an important moment. On one occasion Lin succeeds in holding herself and Marion completely still, both gazing at each other with huge enjoyment. These 'holds' also allow Marion plenty of time to see some of the important facial expressions and other messages which are coming from Lin's face. Even in an interaction as sensitively managed and paced as this one, Marion may miss much in the hurly-burly of it.

Another function of these little pauses may be that they serve the purpose of chopping up into manageable bits, an interaction which is proceeding quite quickly. Marion will not cope well with too much up-tempo activity, though in this illustration, she responds well to the atmosphere of it. Accordingly, one way of managing an up-tempo pace without it becoming too much, is for it to happen in bursts with lots of little pauses.

Summary

- Be flexible and avoid becoming fixed on or attached to one particular activity during interaction.
- It may be your behaviour which is causing the interaction to go well, as much as the quality or worth of the activity at that moment.
- It is better not to try to 'push on' to achieve variety before the student/client is ready.
- Tune in and scan to pick up the smallest of cues or signals from the student/client.
- Gentle and playful dramatisations make staff responses interesting and significant.
- You do not need to be an extrovert to be effective at interacting.
- Staff behaviour needs to be modified to make it attractive and interesting to the student/client.
- Pauses are a very important aspect of interaction sequences.
- It can take time for staff to learn how to use pauses.

Illustration: Marion and Lin (continued)

Lin has now moved to a position directly in front of Marion, kneeling, faces eighteen inches apart. Lin has taken hold of Marion's hands and is moving them together and apart, saying: 'Are you going to clap hands . . . are you going to clap hands?' Lin's voice is full of fun, but you can hear in it also a sense of gentle tease or challenge. You can hear too that there is slight rhythm and a rise in the way that Lin speaks, creating an atmosphere of enjoyable 'tension and expectancy'.

As Lin has adopted this use of voice, she seems to have deliberately reduced the tempo of her physical activity, so for a while things happen more slowly. Marion still seems transfixed by Lin's attentions, face still open, a huge smile evident. As Lin repeats her phrase for the third time, still moving Marion's hands, Marion starts to vocalise, a little soft scream repeated delightedly every second or so, rising in volume and pitch. The fourth one is quite loud and joyful, accompanied by a correspondingly joyful facial expression and a wide separation of her hands, now released by Lin. Lin has moved back slightly on her haunches, and is responding to and illustrating Marion's vocalisation with an escalating change in her facial expression. She is also clapping again, but now in rhythm to Marion's verbalisations. Lin chimes in with the fourth and loudest scream by laughing delightedly.

Marion now seems to take another of her 'rests', removing eye contact and gazing away past Lin, though she is rocking happily and still smiling. Lin falls in with the pause immediately, though she follows Marion's rocking. Lin is clearly in some anxiety to recapture the excitement of the last few moments, and tries two tentative 'ugh?' sounds. These do not regain Marion's full attention, so Lin simply pauses completely, except for her gentle rocking motion in concert with Marion's. Marion has lost the thread for a moment, but Lin does not now add anything more, she is watching and waiting for Marion to restart.

Lin's scanning is so good, that at the moment that Marion's eyeballs are turning back toward her, she is moving into her upright, 'surprised' body language and facial expression. They meet eyes, simply laughing at each other for a few seconds.

'Do you want to clap hands?' Lin whispers excitedly. Marion murmers, a low long noise. Lin takes a turn, 'yes?', she murmurs, extending the 'yes' into a noise like Marion's, but questioning. Marion gazes, murmers again the same noise. 'Yes,' says Lin, long and low again, but confirming their agreement.

Tension and expectancy

During the last illustration, we referred to Lin's use of tension/expectancy. The use of this technique is frequently seen in adult interactions with infants, though not significantly in the illustration of Thomas and Sue. Explaining what is meant by this term is straightforward. 'Peek-a-boo' is a tension/expectancy game. Tension/expectancy games and activities have this gentle and enjoyable sense of 'tease' built into them. We have debated often the meaning of 'tease' here. It is a kind of tease, but benevolent, supportive, reassuring. We are certainly not implying the sorts of emotional manipulation, even unpleasantness, that can be associated with teasing.

Use of tension/expectancy also usually involves a build-up to something. In formalised infant games such as 'peek-a-boo', 'I'm gonna get you', 'round and round the garden' and 'this little piggy', there is a build-up to an enjoyable climax. The cycle of the game is usually repeated several times, and an accomplished adult, using good scanning abilities, can maintain an infant in a state of rapturous attention and concentration for some time. Part of the skill for the adult is not to take the level of arousal over the top, but to maintain the expectancy for as long as possible. The games usually involve a 'hold' period, where there is silence and stillness just before the climax. Casual observation of an adult doing one of these activities with an infant, confirms just how important and crucial the adult use of body language, facial expression and voice is to the effectiveness of the activity. These are the situations where most of us are good at using playful dramatisation in our behaviour.

The importance of such activities for learning seems clear. They all focus on use of face, eyes and body language – 'peek-a-boo', particularly, is marvellous for drawing attention to, and emphasising, use of eye contact. In the classic 'I'm gonna get you' game, the adult holds the fingers which are getting ready to do the tickling, up high, near to the face. These activities also seem to play a role in helping infants to develop the ability to listen, concentrate and attend to another person. The motivation is first and foremost pleasure, the thrill that such a game offers. In being thus motivated to take part, however, a pattern of interaction and exchange of signalling takes place between the two people. The games are elastic, and a skilled adult will make each cycle of the game a little longer and more complex, with an increasingly lengthy 'hold' before the climax.

We have described these formalised 'games' to explain the nature of tension and expectancy, and to emphasise the importance of this type of activity. We need to make clear that use of tension/expectancy can pop up anywhere during an interaction, it is a natural behaviour or atmosphere which we use to emphasise or to highlight what is happening at any given moment. Tension/expectancy is not confined to the formalised games, but occurs as the style or atmosphere used for particular episodes of behaviour between the two people.

In our example, Lin was asking, 'are you clapping hands?' She asked this several times, and as she did so, a certain tone of voice, that atmosphere of rhythm and pause, with a sense of tease, became apparent. She slipped in the use of a little tension/expectancy, just in the flow of an interaction sequence, as it was proceeding. This type of episode is a more frequent use of tension/expectancy than the games. Yes, we do use games such as peek-a-boo with students/clients, and have found them to be effective activities as part of what we are trying to teach. Some practitioners may have particular reservations about using such games with older people, and we again suggest referring to our discussion on age appropriateness in chapter five. Before we return to the description and discussion of Marion and Lin, we include a brief, further illustration of use of tension/expectancy.

120

Illustration: Nella and Dave

The scene is the interior of a minibus. In the minibus are Nella, Dave and two other members of staff. The three staff are all there in order to manage Nella's trip out. Obviously, with such a necessary staff commitment, these trips are carefully planned in advance. During the course of her nineteen years, Nella has achieved a reputation for being violent, hazardous to be near, destructive and disruptive in the extreme, and armed with some impressively off-putting personal habits (see chapter six for a detailed case-study). She is also noted as a person whose concentration-span is virtually non-existent.

For a couple of moments, Nella has been playing with Dave's hands, it is one of her rituals. She is smiling, clearly relaxed and in a good mood. Dave decides to go for a game with an activity selected from his knowledge of the repertoire of successful interactions with her. He leans toward Nella with obvious purposefulness, though it is noticeable that he does so smoothly and not too quickly. He leaves enough time and space to pick up negative signals. Dave puts an arm round Nella's neck and pulls her head toward him, and makes a loud, prolonged, funny-sounding 'owowo-wow' into her cheek. He immediately releases her and they both draw back two feet or so. Nella is laughing and looking around at the other people present, as if to share the laughter, or to pick up their laughter. Dave repeats his activity, this time into Nella's cheek and neck on the other side. Nella laughs more heartily, with Dave chiming in delightedly. She looks around again, but brings her eye contact glitteringly back to rest upon Dave's eyes. Dave has now paused with a silly look on his face which threatens a repeat performance. Nella reaches out for his hands again, and Dave takes that as a cue to behave.

This time his movements are deliberately stylised, almost into slow-motion. He takes hold of one upper arm, then the other, then moves his hands to frame her face, takes a long slow deliberate breath, holds it for a second, then delivers his funny noise on Nella's cheek. The effect that his beha-viour has on her is to cause her to become absolutely still as the build-up starts. She watches him carefully, attending especially to the expression on Dave's face just before the climax. Her subsequent enjoyment is all the greater because of the tension in the build-up. The 'game' is now estab-lished and these 'rules of procedure' are repeated eight more times. With each repetition, the build-up becomes a little longer, the pause before the climax held sustained, until it is seven silent, still, expectant seconds.

During the three minutes that the activity takes, Nella moves away twice for half a minute. After each 'rest' she returns to Dave of her own accord. Her level of commitment to the game and her involvement are clear. She scrutinises Dave's face and body language for signals, she gives clear 'more' signals like holding her cheek forward to do it all again; the vivacious pleasure with which she participates is infectious to the other people in the minibus.

Intentionality

Intentionality is the ability to behave as if what the other person does is meaningful, even if it isn't, and consistently to offer your interpretation of the other person's behaviour in your behaviour.

In the earlier illustration, there is a literal example of Lin using intentionality to take up one of Marion's noises, and behave as though Marion said a word. Lin did this even to the extent of using an imitation of Marion's low noise when saying 'yes', confirming for both of them that Marion wanted to clap again. This is a specific example of a very literal use of intentionality.

However, Lin is using intentionality throughout the sequence, as one of the general driving forces in her own behaviour. Everything that Marion does receives a response and an interpretation. Lin is attentive, minutely flexible. There is no question in her behaviour that Marion is doing anything other than communicating with her. She freely offers her interpretations of Marion's behaviour to Marion.

The ability for staff to behave with intentionality is one of the more powerful aspects of the interactions. In fact intentionality is one of the principles which should quickly be generalised to the wider environment around the student/client. Thus staff can be casually, incidentally responsive to things which the learner does, at any stage of the day. Sometimes this may cause an interaction sequence to get going and lift off. For the learner, there will be the rewarding experience of having initiated an incidental sequence by producing a behaviour which brought about meaningful response, and then further interaction. Even if this does not happen, you can arrive at a happy situation where you may be casually conversing with a student/client by an exchange of noises. The student may not even be intending meaning beyond taking part in the exchange, but you have continuing opportunity to help them shape the meaning.

Chiming in

We have used the phrase 'chiming in' several times now during written illustrations. Lin chimed in laughingly with Marion's little scream. Dave chimed in by laughing with Nella. We hope that what we mean by chiming in has become quite apparent by reading these descriptions. However, we will dwell on some more explanation of this aspect of technique.

The use of the phrase 'chiming in' helps us to understand that first and foremost, it is a way of celebrating sound, of responding with a sound of your own to a sound produced by the student/client. There is also a sense in which we mean that, by chiming in, you will be doing something effective to prolong what is happening at that moment.

Most of all, chiming in with a sound is a way of operating the principle of following a behaviour of the student/client and celebrating it. Secondly, there seems always to be a need not to let a sound go by without a response, and very frequently, but not always, the most appropriate-feeling response to a sound is another sound. The fact that your sound follows that of the other person by a second or so, gives it that feeling of a chime – like bells sounding one after another. The message is affirming and communicating pleasure. There is also this atmosphere of sharing the pleasure fully, by joining in, signalling clearly that you are joining in, thus making it a truly *mutual* experience. With the sounds that you produce, there may also be a sense in which you are trying to help that moment to last a little longer, emphasising the importance of the moment, hoping that one like it will occur again soon.

Long pauses – watching and waiting

Pausing and watching and waiting is one of the more difficult of the techniques within Intensive Interaction.

Many staff, and Lin was one, find the pause difficult to accomplish at first. In our work we tend to be accustomed to dominating and driving activities along, constantly doing things to boost stimulus levels in activities, doing what we can to prevent the atmosphere from sagging. Actually taking it upon yourself to pause and wait for something to happen, seems to contradict all of this.

Nonetheless, as we have stressed, the pause is part of the activity, just as much as any visible excitement. The interaction will be more effective for the learner if her/his need briefly to take time out from it, is respected. It will feel less stressful for the learner and may well cause interactions to last longer the more able you are to use this technique. There are times in the interaction when, if you are not naturally timing your pauses, you have to muster up your will power and hold your own behaviour in check. Once you have first-hand experience of the effectiveness of doing this, of how frequently the learner will return to you and pick up the threads of what you were just doing, it becomes easier.

When to pause

As should now be clear about all decision making during interactions, judgement about pausing is mainly to do with scanning for feedback. There are two main reasons for pausing in your contribution to the activity. One is to allow the student/client to take a rest, and the other is to allow arousal levels to come down.

Getting to the stage where your student/client actually becomes highly aroused and stimulated, may of course be a wonderful achievement for some individuals. Some people are able to proceed well during an interaction at very high levels of excitement. For others, getting that 'high' will quickly become de-arousing, since those levels cannot be maintained for long. Once again, there are more judgements to be made about individual preferences and abilities.

Sometimes, the student/client may launch into a run of quite aroused behaviour within the interaction, which may last a few seconds, but which is more effective if you do not contribute anything to it. An example here is a student, Molly, whose main signal of enjoyment was very rapid rocking. There was a stage with Molly at which the rocking became so frenzied, that contributing more at that moment was actually too arousing for the both her and the member of staff. Experience told us that if we paused, allowing Molly to indulge that expression of excitement, then the pause would be brief. Molly would be carrying out a run of activity solo for a moment, but remain engaged, slowing down and returning to the main theme of the interaction quickly.

How long is a long pause?
During an interaction sequence, a complete pause of five seconds feels like a long time. The pauses vary in length of course, according to all sorts of factors, but three to ten seconds for the student/client's basic removal of eye contact and turning face away, is common.

The sequence with Nella with Dave, from which we took a brief extract, contained two pauses of at least 30 seconds. The pause was made easier for Dave in one sense, because Nella physically moved away from him during it. Thus, the temptation for him to provide stimulus to bring her attention back, was reduced. On the other hand, it became more difficult for him to provide 'still available' signals to Nella, since there may have been a strong possibility that the interaction had finished altogether. A combination of experience and successfully assuming, from scanning her, that all was not yet lost, enabled him to stay put and let her return. A useful working principle here is that until you know a person's signals well from experience, don't assume that the interaction is finished simply because the person has moved away from you. Give it another minute or two of staying where you are, signalling your continuing availability.

Interactions with some people are composed mostly of pauses; at least that can be the sensation. Earlier in this chapter we offered an illustration of Richard and Dave. Richard is a five year old with a great deal of social confidence, but not so much social understanding. Consequently, he doesn't mind you being near him, with him, touching him even, for long periods of time. However, the likelihood is that even with that degree of proximity, he will not be engaged with you, his attention will always be elsewhere. During the early stages of establishing interactive sequences with him, it was possible to stay with him for half-an-hour, and during that time have three or four intermittent engagements of a minute or less. The rest of the time was spent with the staff person remaining relaxed, signalling availability, but looking for an opening which would enable joint focus to be established.

Coming out of the pause

In the last illustration of Marion and Lin, we described a very skilful re-entry from pause by Lin. She had held herself, scanning Marion carefully, and was in action, responding, even as Marion's eyes were swivelling toward her. Getting out of the pause is basically about watching and waiting for the right moment to start up again. Making mistakes is O.K. here, and you can get it wrong several times before being effective. False re-starts are fine as long as you have not completely deterred your partner from finding you interesting. There are two basic methods to the technique:

1. One way is to use your scanning abilities to select a behaviour which the student/client produces during the pause, which may not be referenced to you, but which you may celebrate to bring back the mutuality. Your decision to do this will be based upon some type of judgement that further 'rest' is not essential for the person.

2. Alternatively, watch and wait very patiently for the whole of this decision to be taken by the student/client. You then respond once more as you are sure that s/he has decided to return attention to you.

Lin was using the second technique in the example with Marion, whereas with Richard, it was mostly necessary to use the former as the starting point for a series of brief engagements.

Summary

• Tension and expectancy is a type of gentle 'tease'.

- There are formal tension and expectancy games, but tension/expectancy also occurs throughout interaction activities.
- Tension and expectancy activities help hold the attention of the learner.
- In interaction sequences, it is rare for a noise produced by the student/client not to receive a response from the member of staff.
- Responding to and celebrating noises may be termed 'chiming in'.
- In interaction sequences, the pause is part of the activity.
- Long pauses often enable the student/client to take a rest.
- Interaction sequences are usually more successful and effective if the staff member allows pauses.
- Sometimes during a pause, the learner will physically move away, yet still return to continue.
- The staff skill during pauses is to continue to signal availability.

Illustration: Marion and Lin (continued)
It is more than two minutes into their interaction sequence. They are now paused, gazing at each other, both smiling gleefully. During the 25 seconds prior to the pause they have made a sustained exchange of vocalisations, taking turns eleven times to make a variety of noises in response to each other. During that episode, Marion was clearly experimenting with the responses she could obtain from Lin, and showing obvious delight with the results.

Marion is quite still, her gaze turned away, her head slowly moving forward and downwards. She looks deep in thought, perhaps tired. Lin is relaxed but poised, continuing to signal 'availability', but holding herself back. Marion makes a vague little vocalisation which Lin immediately imitates and reflects back, questioningly.

Very slowly and smoothly, Lin moves her body closer to Marion's, and takes hold of Marion's hands, stroking them. Lin's shoulder and arm are against Marion's side and their faces are very close. The effect is, that though there seems to be nothing active happening at this moment, they are still having an exchange – they are participating in sharing warm physical contact. This exchange continues for some time.

Marion makes another vocalisation, imitated and reflected again by Lin, and this brings Marion's eyes back to Lin's face. Lin is immediately back into her mock surprise expression, though not so dramatically as previously, and without the body language. Instead, she retains her position, which enables her to maintain most of the physical contact. Marion starts her side-to-side rocking motion again, but Lin does not go with it this time, keeping instead to an intense, pleasurable gaze at Marion.

They fall silent and still again, but sustain their exchange of pleasurable gaze once more. This lasts for some time before Marion's head starts to fall forward again and this time it does seem as if she has lost interest or is falling asleep. Lin is clearly still fired up, and tries something new. Moving her head forward in a style and rhythm which echoes the way Marion's head is falling forward, she places her cheek against Marion's and they pause once more in this posture. Marion's eyes are open, waiting, expectant. Then, just audible, can be heard a whispering noise Lin is making into Marion's cheek and ear. Marion suddenly explodes with laughter and delight, throwing her head back once more and clapping her fists together. Like a flash, Lin moves simultaneously back into an upright kneeling posture, chiming in with her own now loud laughter, pointing teasingly at Marion.

Imitation/modified reflecting back

Imitation, or modified reflecting, is one of the more commonly seen aspects of adult interactions with infants at early levels of learning. As we have already observed, it offers a really good way of celebrating episodes of another person's behaviour. When interacting with another person, it is actually difficult not to use imitation of one kind or another, even when sophisticated language users are interacting.

In our example of Marion and Lin, the imitation Lin uses of Marion's side-to-side head movement is a familiar routine for both of them. In the early stages it was a core part of the interactions for them, one of Marion's visible behaviours which the staff could celebrate and join in with. Through this early focus of using imitation or modified reflecting and the establishment of that early game, Marion was able to start learning more about effective communication and social activities. This initial activity enabled Lin and several other members of staff to be increasingly tuned in and available to her. At this later stage, things have moved on and there is a far wider repertoire of activities in the sequences. The use of that early imitation activity is still there, but no longer forms the main focus of an interaction. Rather, it is something which happens almost in passing, or else is happening as well as several other things.

In any event, imitation is rarely the only thing that you do at a given moment. One of the realisations we had at an early stage in work on Intensive Interaction was that if you simply imitate, nothing much happens. That is one reason why we offer the phrase 'modified reflecting'. What usually happens is that you pick up on something the other person is doing, a noise, a movement, a facial expression perhaps. However, as you imitate, you giggle or laugh, or add a different facial expression, some particular type of body language perhaps, add some running commentary, or use a particular tone of voice. It is essential to maintain the sensations of mutual pleasure, participation, interest and to make sure that what you offer with your behaviour is intrinsically interesting to the other person.

Illustration: Adrian and Nikki

Adrian has a lifestyle dominated by his organised self-involvements (see case study in chapter six). He stands and sways, stamps his feet, punctuating this with hand flapping, flicks, facial grimacing and twitching, nodding, spitting onto his hands and the floor and droning verbalisations.

Nikki is standing two feet in front of Adrian. She is joining in with what he is doing as far as she can, but she cannot achieve his expertise or the complexity of his combined movements. She is laughing at her own inadequacies, and this relaxed humour and self-mockery runs through everything that she does during the sequence.

For his part, it is clear that Adrian is interested in what Nikki is reflecting back to him, and that he finds it funny too – he smiles and laughs frequently. More than this though, is that Adrian is clearly enjoying the degree of control that Nikki is offering to him by continually following and joining in with what he does. He watches all of her movements carefully, and he experiments with her every now and again – he does a short burst of very complex movement, then laughs at Nikki's attempts to repeat it.

Nikki is using numerous short bursts of running commentary – partly in acknowledgement that Adrian understands a good deal of spoken language, partly to provide atmosphere with the warmth of her voice: 'Ok, yeah . . . where're we going? . . . I'll scratch my ears as you scratch your ears . . . Is it itchy? . . . I'm getting hot, I'll tell you that . . . my fingers are getting tired clicking as well . . . '

Nikki is also smiling more or less continuously and willingly following Adrian's foot-patterns as he stamps his way across the room. There are frequent episodes of sustained eye contact and warm facial regard, particularly when they laugh together, or when Nikki is saying something.

Imitation/modified reflecting back (continued)

In Adrian's case, he and Nikki are still at a stage when Nikki's modified reflecting of his stereotyped behaviours forms the main focus of the activity. The use of this, for Adrian, highly motivating focus, offers excellent opportunities for episodes which also contain eye contact and warm facial regard. The imitation is the vehicle by which Nikki introduces herself and everything which she has available to Adrian. Her face, voice, body language and warmth come as part of the package. In the early stages of setting up interaction sequences with Adrian, he was significantly attracted by the fact that she and others did what he did and the way they did it. Because of that, he is now interested in Nikki in her own right.

Running commentary and use of spoken language

At various times, we have been making reference to 'running commentary'. Skilled use of running commentary is one of the ways in which adults sensitively expose infants to language during interaction, or on other occasions when they are doing something to, near or around the infant, such as basic care. Though running commentary is presumably an intuitive behaviour among people of all ages, some of the circumstances in our workplaces may cause us to override our intuitions, and for this reason we have got into the habit of defining running commentary. Firstly we emphasise what it is not:

- It is not bombardment.
- It does not demand a response.
- It is not control.
- It does not have to be loud.

Now, more positive statements about what we think running commentary actually should be:

- It has an atmosphere of informality and lightheartedness.
- It is personalised to the student/client.
- It is referenced to what is happening to the student/client at that moment.
- It may be general, and take into account things and occurrences in the environment around the student/client.
- It has an atmosphere of warm participation.
- It usually has loose and ragged edges, open-endedness, half-finished sentences.
- It provides for and suggests that the other person might respond or play a part in the exchange, and leaves spaces for this.
- It contains pauses and silences sensitively referenced to feedback signals from the student/client.

We can tell you something about what running commentary is and how to do it. It is much more difficult to advise when to do it, or more significantly when not to do it. The main principle here is that running commentary should not dominate. Many interaction sequences with certain student/clients may contain little spoken language on the part of the member of staff. The reasons for this may be many, all reflecting intuitive judgements and awareness about the effect of use of language at any given moment.

A good working principle is that you use spoken language with a person even if you know that your student/client will not understand any of it; the *tone* of your voice will transmit warmth, participation and informality. This atmosphere may be picked up even if the understanding of words is not. On the other hand, if an interaction contains many non-verbal utterances, perhaps based on the sounds that the student/client is producing, that might mean that there is less opportunity to use a spoken commentary. Additionally, if an interaction has a particularly quiet and serene atmosphere, and is taking place at a low level of arousal, intuition might tell you not to add anything more in terms of sound.

One member of staff, when asked why she said so little during a particular interaction, could not answer until the next day, when she had thought about it carefully: 'Everything was going well. I was tuned in, being very responsive. We were fairly quiet together, though we used his noises now and again. He was really quite stimulated – active and interested in me. I think I felt that if I said too much more it would make the session too complex for him . . . but I'm not absolutely sure that was the reason.'

At the other extreme, some of the basic interaction principles in Intensive Interaction are useful for communicating with students/clients who have full use of language. Such interactions may have extended use of spoken exchanges as the central focus for what is taking place. It may still be necessary at the same time to give warm encouragement with face, voice and body language to a person who may nonetheless still not be comfortable with some of the fundamentals, such as eye contact and proximity.

Once again we return to issues such as tuning in, developing an intuitive feel for the person you are interacting with, and of course, scanning for feedback signals. Generally we have found that you know fairly quickly if you are using too much spoken language – it tends to diminish the continued effectiveness of the interaction sequence quite quickly.

Physical contact

We hope that the importance of use of physical contact in Intensive Interaction sequences has been made clear. We consider it inevitable that you make physical contact whilst interacting with people with limited understandings. An exception, of course, might be when you do not know the person well, and/or there are clear signals that there will not be consent to physical contact. Physical contact seems like an enjoyable, natural, irreplaceable aspect of communicating with a person who does not use language.

However we find that individual staff in our work vary enormously in their ability and in their willingness to touch their students/clients. Some of this may be to do with consideration of ethics and professionalism, some of it is simply to do with personal and emotional preferences. Once again, we refer you to chapter five for an extended discussion of these issues.

The ways in which physical contact is used, its meanings, the different intensities, these are as varied as many other aspects of interacting. It is difficult indeed to write hard and fast rules for you, instead we try to direct you toward the basic principles. However, if there are any rules, what follows is one.

Any use of physical contact should only be with the consent of the student/client

We recommend that physical contact is used freely and pleasurably, but that it is done only with the permission and participation of the student/client. Thus, if you do not know someone well, if you are starting out, and still thinking about or trying for access, be very cautious with any touch. The principle here is the same as for any other aspect of the approach – if you force physical contact on the person, you will not have achieved participation, you will have compliance from that person at best.

Many staff wonder how consent can be achieved with people who are very remote from human contact, or who seem to have no formal communication behaviours. How do you get a yes or a no?

Illustration: Alex and Veronica
Alex is sitting in his wheelchair. He is distressed and upset, in fact he has just had an outburst, which involved many flailing movements. Veronica, his key-worker, is kneeling on the floor near him attempting to calm him using finely-paced and sensitively timed face, voice and body language. They have a well-established relationship based on sensitive interaction and Veronica is making this comfort available to him. Gradually his state of distress lessens, the noise subsides and Veronica moves a little closer. She is now within touching distance, still giving calming signals, soothing facial regard, her eye-line a little below his. 'Ok,' she says, 'alright . . . yeah . . . that's a bit better now . . .'

Very smoothly and slowly she starts to reach out with her right hand toward Alex's forearm, moving it across the space between them. There is the slightest shrinking away movement of Alex's arm, and a nearly imperceptible increase in the intensity of his grimace. Veronica has been scanning him very minutely as she reaches out. Her hand stops its journey half-way across the space between them, then slowly moves back to her side, 'Okay Alex . . . it's alright'.

The principle of procedure that Veronica uses here is the same one that we mostly use everywhere in life for every situation. As you reach out to make physical contact, you scan carefully and minutely for signals of negativity. If you perceive any, you don't touch.

We find that it is actually easier to use the principle with students/clients, since we can deliberately slow our movements down for them even more. In the complex interactions of a social gathering in a pub or at a party, it is easier to make mistakes and give or receive unwanted touches. Another aspect of the principle is that acceptable social touch is usually to the elbow or forearm. Anywhere else is dodgy territory until you know a person really well. This will be the case usually too, in the early stages of work with someone, even if at a later stage you end up in full-scale romping as part of the interactions. There are exceptions to this – some young children (Diana, for instance, in an earlier illustration) liked to get to know a person by climbing all over them. Sensory disabilities are clearly going to have an effect also on the way in which these principles are operated.

Our experience is that the more sensitively and consistently you use this principle in your work, the more likely it is that the student/client will feel comfortable with your proximity. Over time this will make it increasingly probable that you will start to receive signals of consent. If this makes it sound once more that some of this is a slow process, then yes, that is so. For some students/clients, particularly the ones with the most anxiety about other people, true social participation will take time. It is right that it takes time.

Staff reading this may be wondering what you do about, for instance, basic care activities – washing, shaving, going to the toilet and so on. After all, we don't have any choice in those circumstances but to impose ourselves and our touches – do we? Of course this is true, but we still recommend that as far as possible, you attempt to use these basic principles even then. Work a little more slowly, think about your movements and body language – make them less brisk and business-like perhaps. Work sensitively to have participation rather than compliance in these activities too. Quite often students and clients who have profound sensitivity to other people being near them, will nonetheless have simply got in the habit and routine of receiving touch for basic care. We can be clever, the basic care could be the starting point and focus for interaction sequences. We can decide to make our touches warm and sensitive rather than functional, we can use running commentary and get face in the right place and so on. Basic care activities are a great opportunity for one-to-one interaction.

Types of physical contact

At one extreme, a touch during interaction may be as simple as the hand on another hand. At the other extreme, glorious physical romping with full body contact is not uncommon as an aspect of interactions. Here are some examples to illustrate the point:

Georgiou is a man of 25. His preferred and most effective position for interacting evolved gradually. He is sitting on a mat face to face with Gaynor so that his face is less than two feet from her. His legs overlap hers so that he partially sits on her lap.

Colin has profound visual and hearing impairments. He has been socially remote for nearly all of his life, preferring his own world of rhythmic movements and noises. For him, interactions involving exchanges of behaviour, means romping and rolling on a crash mat, hugging, pulling and especially, spending long periods with faces pressed together.

Michael likes to interact mostly standing up, face-to-face, placing his hands gently on the arms or shoulders of the member of staff. In this way he can exert some slow control over proceedings. After a while it became possible to return the compliment and place hands on his shoulders simultaneously. This has become a very effective situation for the development of face-to-face exchanges.

Caroline and her teacher Stella have a well established relationship and repertoire of interactions. They have constructive activities in all sorts of situations, and a noticeable feature of what they do is the number of 'jiggles' they exchange. 'Jiggles' are brief – one second or so – rhythmic movements. They frequently accompany something else which is happening, like laughter or running commentary. Stella uses her hands to give Caroline jiggles on her arms, shoulders, back, ribcage, and to the side of her head.

Nella, despite her usually vigorous physicality, also enjoys lying quietly with her head in the lap of a member of staff, looking up into that person's face. From this position, the two people can spend quite long periods simply exchanging movements of eyes, nose, mouth, eyebrows.

The purpose of physical contact

As we have stated, whatever the purpose of physical contact may be, we find it difficult not to touch the students/clients we are working with. It seems to us that touch has a deep emotional and psychological significance as an aspect of non-verbal interacting, since the drive to use it seems to us to be so strong. We have met staff who come from workplaces where they have, for various reasons, been forbidden to use physical contact in their work.

In our discussion of broader issues about physical contact in chapter six we make reference to the intellectual significance of physical contact for mammals – it seems to help with the development of cognitive functioning. This is certainly one of the things we are aiming for in developing interaction sequences. Also, if we go back to thoughts about the development of infants in the first year, the use of physical contact seems to be one of the primary techniques used in promoting their development. Infants usually receive massive amounts of physical contact while they are learning communication.

It seems that at its most basic, touch is a fundamental form of communication. You can say things in touch that you can't say in words. This is true we suggest, of all human communication, but must be especially so for people who don't use words. With infants who are distressed or upset, in fact with all people who are distressed or upset, it is the method we wish to use for providing comfort. Once more we suggest, profound things about empathy and sympathy and caring are said more effectively and meaningfully by use of physical contact.

During Intensive Interaction sequences, physical contact of all sorts may be the central focus for what is happening. It may also be a way of commenting on something else which is happening as the central focus. It may be just one of the incidental things which happen throughout the activity. Physical contact also makes good punctuation – 'holding' a pause for instance, literally by means of a gentle hold. A sudden touch can be a way of providing new stimulus during a pause.

Many of the principles and procedures we offer in this book will be helpful to you in your work, even if you are a person who, for whatever reason, cannot use physical contact. Use of burst-pause, intentionality, celebrating and extending behaviours, detailed scanning, all of these may be applied without use of physical contact, especially with more able students/clients. It seems to us though, that for students/clients who are still at the very earliest levels of learning and understanding of other people, physical contact is an essential component of their development.

Stimuli offered – but not insisted upon

As we attempted to make clear in our description of Sue's style in chapter three, there is a sort of dynamic tension between basically following and responding to the behaviour of the student/client, and making carefully judged contributions of your own which are not based upon what happened immediately before. Sue used new stimuli creatively and constructively. When she offered something to the interaction, one of its effects was to provoke a behaviour from Thomas to which she could then respond. Use of running commentary might sometimes be seen to be serving this function. Anything that you say, even in passing, might provoke, for instance, a smile or laughter. You then chime in, and so on.

In the last illustration of Lin and Marion, Lin deliberately and consciously decided to offer a new stimulus in order to see if she could get out of the pause and back into active interacting. This contribution was carefully judged, she moved slowly, kept up her scanning, and if Marion had not responded to her whisper, she could have moved just as gracefully back into her pause position.

Judging the right moment effectively is, as with so much else, subtle. Usually, if the interaction is going well, with plenty of incident and activity, with pauses and re-starts controlled basically by the learner, then you tend not to need to put in too much more. With particular individuals, the interaction sequences may to an extent depend upon a few carefully provided extra stimuli from the staff member.

The main principle is not to offer too much – we are trying to get the learners to explore and develop their behaviours, not to become an audience for ours. For us, the staff, the main psychological difficulties associated with this part of technique are: having the patience to allow pauses to run, and the judgement to know that the student/client has had enough and that the session is over.

Different intensities and levels of arousal

We have to be careful not to think about interaction sequences just in terms of very high arousal and up-beat activities, though this is frequently characteristic. Mutual enjoyment and the engagement that goes with it is just as much seen in very quiet and peaceful exchanges of behaviour between two people. The wide diversity and variety of levels of intensity and corresponding activities is one of the aspects of using the approach which has to be catered for.

For some students/clients, interactions which are properly on their terms need a low level of arousal and intensity throughout. This is limiting of course. It limits the types of activities which can take place, it limits the variety of learning opportunities they are exposed to, it probably imposes limits on the duration or frequency of interactions. However, if the reality is that the student/client can only cope with a certain intensity of experience, that is the reality.

Illustration: Tim and Asif

Tim sits alone on a cushion in the corner of the classroom. No-one else is within two metres of him. He sits cross-legged, head down, rocking gently, but pausing to rub his head rhythmically, or twiddle a piece of string or strands from the edge of an adjacent cushion with his fingers, again rhythmically, repetitively. These activities seem to be carried out with avid, virtually uninterrupted concentration.

Asif joins Tim. His method of approach is to be on the floor before he is within his personal space, covering the last metre on hands and knees, with his face lower than Tim's. Asif's face wears an open, semi-smiling sort of an expression as he leans closer to Tim. Tim smiles slightly and turns his face away, but the smile remains. Asif is talking softly, so softly only Tim can hear it. What he is saying seems to be deeply personal to them. Tim has started twiddling with the edge of the cushion beside him, watching his fingers, but still smiling faintly and rocking just perceptibly. Asif has paused in his commentary, but follows his line of gaze and now murmurs something identifiably to do with this activity. Asif's smile broadens and there is an evident laugh in his voice as he starts to join in with Tim's twiddling. He is still smiling and giving a gentle, murmured commentary, but now with as many pauses as utterances, and during each pause Asif's gaze turns from their fingers to scrutiny of Tim's face.

Tim starts to rock more noticeably, but he also raises his face to look at Asif's, and his smile creases widely. Asif raises his level of activity and his facial expression and body language become 'bigger'. He has moved his face with its open beaming expression very close to Tim's, moving his head simultaneously as Tim tracks to the side. Suddenly Tim is laughing softly, even looking briefly into Asif's eyes.

Ending an interaction sequence

The best ending to an interaction sequence is when it simply peters out. At first, this type of ending to an activity might feel somewhat lame. We may feel better if it had ended dramatically, with something 'snappy' putting a full stop on it, or on some high note. However, from the point of view of the student/client, the fact that it simply peters out means that the session has come to a natural end, no more can be gained from the experience for the time being. Additionally, their arousal level has returned to what is probably normal for them at this moment in time. This normal arousal level may seem low, the

136

student/client once more being disinterested in what is happening around them, particularly other people. However, until you have done a lot more interacting with this person, this is normal arousal. At the end of an interaction, they need to be back there. Sometimes it is necessary to assume some conscious control of endings, so that the student/client is assured a constructive experience.

In the early stages of work with Rebecca, she would interact beautifully and rewardingly for about two minutes. She would then reach a stage where something happened to her, and she simply reached out and hit whoever was interacting with her, hard. Again, careful discussion led to the conclusion that after two minutes or so Rebecca reached a certain 'high' in her arousal. She found this level of arousal difficult to deal with in any way except through use of violence. We decided that for a while we would attempt a policy of deliberately bringing the interaction down and to an end, before the two minute 'threshold' was reached, or before we started to pick up signals of extreme arousal. In this way, Rebecca had the opportunity to engage in sequences which consistently ended positively and with a return to lower levels of arousal. We refer you also to the case study of Matthew in chapter six, for whom particular attention was paid to the issue of ending interactions.

We developed a useful policy of writing narrative records of interactions whilst still 'hands on', immediately the sequence had finished. One reason for this was that it is difficult to write an accurate record several hours later. But it also became increasingly clear that this was an opportunity for both people to rest and relax a little after the sequence – particularly welcome if it had been highly active. We found also that many of our students began to value this part of the experience, staying with us, sitting quietly, perhaps still making physical contact. We became adept at writing the records and giving running commentary on what we were doing. This would simultaneously give good feelings of involving the person in this part of the work with them, and be an opportunity to use calming voice and face.

Summary

- Imitation or modified reflecting is frequently used by staff in interaction sequences.
- Imitations are not enough on their own – they should be accompanied by good use of face, voice and body to signal pleasure and reassurance.

- Imitating or joining in with stereotyped behaviour can be very effective, but not everyone enjoys it.
- Use of spoken language by staff varies enormously according to the abilities of individual students/clients.
- Using spoken language or running commentary is nonetheless a good general principle.
- Physical contact plays a very important role in Intensive Interaction.
- Physical contact occurs in a variety of ways and intensities.
- Any use of physical contact should only be with the consent of the student/client.
- Physical contact seems to have profound significance as a mode of communication.
- A principle of procedure during interaction sequences is for the member of staff to offer new stimuli, but not to insist on them.
- Interaction sequences take place at many different intensities.
- Very low-key sequences are just as important as lively ones.
- The best ending for sequences is when they simply peter out and the learner loses interest.
- With experience, staff can manage the de-arousal of the learner and bring the sequence to an end carefully.

Conclusion to detailed techniques

We have deliberately spent the greater part of this chapter concentrating on what we know to be the difficult bit – making access and establishing constructive routines of interaction sequences with a student/client. It is the most difficult aspect of Intensive Interaction for several reasons. The attitudes and abilities demanded are, for many individual staff, or workplaces, quite different from what is usually viewed as working practice. For some staff groups, working with this approach may necessitate some changes in ethos and atmosphere in the workplace.

It can take time for some staff to become accustomed to working as subjectively and intuitively as we suggest. It may also take time to get used to working with a concept of 'process' and to reduce emphasis, for these activities at least, on the setting of tasks and the pre-setting of objectives for each session. Actually making access can seem, indeed often is, very difficult as an undertaking, until staff have experience of achieving it with several different individuals. By that point, having experienced success with several students/clients, we generally find that the nature of what is being attempted with Intensive Interaction has become very clear to staff.

There is also what may be a major difficulty, and one to which we regularly refer – slowing down. It can be problematic for staff teams to slow down the pace of their work and their movement around the workplace as well as the desire to drive activities along, in order to allow for Intensive Interaction to take place.

Some individual members of staff and their teams may not experience these difficulties to the same degree. One of the comments frequently made to us after an Intensive Interaction workshop is something like: 'I've always naturally worked a bit like that and it's nice to know that I was on the right lines'. Actually, we feel that it would be strange if some of these principles were not present in everyone's work at some stage.

Sometimes we are also asked, 'Well that's fine, but what happens next?' It can be slightly perplexing to be asked that question. It seems to us obvious that once access is achieved, followed by establishment of recognised mutual engagements, then the way is often clear to further developments. The hard bit, accessing and establishing, is done. Of course, there is no reason why the supposedly forthcoming developments and how they occur, should be obvious to staff who have not experienced them.

Consolidating and furthering

Put very briefly, use of the approach carries with it an expectation that much progress occurs through a natural momentum which comes about with doing it. Motivation to take part in activities is primarily provided by the activities being mutually enjoyable, particularly in the early stages. Because students/clients are motivated to take part in this way, they learn at first almost without noticing. They become comfortable with experimenting with their behaviour, and they are enjoyably, yet profoundly exposed to the knowledge and experience which another person has available.

In practical terms, we expect that this early motivation will cause the learner to take part in sessions increasingly more readily. The sequences will gradually start to last longer. The activities which make up sequences will grow and develop. New things will be tried out and kept as part of the sequences. The activities will become more complex, with the learner trying out and using increasingly sophisticated understandings and ways of behaving. Interaction sequences happen more and more frequently. Incidental, unplanned sessions start happening, due to staff responsiveness to something occurring during the general run of activities throughout the day. A milestone will be the student/client intentionally initiating a sequence, then adding this development to the repertoire of activities and understandings. Awareness, the ability to interact, true communication exchanges, these become something that the learner has and does as a normal aspect of their daily existence and who they are. If the student/client is someone who can be 'challenging', we might expect developments in this area too. Without staff specifically focussing on the 'challenging' behaviours, s/he may well have become a person who is easier to be with, more content and fulfilled. In our past work with many of the students at Harperbury School, this degree of success alone might be seen as a terrific achievement for many individuals.

We have known all of these developments occur for students/clients primarily through the 'natural momentum' of Intensive Interaction sequences growing and developing. Yes, there are subtle ways of judiciously guiding events when staff become very experienced and confident, but we have found the main developmental force to be natural momentum.

This may not sit easy with some members of staff, perhaps experienced ones, who are accustomed to working through controlling with some precision what is to be learnt. This realisation was one of the truly hard ones for us at first. Yet nearly all infants learn most of their use and understanding of communication through the snowballing effect of this natural momentum, and borrowing the principles brings about the same effect in our work.

Natural momentum – repetition

Intensive Interaction involves a great deal of repetition of activities. Success is consolidated through repetition – both partners are usually willing to repeat successful and effective episodes. The old adage 'nothing breeds success like success', applies in full measure to Intensive Interaction. Effective sequences which involve repetition are also at the same time likely to promote more diversity. Precisely because sessions with an individual are going well, because they are effective, there is more opportunity for new developments to occur, with the learner being more motivated and confident about trying things out.

Thus, in the first place, progress is achieved through continued reference to and repetition of successful activities. In doing this, more and more opportunities for new activities become available, and the learner adds these, with support and encouragement, to the repertoire. It is the progressive growth in the repertoire of interactive games which is mainly causing the snowballing effect in the early stages.

Natural momentum – repertoires

A repertoire is mostly composed of effective activities which the individual student/client uses comfortably with the available interactive partners. The individual repertoire may vary somewhat for the same student/client with different staff. An activity or game which goes well with one or two members of staff, may not take off at all with another. This is natural, and to be expected. Allowing for our individual differences is part of the approach. In broad terms, though, staff teams working with an individual should work toward a basic sharing of knowledge about the repertoire for each individual student/client.

A repertoire starts its growth with the activity or activities which make up the access. Sometimes this starting point is minute, the merest glance or shared smile. With people who are particularly difficult to reach, the repertoire may remain tiny and limited for a long time. In the early stages, one of the main forces for growth is the celebratory activity of the member of staff. Whilst interacting by focussing on something already established, which works, the member of staff may notice and celebrate something new. If the celebration works to cause mutual pleasure, there is some likelihood that this may become the main focus of the interaction for a period. If that is successful, there is likelihood that one or other of the interactive partners will cause that focus to return to the fore. This new activity is then remembered and tried again during the next interaction between the two people. In the meantime, the staff team have carried out good documentation and evaluation and other staff members are aware of the possibility of a new activity.

It can be seen here that one of the ways in which we can use some intellectual guidance or control over the course of interactions, is by promoting certain activities from repertoires. It is possible gently to focus on eye contact for instance, by deliberately selecting known activities with an individual which rehearse this ability particularly. The principle of sensitive scanning for feedback signals remains the same however. Any sign of boredom should be treated as a negative signal and responded to immediately.

The repertoire remains a secure base for both partners in an inter-action. If something entirely new is being tried out for the first time, it is often the case that there will be frequent returns during this sequence to a known and secure activity. Returning to such an activity remains at all times the main option for staff when in doubt at any time. It is one of the ways of introducing stimulus during the interaction; it is always an available option for coming out of pause.

In the early stages of access and establishment, it may well be possible to record the main items of repertoire in full. We suggest in fact that this is desirable. A good sign of progress and development is when it becomes difficult to record everything that comprises the interactions, or even remember them. At such a stage, the student/clients' communications are truly becoming elaborate.

Individual members of staff, or teams, develop repertoires too. We have found that among any group of students/clients working consistently with the same staff, there may be some aspects of interacting which are shared across all individuals. This may be to do with a team of staff developing a 'house style'. The team members observe each other well, do plenty of sharing of ideas, and as a consequence develop a recognisable style which has some common themes for all the students/clients.

Another reason for this may well be that there are some types of games or activities which are simply naturally good and effective for all human beings. Some examples which seem obvious are tickling, jiggling and raspberries on the side of the face or neck. These types of behaviour between people doing Intensive Interaction arise everywhere.

Natural momentum – plateaux and problems

As with everything else, problems and low periods will be experienced when using this approach. We cannot pretend to have snappy answers to all of the difficulties which may arise. Nor can we claim to have experienced all of the possible difficulties. Our motto, however, has always been that the benefits overwhelm the difficulties and that any difficulties experienced do not make a reason for not using the approach.

One of the main problems we have experienced is that work with an individual may enter a type of 'plateau' period, where for ages nothing more or new seems to happen. You can still do interaction, have good, happy engagements with the student/client, but everything seems a bit routine. One of the effects of this is that you start to lose your sparkle, even some of your optimism. You then start wondering whether this is the end of the line and the student/client has developed as far as she/he can go.

This situation is where quality of teamwork, particularly practical and emotional support, is very helpful. Good discussion amongst staff is needed, together with the will to carry on doing cool, realistic evaluation. One of the possibilities that should be uppermost in discussions, is that it may well not be the student/client who is having the difficulties. It may rather be that the staff team has become bored or depressed, or just lost some sparkle, for all sorts of reasons. Frequently, as we all know, the reasons may not be to do with anything happening in daily work, but more to do with pressure from outside, things we cannot control.

One of the most practical strategies to come out of such evaluation is to just relax and accept that you are having a bad period. That is perfectly acceptable – it will probably pass. There may then be a simple renewed sense of purpose which magically seems to get things going again once you have accepted that you are having a bad period. Neither of these two things will happen, however, without good, open discussion among staff.

Another possibility, of course, is that it *is* the student/client who is having the problems. There may be some things happening in that person's life which you can identify but over which you may not be able to exert control. Good work at this stage may involve simply doing proper maintenance on the interaction sequences, and waiting patiently and hopefully guiltlessly for the situation to improve.

Sometimes of course, work and progress with an individual can be so slow, so long-term seeming, that staff do get bored. There are no special routines for overcoming boredom which are unique to doing Intensive Interaction. If any aspect of the work is boring, then a good staff team will have space and security for people to say so. This is the first approach to dealing with it. Changing working routines can help, changing staff around temporarily can help. For us on one occasion, the arrival of a new member of staff who started doing things with an individual which none of the rest of us were trying, was completely galvanising.

On the whole though, we suggest that with this approach, there is less tendency for a problem such as boredom to arise. It is in the nature of the approach that using it is dynamic. It is fun most of the time, the unexpected frequently happens. Nonetheless, we do not suggest that staff compel themselves to stay in one working situation any longer than is normally considered healthy in this work.

Interactivity

We are not sure if the term 'interactivity' is a grammatically correct one, but we find it useful shorthand to describe a concept. This is a term we developed and used casually at Harperbury School. What we mean by 'Interactivity' is as follows. When we were developing our work on these principles, we firstly thought about the interaction sequences as a special, intense activity which happened at a particular time of the day. We then got on with all the other activities which made up the working day and which were long established. We found some developments occurring naturally however.

First, some students quickly made progress to the point where they were starting to initiate – to look for and ask for interactions. Inconveniently, this would happen incidentally at any time, not just when it was timetabled. We realised quickly that the best thing to do was to be flexible enough to respond to the learner's initiations wherever and whenever possible. It was, after all, an important part of the learning that we respond to their voluntary attempts at communicating. This had the effect on us that we were starting to hold ourselves ready in 'interaction mode' throughout the day. This had the further effect of starting to reduce emphasis on our previous style of doing things. We were starting to change our style of working generally, moving more and more away from being dominating, controlling, forceful.

At the same time, the more we took part in the set-piece interaction sequences, the more we thought about and discussed the power and significance of this way of behaving as members of staff. As a natural process, this style of being with the students started to be influential in everything that we did. We started to relax more and become more lighthearted in the way we organised and led any activity. Again, we were becoming less dominant and forceful, using our behaviour to help our students be motivated to participate.

As this happened we could identify and understand the principles we were using in our behaviour which were having these effects. It was reassuring to have an intellectualised set of principles which explained and guided our basic performance as teachers. More and more we started to realise, articulate and explore our powers as social interactors in all situations. We began to realise fully that assuming ourselves to be dominating authority figures who could compel our students to learn, was not the way forward. We started to talk about the spill-over of interaction principles from the set-piece sessions, to our work generally, as 'interactivity'.

Formerly we might have used an early resort to dominance or even physical force to move a student, say to a different part of the room for a new activity. With our growth in understanding of interactivity, we began to interact the person to the desired place. We would use face and voice to create a participative mood, walk with them in rhythm or use rhythmic noises and laughter. Barring the way to someone attempting to escape the building might become a tension-expectancy game rather than a confrontation. These are gross examples of what became a rich seam in all of our doings around the school. Other pay-offs were things like a reduction in stress levels – staff lost confrontations less frequently by not having them so often – and a reduction in noise levels – staff shouted less. A general, agreeable atmosphere of light-hearted purposefulness became the working atmosphere.

This brings us back to something we have already stated. To learn communication is a paramount learning need for everyone: first, communication is important for personal fulfilment at every level, including crucially developing a sense of emotional well-being; second, there is the simple, practical consideration for all of us in our work, that communication is the basic tool with which we do everything else. Our concept of interactivity helped us to visualise the use of this basic tool in all situations with learners who still had limited understandings. Interaction sequences were established as a need in themselves, but doing this enabled us to develop new and effective ways of attending to many other needs.

Summary

- Student/client progress occurs mainly through the development of the interaction sequences by natural momentum.
- Successful sequences cause a growth in the repertoire of activities available for each individual.
- The growth in the repertoire of activities during interaction, brings with it more options for interacting with and understanding other people.
- As well as natural momentum, there are ways of gently guiding some developments when staff are experienced and confident.
- Effective Intensive Interaction sequences involve repetition of activities in the repertoire.
- Repetition of activities provides increased opportunities for new developments.

- Any sign of boredom from the student/client should be responded to as a signal of negativity.
- Staff teams are likely to develop an interaction style which has features they share.
- With any individual student/client there is unlikely to be uninterrupted progress.
- Some individuals progress very slowly and feelings of tedium may set in.
- Lack of progress may be as much to do with staff state of mind as anything within the student/client.
- Good teamwork, consultation and evaluation, are necessary during periods of slow progress.
- 'Interactivity' is the technique of staff using interaction principles throughout their general work with students/clients.
- The concept of interactivity occurred in our work because the effectiveness of staff behaviour in interaction sequences spilled over into other activities.

Organisational issues

We readily acknowledge that using Intensive Interaction can bring with it some organisational difficulties and it is to these practical considerations that we now turn. These issues will apply most directly to teachers and practitioners involved with day care and developmental work, though some of the practicalities will apply whatever the circumstances. Most of what we offer here are guidelines based on our own experience or on the experience of staff who have worked in other settings and fed back to us. We are less emphatic about these guidelines than about those relating specifically to the interactions, but nonetheless attention to these basics will help if you are considering using Intensive Interaction in your work.

Achieving quality one-to-one time

The importance of being able to concentrate fully on the interactive partner is something with which the reader will by now be familiar. Most caregivers, however busy, usually strive for and attain short periods of time when they can really enjoy their infants. We have come to some understandings in Western culture that it is the quality rather than the quantity of interactions with a familiar caregiver which is important for child development (though this continues to be a controversial issue). If we are to stimulate the development of people with learning difficulties through the intensive use of interactive sequences then we must organise ourselves to allow for quality one-to-one time. We would urge you to look to the possibilities rather than the limitations of your situation here and remind you that this need only be for short periods of time.

An important starting point lies with your attitudes and the attitudes of those around you. In our initial development of the approach we had the benefit of being able to be completely honest with each other and to freely admit that we could not hope to have all of our students doing something useful or educational simultaneously for all of the time. We had tried this and failed, not just as a result of our staffing levels, but as a result of the limited abilities of our students to attend and our limited abilities to find relevant activities for them. No sooner had we got one person settled with some sand and another person doing an inset puzzle than the first person had tipped the sand over and another person had run out of the door. We came to compare this with the poor circus clown attempting to keep numerous plates spinning on poles! We also came to question the purpose of the previously desired constant activity; was it necessary, what did it achieve, did this warrant the pressure it caused to staff and students? Once we had freed ourselves of these expectations we were able to be more creative with the use of our time.

When we began to bring the use of interactive game to the core of our curriculum we began to seek ways of achieving quality one-to-one time. Our staffing ratios meant that for every one person with whom we were interacting there were two who were not receiving staff attention. These people might be rocking in a corner, emptying out a cupboard, dozing, or rushing around the room. We accepted this as part of it and the progress our students made in a very short space of time reassured us that this was fair judgement and the right way to be proceeding.

We organised ourselves so that we had someone playing the role of 'room manager'. It was the room manager's task to ensure that everyone was safe and contained, that people were stimulated where possible, and that intensive interactions were not interrupted unless absolutely necessary. It was not expected that the room manager would spend time teaching; she might put on music, or offer equipment, but her primary purpose was to enable the other staff members to be most effective. The policy of room management was a basic organisational tool which enabled us to work in the way we wanted. We all took a turn at the room manager role and we all recognised that on some days the system would fail us and we would all have to be involved with one or two disturbed students. Days like this though, when no one got any contact of any quality, were less frequent with our newer practices.

Mostly we worked with two teachers and two assistants with ten students, but room management can be utilised with different staffing ratios as long as there is more than one member of staff, as long as staff are prepared to experiment with and share roles, and as long as they are prepared to make difficult-seeming judgements. We reiterate that it is the attitude of accepting that the value of quality one-to-one time outweighs the accompanying problems which will be the key to enabling you to creatively find your own solution to achieving it.

Team working

We would suggest that team working is important to Intensive Interaction. One can argue that frequently caregivers engage in wonderful interactions with their infants in the absence of a supportive team, but using interaction in developmental work with people with severe learning difficulties can have some different prerequisites. Team working is not only important for achieving quality one-to-one time, but for sharing ideas and workload, for analysing feedback, and for recognising progress.

As we have described earlier in the chapter, making access with the person can take a long time. Sometimes one person can make initial access with a student and then share with team members how this was achieved. With a small team of staff working together there can be a pooling of experience and ideas about making access, the person's preferred tempo, the best times to approach them, what they respond to. When it is very physical rough and tumble play or synchronised rocking and head-bobbing that the person responds to, it can be essential to share the workload!

In using Intensive Interaction we become very sensitive observers and we learn to pick up on the finest signals of pleasure and negativity. It can still be helpful, however, to have other people to mull these over with and to point out aspects of signalling we may have missed. Similarly, we can learn a lot from watching each other and from hearing about each other's interactions and interpretations of what they involve. We were helped enormously in developing Intensive Interaction by the fact that we were working together in teams towards a common goal.

There is of course a need for the team to have times in which team members can get together to discuss, plan and evaluate. Although our teaching was not pre-planned and structured in the traditional sense we always started the day with a mini-conference. Here we would reflect on the previous day, allocate roles for the room management and make priorities. We organised ourselves so that we were each allocated to room manager role, to working with one person with particular needs, or to a group of three students (each hopefully to get a quality one-to-one session within the time). Intensive Interaction can require you to give more personally than other approaches and this staffing allocation could be affected by who was feeling tired or whose back was aching most! Usually though, we rotated roles so that everyone worked with every student over the course of the week.

We would recommend some kind of organisational structure which blends this flexibility with the need to give the students/clients equal access to the qualities of different members of staff. We need to make explicit that the approach is not about achieving strong, exclusive bonds, but about facilitating development. There will always be personalities that blend particularly well, but we want our clients to be able to relate to a range of people. We need to ensure also that we spend quality time with everyone. Without safeguards an interactive approach could be very good for those clients who are able to reward us for being with them, or who have qualities which attract us to try to reach them, but those students who give very little positive feedback or who have more offputting behaviours can continue to miss out.

The length of sessions

We are frequently asked how long an interactive session lasts, to which we always have to reply 'it depends'. In terms of organisational practicalities a certain amount of flexibility is necessary to allow for the possibility that the session might last for 30 seconds or for 20 minutes. We found that allowing 30 minutes to work with three people worked for us. This meant that there was time and flexibility to decide which of the three people we might approach first, to spend longer with some students than with others, and to return to someone who had earlier been rejecting. Other practitioners have found that they need longer time slots or a more open structure.

Whichever way you organise yourself you need to avoid working to the clock and unnecessary pressures to finish an interaction session prematurely. You also need to avoid feeling pressured to spend too long with one client. Interactions like this invariably take the form of short bursts. We need to respect the signals of the other person and all attempts at lengthening the sessions will need to be done with the person's consent. Dragging a session out or staying with a student who has lost interest is likely to be counterproductive. It is better to have short, quality interactions interspersed with short periods of rest and reflection. As practitioners we will also need breaks from the intensity of the experiences.

The intensity of the sessions

Intensive Interaction is about promoting the kinds of interactions which are mutually pleasurable, reciprocal, and increasingly complex and communicative. This does not mean that every interaction you have with a client will be brilliantly enjoyable, include a lot of activity, or be a bit more involved than the last one. All sorts of factors will affect the nature of each interactive sequence, not least of all how you and the other person are feeling at the time.

We found that some of the interactions which took place when we had set up time for quality one-to-one, were actually of a lesser quality than some of the peripheral interactions which took place in a snatched couple of minutes between other activities. The intensity and quality of interactions vary just as much as the content of the interactive games. We have also come to realise that the very gentle interactions in which we might just enjoy sharing the sofa and humming together play an important bolstering role alongside the more intense sessions. They help to provide a context of positive social experience and to facilitate the process of getting to know and feel comfortable with each other.

For some people it might be our aim to widen the range of interactive experiences they can cope with. We have had students where we have had to always be very dramatic and overt with our faces and voices and actions in order to attract their attention. In contrast, we have worked with people where the interactions had to be very low key or very short to prevent them becoming over-aroused and then aggressive. The art is to be aware of such limitations whilst always looking for ways of moving on.

The physical environment

Intensive Interaction was for us born in a dreary converted ward in a long stay hospital where the rooms were large and cold and not very well equipped. This is not one of those approaches which requires a massive cash input to get the environment right. We hope that this is reassuring as we recognise how demoralising it can be to try to work in surroundings which are clearly inappropriate. Having said this, there are changes we can make to the physical environment to support the social and learning processes.

Initially our classrooms looked and felt like traditional classrooms. They were dominated by tables and chairs and the inherited table-top equipment. Acting on the theory that we should start where the student is at, both physically as well as developmentally, we found that we rarely used the tables and chairs. Instead we would join the students in their preferred or safe places – in the corners of the room, often on the floor, and sometimes in the corridor or doorway! This led us to do away with much of the table space and to invest in some carpets and soft, comfortable furniture. The rocking chair became our most used piece of equipment.

Readers who work in home environments will be at an advantage in this respect. The physical environment can influence the way we behave and it is likely that homely atmospheres are most conducive for the optimal style of interaction we described in chapter two. In contrast, classrooms that look and feel like traditional classrooms can encourage us to be loud and dominating and to do tasks. Intensive Interaction is more suited to environments in which the learner as well as the staff member can feel comfortable and relaxed. This might be a different environment for different people. We have enjoyed some wonderful interactions in the school therapy pool which is warm and relaxing and where physical contact is most often welcomed. We have also, however, enjoyed very purposeful and pleasurable interactions in the bathroom, the sandpit, the corridor, on a garden swing, and in the minibus in a queue of traffic. One of the beauties of this approach is that it can take place anywhere.

With the group or on your own?

While this is less of an issue for parents and caregivers, one question for practitioners concerns whether or not you should endeavour to set aside a quiet space or room where you and your student/client can withdraw to enjoy quality one-to-one time. This would certainly offer the advantages of enabling you to be uninterrupted and to feel unin-hibited and for some clients it would be a nice environment. In a very mixed ability group, or with other staff who would disparage your interactions, the only option might be to go to the soft room or the quiet room. We would, however, strongly put forward the case for Intensive Interaction taking place in the everyday environment with others around you.

Firstly, when we are working with people who are pre-verbal and whose learning needs are in the areas of fundamental communication and sociability, an interactive approach like this at the core of their education or day care is highly appropriate. We feel this should be recognised by the interactions occuring as a valued part of the usual routine, not being marginalised. Every effort should be made to ensure that all staff understand what the approach is about (we acknowledge that this can be difficult) and they should have opportunities to see this at work. The qualities we use in interactive sequences should and will inevitably be used in everyday relating and in doing the mundane tasks; they should not be seen as special and separate.

Secondly, Intensive Interaction works best as team work; we can benefit so much from watching each other's interactions and from sharing feedback. Our students/clients will also benefit from being in an environment with interactive games going on around them. Our experience was that once you had a couple of pairs of people in a room interacting playfully, this had a positive effect on the overall atmosphere.

Thirdly, Intensive Interaction can involve you in warm physical contact with your client. You might hug and romp together and this is an essential part of it. Bearing in mind the issues around abuse, however, it is a sensible safeguard for all concerned to place such interactions in a room with other staff around.

We recommend using Intensive Interaction within the group environment, then, to emphasise that it is everyday teaching, to enable a sharing of good practice and as a precaution in the light of possible allegations of abuse. If, however, bearing these factors in mind, you still feel the need to withdraw from the classroom to do Intensive Interaction then you should do so and find other ways of addressing these factors. We are aware of examples of this being the case in classrooms where the majority of the students were more able and the students needing Intensive Interaction had sessions in the sensory room and sessions in the classroom when the others had library trips and integration sessions. There were efforts to ensure that there were always two staff involved in the interaction sessions, that all of the staff were involved with Intensive Interaction at some time, and that opportunities for communication were built in.

The whole day

One of the organisational issues concerns how much of your day should be given over to Intensive Interaction and how well Intensive Interaction can fit alongside other activities in the day. In our school the approach began as an activity very much on the periphery of the main action. We would enjoy playful interactions with students at odd moments between sessions, while waiting for something else to happen, or when moving around the building or grounds. It was the recognition of the value of these peripheral interactions that led us to make them more central to our work. With many students Intensive Interactions became the core of the curriculum. The most intense part of the day, when we would work towards the students' individual aims, became a time taken up with promoting powerful interactive sequences. This was only one hour of a three hour session, however, and we were aware that we needed to continue with other aspects of our curriculum. The intensive one-to-one sessions, therefore, were followed by a relaxed group 'hello' session, some time to have a drink, and a time without any demands being made, perhaps in the garden or with music playing. The day was completed with an activity-focussed session, this might be art or music, 'cooking', movement, swimming, or a trip out on the minibus.

In the classes which were entirely dominated by students who were pre-verbal and yet able to develop fundamental social and communication abilities, Intensive Interaction became the central focus. The first, intensive part of the day was highly valued and very purposeful. How we behaved for the other sessions was affected by this. In our interaction sequences with the students we got to know them well, their signals, what made them anxious and what they enjoyed. This obviously influenced our interactions with them at other times in the day. We also became more effective at involving the students in other activities because we learnt new abilities to attract and hold their attention – the 'interactivity' described earlier. A useful way to describe this might be that we were using 'interactivity' throughout the day. We did not turn on and turn off our abilities to be playful, sensitive, engaging; these were present throughout and helped to make the other activities more enjoyable and worthwhile.

In our travels around other workplaces where there is interest in this approach we have found a range of ways in which Intensive Interaction is used. In some places the approach is used across the day as it was at Harperbury. In some places where staff were experiencing difficulty in convincing their managers of the value of the approach, it was almost sneaked into the day under the guise of movement or drama. We have also seen Intensive Interaction incorporated into relaxation sessions, massage, free play times, times in the therapy pool or sensory room. There is a sense in which it can be done at certain times in the day, but we very much doubt whether it can be kept entirely within these artificial boundaries. Staff who are keen to intellectualise and analyse the processes of interaction in the interests of their client's development, are likely to be staff who already use playful, positive interactions as a way of relating with the clients throughout the day anyway. In our experience even if staff do initially switch back to a different way of interacting outside interaction sessions, it is unlikely that they will continue to be able to, or even want to. Just as taking part in these powerful interactions can have a lasting effect on the student/client, the effect on the staff member can also be irreversible.

Mixed-ability groupings

At the hospital school we had classes in which all of the students were at a level of development such that their primary needs were concerned with the very early development of sociability and communication. This concentrated our minds wonderfully on the task of developing an approach to respond to these needs. It is perhaps more usual that a school, day centre or residential setting will have groups of people with learning difficulties whose needs and abilities are more diverse.

Teachers with mixed-ability classes have often expressed concern that having some students doing Intensive Interaction will lead to other more able students behaving inappropriately, perhaps wanting too much attention, wanting physical contact, or even copying games deemed to be child-like. We would not want to devalue these issues and we appreciate that these mixed settings present problems that we did not have to face when developing the approach. We would suggest, however, that these problems are not insurmountable. With peers who are much more able, it might be possible to explain that it is now time for Maria's favourite activity with you, and that you will spend time with them on something really nice later. Perhaps giving and receiving physical contact might be appropriate in some form for all of the clients anyway. The issue of copying might not be problematic either. It might be that more able students can observe and learn effective ways of relating to their less able peers. If other clients don't seem able enough for these kinds of solutions, but still seek out attention, physical contact and interactions like this, it might be that despite other superficial abilities, their emotional and social development is such that they are needy of Intensive Interaction also.

With very mixed groups Intensive Interaction may have a different role to play. It may not dominate the atmosphere and the day as it did for us, but merely be one of many available approaches. It might be that the students/clients need to be divided up for different activities at different times, and that Intensive Interaction will offer a very relevant activity for those people for whom you have previously been short of ideas. It is worth considering, however, how much the principles of the approach can be usefully applied to any learner, and we will discuss this more fully in chapter five.

Planning and recording

Accountability

Demands for accountability are currently a feature of most disciplines and we cannot ignore them. Even if we are cynical about some of the systems associated with this, we can be sincere about our need to be accountable to our clients at least. We need to make very clear to staff, managers, parents and employers that Intensive Interaction is not just about having a good time. It does require mutual enjoyment, but it is much more than just the fun slots alongside another activity which is seen as the real work. Intensive Interaction is about facilitating development; it is effective, relevant and purposeful. This needs to be clear at all levels and to be reflected in our paperwork.

Structure of planning and recording

Some practitioners and managers will feel uncomfortable with the fact that working in this way is not compatible with rigid structures, tight objectives, and tick-lists. It is important to resist pressures to impose such systems of planning and recording which are at odds with the way of working itself.

One of the elements of Intensive Interaction is that the staff member bases her/his activity on that of the student/client. A consequence of this is that we can never accurately predict what form a session might take nor specify in advance what the outcomes might be. Staff accustomed to more behavioural ways of working will be in the habit of specifying objectives for a session in a way which we cannot do here. This does not mean that the session lacks purpose, however, and we can plan in terms of the strategies we might use and the abilities we might want to see the client develop.

At Harperbury School the individual programmes which stated our aims and objectives for a student were replaced by programmes detailing our aims and our strategies and intentions for working with them. In this way we planned what we hoped to achieve with a student and how we were going to go about it. The strategies referred to the particular aspects of interactive style which we might find or had found to be useful in making access with the student and the elements of her/his behaviour and preferences which could be utilised. We might, for example, aim to increase the student's tolerance of the proximity or touch of the staff, or to develop a repertoire of simple interactive games. Strategies might include experimenting with various approaches to the student's proximity, capitalising on the knowledge that she likes to have her neck stroked, or building on some signs of pleasure shown in response to having her stereotyped behaviours imitated in a playful and dramatic way. Figure 1 provides an example of one of these individual programmes.

We moved away from checklists of skills and behaviours towards anecdotal, unstructured discussion of progress together with written

Figure 1: *Example of Curricular Programme: Desmond*

Aims:

To increase Desmond's tolerance of the proximity of all the staff group.
To establish and consolidate the use of eye contact.
To reassure him of the gentle nature of our touch.
To develop a repertoire of simple interactive games.
To extend the timespan for which he is willing and able to be involved with staff or in activities.

Strategies:

Experiment with a range of different kinds of interaction to begin to identify Desmond's preferences.
Utilise what we already know about him liking to have his neck stroked and to rest his head on our laps while lying on the soft furniture.
Follow up on his positive responses to playful approaches including having his nose tweaked and imitation work at a distance.

narrative recordings (see figure 2). These narrative records were completed immediately after the session took place as we found that if we waited until the end of a morning or afternoon too much else had happened in between for us to remember properly. While this took up some of our valuable contact time with the students, we saw it as an essential part of the process and we valued the opportunity to reflect and to clear our minds before moving on to work with someone else. We trained ourselves to become analytical thinkers about what we were doing, while not letting this spoil our enjoyment of the interactions. Indeed the recording process itself trained our perceptions and analysis. In addition to recording the main sessions we found ourselves motivated to record incidental interactions which were especially good or informative in some way.

We were concerned with describing what we did and why we did it as well as with noting anything new that happened. We deliberately did not limit ourselves to what was observable (and objective?), we wanted to record also our thoughts, feelings and suppositions, valuing this subjective information. We asked of ourselves three important questions: What happened in the sequence? What was significant? How did we feel? We can recommend this kind of recording and evaluation as both useful and satisfying to do. You may, as we did, become highly interested in reading each others' recordings, and in reflecting on the process. You may want to dwell on such issues as the degree to which you were working from intuition, the decisions you were conscious of making, how effective the signalling system was, how your mood affected your performance and what you learnt from the session.

Evaluation

It is important, of course, that records are kept for the purpose of informing the teaching activity and for illustrating what progress is being made by the learner. Simply analysing and writing down in this way goes some way towards this, but we need to take this further. At the end of each term at Harperbury School we would complete evaluations of the programmes, commenting on where significant progress had been made, which aims had been achieved and which strategies had been useful. Looking forward we would think about where we needed to go next and what new strategies were needed. Another way in which we evaluated involved us in pulling together the records of the individual sessions and drawing out common themes and crucial pointers. We had a good system for this with the members

Figure 2: *Example of record form*

Student: Kevin   *Date*:   *Place*: classroom

Staff member:

Description, type of sequence:

Very varied – lots of different activities – jiggling, stroking, using lots of commentary. Very over-dramatised behaviour from me in response to any behaviour from K. Used the game where I respond with a huge exclamation every time K. looked in my eyes. Lots of teasing voice 'show me your tongue – where's your tongue?' Got a game of turn-taking with short turns.

Significant occurrences:

Very good, sustained eye contact. Activities went easily between very gentle and quite dramatic. K. controlled this. I asked K. to stick his tongue out. He did this quickly and watched me smiling. Turn-taking game with voice.

Brief comment on your own performance:

Felt rough. Quickly 'tuned in' and forgot this though. Felt all the time like something was about to happen. Felt that K. was very much with me and to some extent alive to what might happen. He has sat down beside me to watch me write this. He keeps trying to get eye contact.

Other comments:

Voice is important with K. I feel also like he is sometimes almost saying something and I work on that with expectancy and intentionality. Feel good about prospects.

of one staff team, classroom assistants included, in turns taking home the records each weekend, reading them through and writing a short evaluative summary on each of the students and on each of the staff, reporting this back on a Monday morning. You have to have a very committed team who are very trusting of each other to do this, but it is worth it. This is again a challenge to the traditional boundaries between staff and students and between the staff themselves.

This kind of approach to record-keeping and evaluation provides a wealth of insights into the teaching and learning process and into the students' development. We were able to use this to highlight when one of us had made a breakthrough, when one of us was spending too much time with one particular student, when a student was not experiencing very positive interactions with any of us, and when subtle but significant progress was being made. Such systems are based on observations which are highly subjective, but the team approach to analysing them brings with it a kind of layer of objectivity.

Supporting the observations with video records

In addition, narrative and anecdotal records can be supported by regular and frequent video recordings. Again, however, there needs to be an element of team analysis with this. We found it useful, especially when we were first setting out, to make fortnightly video recordings of the students, both in interaction and when they were alone. We looked back on these aiming to identify new developments in the students' behaviour, new developments in the interaction sequences, and new developments in the teaching approach itself.

Videos can be particularly useful in trying to understand various patterns. Examples of this might include situations when you cannot make out what one person in the team is successfully doing which is different from what everyone else does, or why sometimes a particular approach to a student gains a favourable response and sometimes no response at all. Periodic video analysis can also provide some completely new insights. It is true that sometimes signalling systems are sensed by the staff but not observable to onlookers, it can also be the case, however, that signals are not picked up at the time but can be detected later on video. Observing signals can be particularly difficult when the student/client is very active or else very passive and video tape gives us the opportunity to observe a sequence slowed down or speeded up or else to re-run it over and over again.

Videos can also be made and kept to compare someone's responses over time. As part of a research project, we made video recordings on a fortnightly basis for eighteen months (see Nind 1992). We analysed them for changes in the students' repertoires of behaviour when alone, and for changes in their interactive behaviours such as the development of eye contact, contingent smiling, vocalisation or movement, reaching to touch and nestling in. We acknowledge that this procedure is time-consuming and expensive, but the record of development it produces is highly detailed and informative.

Structured observation and assessment schedules

More objective recording can also involve the use of structured observations and published assessment schedules. In researching the efficacy of the method we needed this backup and we made good use of both. The Sociability Observation Schedule (Nind 1992) was developed to provide a format for quickly-administered, structured observation in the natural classroom setting. We were able to use this to measure changes in the students' ability and motivation to make contact with others, and in the extent to which their responses could encourage others to interact with and be near them. It involved taking samples of time and allocating the students' responses to various categories of behaviour, based on whether or not they had an initiating or encouraging effect. We thus looked at changes in students' body posture, head inclination, facial expression, glances, eye contact and movements. This kind of structured observation can be applied whenever such careful scrutiny is necessary.

Published assessment schedules can also provide supporting evidence of student/client change. This can give another angle on development and be quite convincing for the sceptics. Many of the available schedules, however, will not be basic or sensitive enough to illustrate progress at this very early stage of development. Few schedules will cover the social and communication areas with which we are concerned. Having said this, we found that the Pre-Verbal Communication Schedule (Kiernan and Reid 1987) was pertinent and useful, as it was concerned not just with formal communication skills, but with informal and pre-communication behaviours. Using this we were able to keep supporting records of developments in the students' enjoyment and interest in other people and the beginnings of their use of gesture and vocalisation.

You might also find that the Affective Communication Assessment (Coupe and Goldbart 1988) provides useful support in the tasks of assessing, record-keeping and evaluation. We would emphasise, however, that none of these more structured and formal approaches can replace the day-to-day subjective observations, records and analyses of the staff themselves.

Cautions

We have used this chapter to focus on the practical application of Intensive Interaction. We hope that we have provided useful guidelines on how to begin and how to proceed as well as guidance on organisational matters. Before moving on to a discussion of some of the wider issues in chapter five we would like to offer some cautions. We are simply making you aware here of some of the mistakes we find people starting out on this approach are vulnerable to and of those traps we fell into ourselves.

Beware of being too passive

We cannot emphasise enough that Intensive Interaction is not about leaving them to it. Even when you are observing you should be actively involved in developing some empathy or giving some analytical thought to how it feels to be that person. Even when you are sharing a relaxed embrace with a student/client you should be alert to her/his signals. There will be times when you are exhausted or simply not in the mood and you just flop down on a mattress beside a passive student. This is inevitable and might have some value, but if it is all that is happening it is probably not Intensive Interaction.

Beware of not moving on

Some of you may share the experience that we often had of finding that your learners respond to this way of working very quickly. You may soon have a warm rapport and a range of pleasurable interactive games. If you are lucky the process of interaction will have its own momentum and you will find yourselves in a positive spiral, increasingly motivated to take part in increasingly sophisticated interactive sequences. Often, though, moving on will require much reflection, discussion and analysis. If you and the student/client are enjoying your time together more than ever before you may find that this is enough. The danger here is that the interactions will become stilted and that you will become bored and de-motivated by the limitations of the range of games and responses. It is easy to use a sensitive style of interacting to bring quality to your everyday practice without using it more fully to facilitate ongoing social and communication development.

Beware of forcing the pace

Taking care to make the most of your interactions to promote development does not mean that you have to force the pace. You can work towards keeping things moving on without there ever being a sense of you driving on in the interactions themselves. These should still reflect the pace and rhythms with which the learner is most comfortable. Remember also, that when you start from where the learner is comfortable and familiar, your responses will be celebratory, but also very slightly challenging. You will need the gap between what s/he can already do, and the new abilities you are expecting, to be very small and unthreatening.

Beware of doing 'to' rather than doing 'with'

When we give staff development sessions on Intensive Interaction in various workplaces a common response is that the staff comment that they already do this anyway. We find this immensely reassuring and staff groups are reassured also that they are along the right lines. Sometimes, however, staff will claim to be doing this with clients with profound and multiple learning difficulties in their movement or massage sessions. At their best, movement therapy and massage sessions will be interactive, with the practitioner highly sensitive to the signals of the client. More often though, the client can be very passive while we roll or stroke or massage them. This may be extremely beneficial and extremely relaxing, but we need to be aware that this is something we do *to* rather than *with* our clients. Interaction is more mutual and reciprocal than this.

Beware of using Intensive Interaction to modify behaviour

Another very common response during staff development sessions is for staff to quote their most difficult clients and to seek help in stopping or modifying their 'anti-social' behaviours. This is entirely understandable and we often wish that we could be more helpful. One of the consequences of using Intensive Interaction at Harperbury School was that much of the difficult behaviour faded, becoming less apparent and less significant. We cannot know exactly why that was and many factors are likely to have been influential. It must have helped that the staff team were feeling positive and much less stressed and that the atmosphere was more fun and purposeful and less confrontational.

When we started to use Intensive Interaction we never set out to deal with the students' various challenging and ritualistic behaviours, we were setting out to promote the development of fundamental social and communication abilities. With these developments came improvements in behaviour. We now often find it useful to think of behavioural difficulties as communication difficulties and conclude that much of the difficult behaviour was a response to the anxiety and pressures associated with lacking the abilities to understand or communicate. We recommend starting from the stance of promoting positive behaviour positively, rather than diminishing negative behaviour negatively. It is more respectful and altogether more sound to set about facilitating development than to seek to change a person's way of behaving without understanding the motivations behind it. Intensive Interaction should be a very positive process, not a negative one.

Beware of not explaining what you are doing

It is possible to use elements of Intensive Interaction quite successfully. It is also possible that parts of the approach can be applied without fully understanding the underlying thinking, with detrimental effect. It is vital, therefore, if you want to work in this way, that your colleagues fully understand what it is all about. On a different note Intensive Interaction will involve you in what can appear quite bizarre behaviour. You may find yourself imitating strange rituals, joining in with rhythmic sounds, romping and behaving in ways which some people would view as inappropriate. Your good practice could easily be misconstrued and it is in your interests to ensure that others understand it. This is particularly important for managers, parents and visitors to your workplace.

Beware of giving contradictory messages

With all approaches there is good practice and there is bad practice. Very often the way in which staff work with an individual will involve an eclectic combination of a number of approaches. Your reading about Intensive Interaction may lead you to add this to your 'tool box' to be used in this way. Our main caution with this is that you may then give mixed messages. Intensive Interaction is about valuing the person just the way they are. It views ritualistic behaviour as important to the person and not as something to be taken away because it seems meaningless and worthless. It involves treating the person with respect as a social and communicative being. It involves following their lead, enjoying and sharing control of the learning. There are other approaches which have a philosophical basis which differs greatly from this. Intensive Interaction may not be compatible with these and mixing the elements may leave the learner very unsure of her/his position.

CHAPTER 5

Wider and Related Issues

Introduction

We have advised readers to use this chapter for reference, particularly whilst reading the previous two chapters on practical techniques. We are aware that certain issues – 'age-appropriateness' or physical contact, say – may be a stumbling block to certain readers. It might be necessary to give detailed thought to one of these topics, before continuing to read on about matters of practical technique. For other readers, it may be something of a relief to have reached this point, since we have referred to its presence so many times.

Here we present an assortment of topics which we know from our work are important to practitioners, and about which we are likely to have significant views too. There is no particular theme unifying the topics, they are a variety of somewhat wider issues which have an effect on working by use of Intensive Interaction. We have given them all varying amounts of space, but this should not necessarily be taken as a rating system of their degree of comparative importance in our eyes. 'Age-appropriateness' wins the largest chunk, due to the complexity and diversity of the arguments and considerations involved. This topic does also bring about thoughts on a wider sociological perspective which we felt nonetheless had direct bearing on Intensive Interaction.

We decided at the outset to use plain speaking in setting out our own views on some topics. We do have strong opinions about our work and we decided that readers should be quite clear about what they are. We do not intend any degree of provocativeness by doing this, simply clarity and honest discussion.

What evidence is there that Intensive Interaction works?

Some readers might respond to reading about the background to Intensive Interaction at Harperbury School with the comment that any approach we might have tried would have worked. This might be so. We were a highly committed team who worked extremely well together and who wanted very much to reach our students. Some of the initial access we made with students could have been as much about a positive blending of personalities, as about the methods we were using. This is unlikely to be the case for the students for whom making access was a long and difficult process and for those students who were very unresponsive.

The formal research we undertook was a response to our seeking to understand more about the method of Intensive Interaction (Dave), and to show that it was effective in facilitating social and communication development (Melanie). The study of its effectiveness (Nind 1992) involved rigorous fortnightly observations over a prolonged period, firstly looking at the students' responses before Intensive Interaction was used with them and then for about a year afterwards. We used structured observations to look at initiation of social contact and responses to the physical proximity and physical contact of familiar staff. We analysed video recordings to compare over time the students' behaviours when alone as well as their interactive behaviours and their ability to become engaged in interactive game. There were various checks with other assessments and assessors.

We involved different class teachers in the formal research and six very different students. All the subjects were pre-verbal and lived in the institution, but the differences came with one having additional profound physical disabilities, one having sensory impairment, one having a history of self-injury, one with additional mental health problems, one with autism and hyperactive behaviour and one who was very passive apart from some sexual behaviour. We wanted to look at Intensive Interaction at work with a cross-section of our school population. The findings were complex, but all six students were shown to make progress, with Intensive Interaction the most likely linking factor.

While each of the students changed in different ways and to differing degrees, initiation of social contact increased or emerged for all of them. Their responses to the proximity and physical contact of staff became more encouraging with new developments including looking at the teacher's face, making eye contact, exhibiting a happy facial expression and making happy vocalisations. Four of the subjects developed new or increased ability to be still or occupied other than in organised self-involvement or stereotypy.

Common developments in the subjects' interactive abilities included more smiling contingent on the activity of the teacher and more time spent in interactive behaviours and being engaged in interactive game. They all showed improved ability to reciprocate warm physical contact as measured on the Cuddliness Scale (Brazelton 1984) and advances in their communication abilities as measured on the Pre-Verbal Communication Shedule (Kiernan and Reid 1987). Interestingly, the P.V.C.S. highlighted developments in the subjects' abilities to visually examine people's faces, to interpret visual cues, to show evidence of enjoying being with people, to distinguish familiar people from strangers, to respond to comfort, to experiment with vocalisation and to express emotion.

This study was really just an initial inquiry into how Intensive Interaction can aid development, with particular reference to sociability and communication. More in-depth, widespread and long-term investigation is needed, but we know enough about the effectiveness of the approach to make this research and continued use of Intensive Interaction worthwhile. Case studies of four of the subjects, Marion, Kevin, Georgiou and Victor, can be seen in chapter six.

Progression – what next?

Intensive Interaction takes us back to the very beginnings of learning about communication and sociability. We have probably all met people with learning difficulties who seem somehow to have missed learning these basics. We are thinking particularly of those individuals who do not seem to understand that communication is reciprocal, that it helps to look at people when you talk to them, or that there are facial expressions which go with various emotions and messages. Using this approach will help to ensure that the learner gets these fundamentals established and therefore has a sound basis for further learning. Intensive Interaction teaches the basics, but this includes the complexities of these basics.

Although we are very clear about where Intensive Interaction begins we are less clear about where it ends. It differs in many respects from those programmes of teaching and learning which take the learner from one clearly defined point to another, with the criteria for completion and the next step well defined. We have stressed that Intensive Interaction does not have this kind of pre-planned structure and that the experiences cannot be easily compartmentalised. The lack of a clear end-point is part of this.

When we look to the roots of Intensive Interaction in terms of the natural model of caregiver-infant interaction we can see this untidiness. Caregivers do not suddenly change the way they interact from an infant style, to a child style, to an adult style. The changes are more subtle than this. The amount and kind of support the caregiver provides may change as the infant develops (we refer you back to the literature about Bruner's 'scaffolding', see chapter two). The caregiver may take less responsibility for the interactions and increasingly hand over control to the developing infant. The caregiver may have less need to mediate the physical environment as the infant gains the confidence and competence to explore things for her/himself. The caregiver will become just one of many people to interact with, other children becoming increasingly important and influential. These changes in adult role and input change in response to changes in the infant; they are usually very well matched to the pace of infant learning and ensure that progress is continuing.

When we borrow from this natural model in using Intensive Interaction we need to remember about progression. We must be wary of pressing on with changes in our style of interaction without referring this to the developments of our learners. We need to pay constant attention to the match between what we do and where the learner is at. This should help to guide us to know what do do next and what are the progression routes.

With people with very severe learning difficulties it is unlikely that they will altogether outgrow this kind of approach. It may also be unlikely that they will become sophisticated and subtle enough in their interactive abilities to learn to socialise and play together. It is more probable that we will need to continue to be supersensitive interactive partners for our learners and that we will adapt our behaviour accordingly. It may also be that we can successfully introduce other activities and that we can begin to teach other skills by use of Intensive Interaction or through using other approaches. Intensive Interaction can certainly be supplemented by more diverse experiences as the learner becomes more able to make sense of the world and of the control they can have over it.

At the end of the five years we worked together using Intensive Interaction at Harperbury School some of the students were still in the early stages of gaining access, some had only a limited range of simple interactive games whilst others had made huge gains in terms of communication and sociability. We had direct experience of students moving away from having exclusion zones and violently defending their isolation, of students learning to enjoy, reciprocate and initiate interactive games, of students beginning to enter dialogue-like exchanges of vocalisations, and of students effectively using eye contact, facial expression and gesture to communicate. The students there, however, mostly began from a very basic starting point with the effects of institutionalisation to overcome. It was unlikely that five years would be sufficient to make Intensive Interaction redundant. There was often the frustration though, that for moving on further a different environment was needed.

In the natural model infants move on to develop formal language, usually speech. There is some, admittedly meagre, evidence to suggest that once the person is beyond childhood, full language use is unlikely to develop however good the teaching and preparation for it (Gardner, 1983). We did not see speech emerge in the adults at Harperbury School, but we know of colleagues using Intensive Interaction with children who are experiencing this exciting development in their learners.

We would urge you to not let any lack of clarity about the future after Intensive Interaction hold you back from beginning. The processes are worthwhile in themselves and whatever the outcomes, using Intensive Interaction will affect the quality of life of the learner and the quality of what you do together.

Progression – the content and method of Intensive Interaction

When we have described Intensive Interaction we have deliberately kept together the content and the method (or processes) of the approach. We have tended not to separate out what happens from how or why. This is because in actual practice these aspects are inseparable and it does not usually aid our understanding of Intensive Interaction to separate them on paper. There is, however, a useful broad distinction to be made when we think of progression and using the approach with people of different abilities.

In all the examples we have given so far we have been concerned with applying and borrowing from the natural model, aspects of both the content and method of caregiver-infant interaction. This is because both are relevant in terms of a good 'fit' with the abilities and interests of the learners. In most of our work at Harperbury it was games like 'peek-a-boo' and 'I'm going to get you . . .' that captured and held the students' interest. We have been able to identify, however, that there are good general principles of teaching and learning to be found in the caregiver-infant interaction model which can be applied to anyone.

168

We would suggest that with early levels of social and communication development both the content and method are relevant. With learners who have greater abilities or awareness, the teaching and learning experiences may usefully include the same methods, but with different content. The games typical of infancy will be replaced by other games, even to the extent of games which teach the basics of mathematics (see McConkey 1989).

Age-appropriateness

In our work we meet practitioners with a wide variety of attitudes towards their work. This issue is no different in that respect and it is inevitable that in discussing it we will probably not properly do justice to the wide range of possible views.

Mostly, we meet staff for whom the issue of age-appropriateness does not present massive problems. They seem to be able to address both the chronological age and the developmental age of their students/clients happily, without any sensation of contradiction between the two notions.

However, a noticeable proportion of the staff we meet seem to operate within a view of the 'age-appropriateness' notion which is overwhelming. Everything that takes place in the workplace, every act by a member of staff with a student/client, seems to be judged first of all for whether it is something that a person of this or that age would or should be doing. We do not meet those staff as frequently as was the case five years ago. However, on first introduction to the principles of Intensive Interaction some staff say that they would not use the approach because it is not age-appropriate. Others say that their boss would not let them use the approach on these grounds.

We shall work our way through this topic as carefully as we can, examining all of the issues as far as possible as we understand them. Naturally, we have views which are important to us and which are reflected in our work. Thus, before proceeding, we will make our views clear, so that at all times the reader is in no doubt about our standpoint. We will commence with a simple statement of our views, and allow the justification for our standpoint to unfold as we proceed.

Our view

The chronological age of the student/client is one of the aspects of that person's life to be considered when making judgements as to how to meet that person's individual needs. However, it is not the only aspect, and is arguably not the most important one. Much more important in our view is that the person has experiences which we might describe as person-appropriate and which therefore, as far as possible, meet that person's needs in terms of lifestyle, personal development, emotional security and so on. In fact, we would say that the person's age in years is one of the considerations when thinking about person-appropriateness. Our primary judgement, for instance for clients who are pre-verbal, is that they have needs in the areas of communication, personal development and emotional security which must be met at all costs. Critical in our view is the continuing development of communication abilities and emotional well-being. We offer experiences to the person with that end in view. We do not deny the person those experiences because other people of similar age may not have them.

In company with virtually all other practitioners we have met, we have concern for the status of people with learning disabilities within our society. We have not been convinced, however, that the interpretations of normalisation and age-appropriateness advocated by some people in our work will meet that end.

Age-appropriateness – the arguments

We offer here a list of the sorts of statements we have heard, or which have been presented to us on these issues. We fully agree with some of these statements. Where we do not agree, there is inevitably some risk that we will not present these arguments well, or that in discussion with other practitioners we have not fully understood their point of view. Nonetheless, in so far as we understand them, we will set out the main themes of the argument as they are sometimes presented to us in workshop sessions on Intensive Interaction.

- It is disrespectful to allow a person with learning difficulties to take part in activities which other people of a similar who age would not do.
- It is disrespectful to provide adult learners with materials or experiences which would normally be offered to children.
- People with learning difficulties will never 'grow up' unless we view them and treat them as adults.
- We have to combat the image of people with learning difficulties as life-long children.

- We must do everything we can to make sure that people with learning difficulties have a status in society which means that they are respected.
- It is our job to make people with learning difficulties acceptable to society. Causing them to behave according to their chronological age is one way of doing this.
- People with learning difficulties will better learn how to behave as adults if they are treated only in ways which conform to how another person of that age who does not have learning disabilities would be treated.

As far as we can judge, there is a spectrum between quite an extreme attitude and one that is similar philosophically, but pragmatic in practice. The extreme attitude suggests that nothing around the student/client, nothing they are given, nothing which happens to them or near them, should be anything other than an experience conforming with their chronological age. Everything which happens in the workplace should be viewed and assessed through that focus, before it happens. Failing to do this is a mark of disrespect.

Those whom we think of as the pragmatists, assume that it is often possible to do this, but that on many occasions some compromises are necessary. The staff at this end of the spectrum may also suggest that activities or experiences which are not age-appropriate can take place in private.

At the extreme end of the spectrum, there are frequent accounts of people with learning difficulties being denied cuddly toys, denied access to physical comfort from another person when distressed, barred from exhibiting distress, prevented from indulging interests in Disney cartoons, forbidden from enjoying swings or from going to a pantomime. The more pragmatic practitioners would frequently agree that some of these effects are undesirable.

Age-appropriateness: discussion

We have seen establishments where, in our view, the imposition of rules generated by someone's notion of age-appropriateness resulted in a tyranny for the students/clients. It may have been a tyranny resulting from the very highest and most laudable of intentions, but it was a tyranny nonetheless. We find it ironical that a concept implemented mainly in order to improve respect and status for a group, may in practice have the effect of reducing personal choice, limiting access to needs and preferences and preventing expression of emotional needs and feelings. All of these are consequences which we would judge would have a profound effect on an individual's self regard and sense of worth.

When we have discussions on this topic with groups of staff, many of them will frequently own up to their own childishness, their own emotional needs which may seem to be at odds with their chronological age. They will often point out that they nonetheless have complete freedom to indulge these needs and preferences, yet their clients may be denied the same freedoms. As Corbett and Barton (1992) contend, 'adulthood is a process not a state . . . adulthood can also be contradictory in its expression.' (p.24).

Another frequent observation, shared and endorsed by us, is that it rarely happens in everyday life that you assess something you want to do for whether it is something someone of your age should do. The counter-argument to this is, of course, that most of us have already been 'normalised' to those judgements by our cultural experiences, and many of our students/clients have not. But this returns us to the issue that one of the realities of being a culturally 'normal' adult, is that all adults seem to have desires or needs which are essentially childish, and are free to indulge them. The view that adults do not play, for instance, is clearly not accurate.

This may bring us to one of the views held by those we call pragmatists, that most adults indulge their less adult behaviours in private situations or specific contexts. This seems to be the case to some extent. Those members of staff we have met who own up to a bedroom full of cuddly toys, rarely admit to taking them out of their home, or cuddling them in front of visitors. On the other hand, many adults freely exhibit favoured cuddly toys in their cars. We find much room for agreement with staff who may not mind romping with their students/clients in the home, day centre room, or other private context. All of us, in all walks of life, are much more likely to be relaxed and informal in certain contexts, many of them private. In any event, we usually point out that being out and about in the public eye, rarely provides a context where it occurs to you to do, for instance, full-scale Intensive Interaction sequences. However, it is inevitable that you will use 'interactivity', be lighthearted and adopt a playful manner, if that is the way you relate effectively with a student/client. Does doing this devalue the person in the eyes of onlookers, and what should be our attitude toward that possibility?

172

Does 'age-appropriateness' enhance respect?
The most often quoted argument put forward, it seems to us, is that we must do everything possible to enable people with learning difficulties to be respected and held in esteem by people in the world at large. We agree with that sentiment, but not with some of the practices which may arise from it. In our view these practices embody a misinterpretation of normalisation principles. One of the consequences is that there there often seems to be a major drive by staff to compel a student/client to be 'normal', or at least look and behave 'normally'. This may mean a stern and devaluing attitude toward behaviours which may be important and even central to that person, but are not deemed 'normal'. On the one hand this may be done out of genuine concern for the perceived status of that individual by people in public. On the other, a more extreme view, and one which we have had expressed to us as a legitimate working stance, is that it is our job to make them acceptable to society, for the sake of society.

Our view here is that this approach, arising either from genuine concern for an individual, or for the society, can be dangerous. There is an atmosphere within it of holding the individual responsible for her/his disabilities. It seems to be less society's responsibility to allow for the differences of people with disabilities, and more the responsibility of the individual to seem less disabled. Corbett and Barton (1992) argue that the influential writing of Wolfensburger on normalisation, rests responsibility on the individual to learn to be more 'normal' than the norm.

To put it another way, expressed succinctly by a member of staff we met: 'What is wrong with respecting people with learning difficulties for what they are?' We feel we must challenge the view that people with learning difficulties must change in order to earn culturally valued roles, respect and status.

A principle of Intensive Interaction already forcefully expressed in this book, is that the first basis for helping an individual to progress and develop, is that they be accepted and valued unequivocally for what they are, at this moment in time. This surely is a working principle embodying decency, humanity, even spirituality. It is also highly practical. Is it too much to expect our society to achieve an understanding of this necessity during the next few decades? If it is, do we then load the responsibility on to people with learning difficulties and urge them to be 'normal'.

A further problem with approaches which ask people with learning difficulties to behave as normally as possible in order to earn respect, is that in itself, this further excludes many students/clients. We all must already be quite aware of the extent to which it is possible to use power and authority to obtain compliance from many students/clients. Many people with learning difficulties have been coerced and trained to be heart-breakingly eager to please. In so doing, we can achieve, for many, the goals of causing them to behave as 'normally' as possible in order to earn status. We suggest that the degree of compliance and conformity attained is in itself in conflict with good normalisation principles. However, the further problem is that we know very many individuals for whom this could never be achieved, though they may yet make all sorts of progress. Their needs and understandings are too fundamental, their behaviour is too extreme, their drives to indulge in certain types of behaviour too great. Unless people everywhere are aware of their existence, and that however much we may desire them to be different, they do nonetheless behave in these ways, then their behaviour will always appear daunting and alarming. A society which expects that all people with learning difficulties are polite and behave well, will always reject and devalue these others.

Our position as stated so far makes it seem as if we are at odds with the often quoted Wolfensburger view of normalisation principles (see Wolfensburger 1980, 1983). This is so, but only to an extent, there is at least as much of Wolfensburger's views with which we agree. Wolfensburger is perhaps the most well-known of the theorists on normalisation principles, though the complexities of his arguments are probably one of the contributing factors to 'bad' normalisation, such as imposing a notion of 'age-appropriateness' at all costs. His work also leaves the nagging sensation that he is more concerned with the image of people with learning difficulties than the actuality of their individual needs. This view of his work is shared by Szivos and Griffiths (1990) and as we have quoted, Corbett and Barton (1992). Emerson (1992), points out that Wolfensburger clearly states (Wolfensburger 1980) that the social status of the group as a whole is more important as an issue than any consequent 'restriction of individual choice'.

Perrin and Nirje (1985) attempt to set the record straight on some of the misapprehensions about normalisation, including the view that normalisation is about making people normal. In Nirje's (1976) view, normalisation is simply and elegantly about making normalising experiences available:

> The normalization principle means making available to all mentally retarded people patterns of life and conditions of everyday living which

are as close as possible to the regular circumstances and ways of life of society. (p.231)

We see a world of difference between making experiences available, and denying access to experiences. Nirje's definition does not ask us to disregard an individual's needs to be apparently abnormal, but rather, to make available the same normalising experiences enjoyed by most of us. We would include within those experiences the freedom and opportunity to be childish when you have a need or desire, and/or to indulge those behaviours which are an expression of you as a person. We would include also, and this is crucial in every respect, the opportunity to communicate with other human beings at a level which may be comprehended with your present abilities. The less an individual has opportunities to do this, the more likely it is that s/he will behave in ways which look strange and are socially remote, or ritualistic.

Normalisation and (hopefully), even the most severe of 'age-appropriateness' notions, are about respect and the giving and receiving of it. Surely one of the most disrespectful things that can be done to an individual, is to fail to communicate with and thus relate to, that person in a style which that person can comprehend.

Another of the points often put to us is that we need to guard against the attitudes of many people who have been visible in our work, who seem commited to maintaining students/clients as perpetual children. These people often have a manner of going about their work which is particularly disturbing and in the judgement of most of us, devaluing. We fully agree with the need to guard against them, but a notion of 'age-appropriateness' is rather a clumsy instrument to this end. It might occur for instance, as a result, that we observe a member of staff talking calmy, soberly and correctly in full sentences to a student/client. Very respectful it seems. However, if that student/client is Nella (see the case study in chapter six and the illustration in chapter four) and this attempt at communication does not even attract her attention, it is disrespectful, in our view, to carry on in that style. However, that member of staff's definition of respect may not allow use of a different one.

Writing 'rules' for the giving and receiving of respect is a particularly troublesome undertaking. Whether or not something is respectful is partly an emotional judgement in the eye of the beholder. It is difficult to legislate for it, yet in a way 'age-appropriateness' is an attempt. That it is fraught with difficulty is surely borne out by the nature of the arguments set out in this section.

What is wrong with childishness?

It is worth viewing the issue from another focus. What is it about behaving in a manner which is apparently younger than your chronological age, which is so unacceptable? In a sense, why is there any difficulty with this at all? What is inappropriate about this situation, since it occurs naturally, or through injury, to a visible minority of people in our society?

We suggest that the apparent problems we experience with this situation are partly related to fundamental issues concerning our culture's attitude to childhood itself. Sometimes it seems as if it is not acceptable to be a child, even when you are one. We perceive in our culture an inherent disrespect of, and for, children. Many of us must share the general perception of Kitzinger and Kitzinger (1989), that it is amazing how 'rudely adults can themselves behave in front of children, and yet expect them to grow up polite'. Adults, they say, are often 'especially rude' to children, adopting an 'insulting tone of voice' and generally treating them as 'social inferiors' (p.13). This is a generalisation, of course, but unfortunately the most cursory observations of adults out and about with their children in England, can confirm much of it.

O'Hagan (1993) and Newson and Newson (1974) chronicle the development of the child-rearing practices which are labelled the 'Hygienist Movement'. Here appropriate behaviour at almost any cost is the paramount consideration, with any vices the subject of vigorous eradication. This tendency, they suggest, has been a powerful influence in child-rearing in our culture during this century, and even, according to O'Hagan, constitutes a form of commonplace and legitimised emotional abuse.

The perception of children as being prey first and foremost to some kind of 'original sin' may sound familiar to many of us who have grown up in a white, English culture. This concept brings with it powerful adult forces demanding that children behave in ways which are 'good' and stifle or set aside desires to be 'bad'. A classic exhortation used on children and which relates to our discussion is the familiar 'act your age!'. This seems a strange thing to say to a child, yet its use is commonplace. Miller's work (1986, 1990) has done much to bring to light the later effects, in adulthood, of being nurtured in an atmosphere where conformity of behaviour and emotion is all-important.

Is it not a strange culture, where use of violence is generally disapproved of, even illegal, except where it is used on children? In fact many people in our society still consider it a matter of virtue that children be the subjects of violence from adults in order to regulate their behaviour. There must be something socially inferior about those citizens who are the recipients of legitimate and legal violence from other citizens.

We do not find it surprising that in our society, visions of adult behaviour mean disregarding, or apparently disregarding, any sense of the child within the adult. Since children are such second-class citizens, the only way to be 'adult' and gain esteem and respect, is to deny childhood altogether.

Of course, these are not the realities shared by all of us, and many of us are fortunate and have been brought up in our society in ways which make the above sound unfamiliar. Yet we believe that what we have all too briefly described is a reality for many children, and a powerful force in our society. Its effects are powerful enough to spill over into the way we treat other socially devalued groups such as people with learning difficulties. According to many, there is this need for people with learning difficulties to achieve apparent adulthood at all costs, in order that they may be socially valued. Such a concept is unfortunately implicit in Wolfensburger's (1983) alternative set of principles for normalisation, 'Social Role Valorisation'

Treat them older and they will develop better?
How about the suggestion that treating people as being older than the way they behave, helps them to develop and learn how to behave as an older person?

Norris (1991) found that intervention strategies commonly used to teach even young children with handicaps were often 'too developmentally advanced . . . for optimal learning.' In other words, if an offered activity is pitched too far in advance of the cognitive ability or understanding of the learner, s/he is unlikely to be interested and engaged by the activity and will not learn from it. This seems like plain common sense that hardly needs research to be confirmed; we all operate this knowledge with infants. We know intuitively that an infant of, say, nine months, does not progress toward the behaviour, knowledge and understanding of a five-year-old, by being treated as, or given experiences typical of, a five-year-old. A nine-month-old makes good progress by being given experiences which are pertinent to her/his level of ability. That doesn't mean that we should not have all sorts of high aspirations for what that person might achieve, but that the techniques used realistically take present ability into account.

We see this theme as a problem in much developmental work with people with learning difficulties. Our strong desire for what a person, in our view, should achieve, has the potential to dominate the reality of whether it can be achieved. One of us writing here must own up to having worked in such a way for a long period of time. An example of this from our own work is attempting to teach self-care – putting on a coat – by backward chaining. Whilst carrying out the programme, it was necessary to hold on to a particular student/client for dear life, because this person lacked the ability to be social and did not want to be with anyone. This was a confusion, on our part, of need and ability. We judged that this person had a need to learn this skill, but did not give proper recognition to the fact that he did not yet have the ability to learn it. The gap between what he knew, and what he was being asked to learn, was too great to be crossed.

Of course, the above is a crude example of the point we are trying to make here, but not so crude as to be atypical. People, particularly at the early levels of learning, learn better by having a small gap between what they know, and what they are being asked to learn. The processes and principles of adult-infant interaction ensure that this is the way that communication and sociability develop. The more experienced and knowledgeable a learner becomes, however, the more likely it is that the gap between what is known and what is to be learnt, can be wider.

Let us take as an example an eighteen-year-old man whose communication ability is identifiably pre-verbal. Addressing him always with the syntax, vocabulary, and conversation style used with other eighteen-year-olds can hardly be expected to be a force in the development of his fundamental communication abilities. The detailed personal attention of Intensive Interaction and the rehearsal of fundamentals such as turn-taking, non-verbal signalling and so on, is a more rational approach. This by no means is to imply that the young man should not be exposed to the apparently normalising experiences of the presence and style of eighteen-year-old full language users. Nor is it to imply that we think such experiences would not be beneficial in various ways. We simply mean that it is important not to confuse aspirations for what should be achieved with appropriate techniques for achieving it.

We have already used Nella as an example of this, and the difficulty of even attracting her attention by use of 'adult' styles of interaction. We can take this point even further. In our work with her, one of the breakthroughs for us was when we started to acknowledge her inherent babyishness. In particular we constructively began to view her violent behaviour as partly the reactions of someone who consistently, throughout her life, was subjected to demands she could not understand. Life for her, and for us, became better when we openly acknowledged these truths and worked with her from that standpoint. Facing the reality of her abilities, of her inherent babyishness, was a liberation.

And here we come back to the question of the hazards of notions of age-appropriateness. Our desire to give respect in this way can seem so imperative that many people in our work are not able to take a realistic view of individual clients' actual abilities.

We do not feel that any of the points we have made in this section are at odds with giving maximum respect to an individual and considering chronological age. As we have stated, this is one of the considerations when thinking about meeting the person's individual needs. Matters of dress, of surroundings, many aspects of lifestyle, can be considered from the viewpoint of the actual age of the student/client. Our main concern is that none of that is paramount over meeting the person's needs based on a proper recognition of ability and the consequent techniques for helping that person to develop. To do otherwise is not only disrespectful, but will not ultimately enhance the status of people with learning difficulties in our society.

How is stereotypy affected by Intensive Interaction?

Many of the students with whom we worked had behavioural repertoires characterised by stereotypy. We came to view these stereotyped behaviours as organised self-involvement. To explain this further, we saw the students as stimulating and interacting with themselves in a way which was repetitive and familiar. As we have described in chapter four, we regarded such behaviours as important to the students and not as something to be eradicated on the grounds that they were meaningless to us. We often used the behaviours, particularly rhythmic body movements like rocking and swaying, as a way of joining in and making access with the student.

At the same time as celebrating the students' behaviours and enjoying them as they were, we did have long-term hopes that they would develop other ways of interacting with the world. In common with other practitioners we wanted our students to learn to explore with all their senses, to have the confidence to try new things, to move on from the stages of development at which they seemed stuck. We want to look in this section at just what happens to stereotyped behaviours when Intensive Interaction is used.

At Harperbury Hospital School we did not concern ourselves with worries about whether our imitation and celebration of people's stereotyped behaviours might reinforce them and cause them to increase. This was partly because in this setting these behaviours had become established over a period of some years, and had survived a range of interventions to treat and eradicate them. We did not really think therefore, that we could have that much impact in affecting stereotypy either way. We acknowledge the point made by practitioners in our workshops that the issue of whether we reinforce stereotypy may seem to be more crucial when working, for example, with a five-year-old who might be just beginning to display this organised self-involvement. We have to question though whether the principle remains the same.

As part of the research into the effectiveness of Intensive Interaction we gathered data on the incidence of organised self-involvement, both when the subjects were alone, and when their teachers were attempting to engage them in interaction. With Georgiou (see the case study of Georgiou in chapter six), Gaynor and the staff team established mutuality, empathy and joint focus by blending their behaviours with those of Georgiou. This frequently involved the staff in joining in with his range of stereotyped behaviours, and with his rocking, patting, and rhythmic mouth movements in particular. The data show that early on Georgiou developed a new and more sophisticated kind of stereotyped finger play. The data also show that this later faded out and that the incidence of his having two or more self-involved behaviours going at the same time decreased. There was evidence of a functional relationship between this decrease and the intervention of Intensive Interaction. Georgiou at first involved the staff in his organised self-involvement in the form of hand games, but again this later gave way to other, more reciprocal kinds of interaction.

Data for three of the other subjects also show patterns of their organised self-involvement decreasing. To some extent our research verified the understandings we were gaining from analysing our work in the classrooms. From our experience we suggest that stereotypy may increase at first with Intensive Interaction, but that this trend will only be transitory. In the long term such displays of organised self-involvement are likely to decrease as the staff member and client together move on to find new ways of relating, and as the client learns new ways of interacting with the environment and gains new understandings of her/his world.

Issues concerning challenging behaviour

As we have tried to illustrate throughout, Intensive Interaction is an approach designed for learners who are pre-verbal and who lack the fundamentals of sociability and communication. The reality of this for us, and for many of the client groups whose staff we have supported, is that these learners also often have behaviours which we find challenging. We refer here to behaviours beyond the scope of just the stereotyped or self-involved behaviours discussed above. We refer to such behaviours as physical aggression, furniture throwing, self-injury, inappropriate sexual behaviour and obsessive behaviour.

Many of the students we worked with at Harperbury Hospital School were very challenging in some or even all of these ways. They were people for whom drug intervention and behaviour modification were regularly used. Sometimes therapeutic or educational interventions were not seen by hospital staff as viable until their behaviour became less challenging. Intensive Interaction was never developed as a means of altering or managing these behaviours, nor is it required that these behaviours are improved first. Intensive Interaction is an approach to working with the person as s/he is and to a large extent that person's behaviours are accepted as part of them at this moment in time. The aim is not about behaviour as such, but to develop a relationship with that person, to facilitate her/his social and communication development and develop the behaviours which go with this.

Our experience has often informed us that a beneficial side effect of using Intensive Interaction is improved behaviour. Student after student we worked with became more tolerant, more relaxed, less obsessive and less aggressive. This pattern was partly verified by the more formal evaluation and research; the video recordings made at regular intervals over time graphically illustrated the emergence of calmer states and a tempo of behaviour more in harmony with the rest of us. The case studies of Nella, Dominic, Betty, Adrian, Jerry and Victor all offer examples of students' behaviours becoming less challenging with the use of Intensive Interaction. We are very well aware of the potential of the approach to have this effect and we are aware also of the interest of practitioners everywhere in this aspect of it.

We highlight this as an issue for this chapter as there are ethical and practical considerations. It could be argued that if we as practitioners know that this approach can facilitate welcome changes in behaviour then we have a duty to use it to do this job. We firstly need to explore, however, how and why Intensive Interaction might affect behaviour.

It is our understanding that the student/client's behaviour changes because s/he has learned new ways of relating to the environment and to the people within it. The student/client may have established a way of communicating needs or moods, when these communications are responded to, s/he no longer has the need to behave in the same ways. It may be that the individual's level of anxiety is much reduced because all contact with her/him is respectful of signals of negativity or rising anxiety. It may be that the individual feels safe to explore with new behaviours. S/he may have learned through a kind of apprenticeship the tempo of others' behaviour. There may be a new desire to employ self-control rather than to hit out at someone with whom a relationship has been made. It may be that new ways of interacting simply take over. We are not in a position to do more than hypothesise at this stage. It is our belief, though, that the changes in behaviour come out of the developments in trust, relationship and social and communication abilities. We must set out to facilitate these developments first and foremost. We need to have the order and the aims right. If we set out primarily to alter behaviour then we are missing what this is all about and we are likely to be unsuccessful.

A further problem is that if Intensive Interaction is used with the aim of altering behaviour, this will entail the wrong attitude to the behaviours. As we have tried to convey in chapters three and four a major part of the method is the attitude of the practitioner. We do not deny that we make some value judgements about the behaviour of our clients and about which behaviours we see as affecting their quality of life. At the same time we do not set out to impose these value judgements. The attitude of unconditional acceptance of the person is important and the willingness to find aspects of the person's behaviour to celebrate is vital. Very often staff in our workshops present us with their most difficult client and ask us how we would going about getting her/him to stop this or that behaviour. We ask people to stop and rethink. Let us reiterate that Intensive Interaction is about using positive attitudes and behaviours to promote positive developments; it is not about using negative attitudes to stop behaviours.

Emotional involvement

Our training has instilled in many of us the need to retain professional distance from our clients, with cautions not to get too involved. What constitutes 'too' involved, however, would probably be defined differently by each and every one of us. Emotional involvement is more of an issue with some approaches than with others, and when we started out on the development work at Harperbury, emotional bonding was an issue at the forefront of our minds.

We have stressed the similarities which exist between Intensive Interaction and the interactions between caregivers and infants, but we have also stressed the different intentions. Intensive Interaction is not about re-parenting, it is about facilitating development. Are these different intentions reflected in the actual practice? Analysis of videos of mother-infant interaction makes the observer strongly aware of the intense emotional involvement, often you can quite literally see the transmission of love from the mother to the infant. The intensity of the eye contact, the intimacy, the nodding and cooing, the verbal praising and celebrating all add up to powerful communication of the emotional involvement. These loving behaviours must also be very effective in communicating to the infant that she/he is valued, worthwhile and good to be with. It is this message that we want to communicate to our learners, to build their self-esteem in readiness for taking the risky steps of exploring, communicating and being social.

The issues are of course complex. We want to borrow from the style of interaction we know to be effective for facilitating development. We cannot just eradicate from this the aspects which involve physical contact, intimacy or emotional involvement. What we can do, however, is build in safeguards and this is the approach we decided to take at Harperbury.

A fundamental safeguard concerns creating an atmosphere of trust in which members of a staff team feel able to talk to each other about the issues which arise. This is a necessity. Many of the discussions which arose from the weekly evaluations of the students and ourselves (see chapter four) centred around issues of involvement. We found it highly useful to say when we were feeling involved and to check out for feedback as to whether there was evidence of this in our behaviour. 'Am I spending too much time with X?' was a frequent question. As we have said, inevitably one member of a team will make initial access with a student/client and this can give rise to a feeling of bonding. We must be encouraged to say how this feels, to share with our colleagues the insights we have, so that they too can enjoy positive interactions with that person, and to say how it feels to 'share' the person and the relationship. This may not sound like professional distance, but we believe that there is a professional honesty here that is lacking in pretending that bonds do not exist.

183

Another safeguard surrounds the whole idea of teamworking. Emotional bonding with a student/client can be problematic for that person when the member of staff moves on. With a team of staff working closely with the person it is likely that other staff will enjoy a good relationship with them also and this can be helpful with feelings such as loss that might be experienced. Another benefit of having a team of staff is that the chances are increased of every student/client finding someone to bond with in some way. We all make relationships in our lives, some transitory, some longer lasting. We would argue that it is wrong to deny someone this because they have severe learning difficulties. Instead we should work to ensure that there are protections for the person with learning difficulties because of the power imbalance. We have had people question the ethics of using Intensive Interaction with our students, because it cruelly awakens them to feelings and relationships which they have been denied. Some people would find it preferable and more 'kind' to 'leave them be'. In contrast, we would find it unethical to know of a way of working with people which could open up for them the world of sociability and communication and then not use it.

Returning to our claim that this is not pseudo-parenting leads us to think about the nature of the relationships that develop. They are likely to be built on feelings of mutual pleasure and mutual involvement, with feelings of efficacy generated from the success of the interactive games. There is likely to be an element of protectiveness also, but not those deep feelings which come from the responsibilities of having someone totally dependent on your care and love.

Staff selection

We have often been asked about the implications of the use of Intensive Interaction for issues of staff selection. One of the reassuring things we like to say about this approach, is that it utilises abilities and behaviours natural to most adults. In this sense, the basic techniques are non-technical and thus non-qualified staff can also be highly effective teachers.

The difficulty with this statement is that we have met individuals for whom using this approach presents massive problems. Some people are clearly unwilling to offer themselves to the students/clients in this way, and unfortunately, some people seem incapable of attaining the sensitivity necessary.

Some of the reasons why certain individuals may be unwilling to work in this way seem clear to us, and we have taken a carefully considered decision to include the sentiments we set out in this paragraph. It is a depressing reality that it is possible to meet members of staff in our work, who clearly do not like their students/clients, either as individuals or as a group. These people do not seem to value or respect the students/clients at any level. The reasons why they have come into the work, and stay in it, do not seem at all apparent. These people are mercifully few, but their presence in a staff group is often a powerful one. We have elsewhere set out our views on the likelihood that negative behaviours and attitudes have the potential to be more powerful than positive ones.

There are many other reasons why an individual may be unwilling to use the approach, and no doubt we are not even aware of some of those reasons. Intensive Interaction is a profoundly personal way of working with another person, and the question of staff having 'emotional fit' with the working technique is therefore crucial.

We cannot claim to understand why it is that some people we have met are enthusiastic to work in this way, but despite their best efforts, are unable to. Many practitioners experience difficulties at first, but grow into confident interactors over a period of time, especially with good support and encouragement from colleagues. We might guess that for those who cannot, it has something to do with their own experience of learning, particularly perhaps their learning of these fundamentals. That is only a guess, however, and we quite honestly do not have wisdom to impart on this issue.

Thus, for us, the main issue was always one of staff selection. Naturally, any establishment looks for the best possible qualities in the individuals from whom they are selecting. For us, the paramount issue in the selection criteria was that the person should be a good social interactor, or have the basics of being a good social interactor. We have to admit straight away that 'good social interactor' is a vague term which may imply a wealth of meanings and interpretations for different people. However, we would say that most of the people we meet in our work are good social interactors. We mostly self-select ourselves; being with people with learning disabilities is genuinely not the sort of work to be undertaking if you lack this facility or do not desire to develop it.

In our sense of the term, we mean something more than a person being extrovert or outgoing, confident, speaking in full sentences, having a strong handshake and adopting the right posture in the interview. We are thinking toward some deeper and harder to define issues like genuinely and simply liking people, naturally giving off warmth and affection, being good to be near without having to do anything too dynamic, rewarding other people with their presence. In addition to this, there are the important 'mechanics' of interacting – use of eyes and face, body language, posture, use of personal space, ability to read and be sensitive to other people's signals and so on. These too need to be in place, or at least their potential to grow and develop.

As we have asserted, the above description applies to most people, but not all. We cannot go on to give the definitive interview person-specification. Some of the things which we have mentioned above will defy satisfactory definition as selection criteria under equal opportunities. What we do suggest, however, is that these issues should be taken into account, and the difficulties of definition faced and met.

We have always been puzzled by the way in which staff may be selected for subtle and demanding face-to-face work with other people, by means of a formal interview. We are teachers, and in education this style of interview is staggeringly the norm. In our view, the formal interview is usually not a good forum for making the sorts of judgements about people with which we are concerned here. It is all too easy to rehearse a highly effective performance for this artificial setting. Indeed, we know quite well the principles for doing this. Perceptive and experienced interviewers may well be able to judge some of the social interaction aspects of a person in such a setting, but this one setting is not enough. We need to see the person that the students/clients will meet, not the persona designed for the interview. Thus, we always used as part of the selection process, the practice of placing the applicant with the students for a period of time and observing them for appropriate personal qualities. This can be difficult to do satisfactorily under some interpretations of equal opportunities procedures, but surely not out of the question?

However, let us return to the main issue of this section which is simply to acknowledge honestly that this is not an approach which everyone will wish, or be able, to use. This sense of personality 'fit' probably applies to all approaches or techniques in our work, but the personal and intense nature of Intensive Interaction can seem to magnify this difficulty when it arises.

Tasklessness

We had been working on Intensive Interaction for several years before we started to formalise thoughts around the concept of tasklessness.

We had been using the concept for most of that time, without finding a name to describe and define it. One of the reasons for our lack of attention to it, is the same as the degree of difficulty many practitioners have with it on first acquaintanceship. Basically, even after we had long since stopped working with a sense of task for communication activities, we could not think clearly about this lack of task, because we were teachers. Our experiences previously – our, if you like, up-bringing in our work – had developed us to be people who dominated and controlled the learning. It was our job to set tasks and objectives for sessions and make sure that they were fulfilled. This working posture is familiar to many staff we have met, particularly teachers, and it is difficult to unthink it. One thoughtful practitioner likened it to a violinist who had been trained in the disciplines and formal structures of the classical repertoire, suddenly being asked to play improvised jazz. That is a bit extreme as a comparison perhaps, but it does have an authentic ring.

Our concept of tasklessness is deeply rooted in the way in which infant learners operate in interactions, and we drew this point out from the illustrations of Sue and Thomas in chapter three. To reiterate, Sue did not set tasks for Thomas during their activity together. The activity flowed, with the major visible aspects of the structure being the emotional and practical support being given by Sue, and crucially, the way in which she continually worked from Thomas' behaviour by celebrating and extending. Sue probably could not have intellec-tualised about the lack of task, had she been asked. She simply seemed to have an intuitive understanding about how to use herself to best effect, and a reliance on, and confidence in, the process of the activity. We can intellectualise however.

We have pointed out that a lack of a sense of task would seem to provide a good atmosphere in which learners can experiment with their own social behaviour and understandings. If there is an atmos-phere of tasklessness, and Sue, or a member of staff, is effectively celebrating and extending, there must be a marvellous and reassuring sensation for the learner, of operating within a failure-free environ-ment. There may be nothing wrong with human beings receiving constructive criticism, but what we need to assume and remember about people who are still learning the absolute fundamentals, is that they are probably not yet sophisticated enough to deal with too much negativity. Most people seem to be generally successful in assuming this about infants in the first year.

We have to offer some extra care about what we mean by 'task' and 'tasklessness'. A task includes formal notions about things like defining what will be achieved and communicating this to the learner. Tasklessness includes also more subtle things such as taking care in interactions that your own emotional needs for the person to do this or that are not communicated to the learner. Our own needs can arise in various ways. Classically, a sceptical boss may ask you to prove that so and so now makes eye contact. The session with the boss watching has a drive toward eye contact which may come out as a task. Any atmosphere which conveys to the learner that s/he has to do something to perform, to please you, can become task fulfilment. This is quite hard for us, but remember, one of the ideas is that we, the staff, make ourselves available to the student/client on their terms. We then assist the learner to move forward by this process of experimenting with and developing their social and communicative repertoire. We have stated that with experience of the approach and individual students/clients, some judicious, and quite minor, guidance within interaction sequences is possible. We suggest that this is only done with experience of both the practical activity and the way in which the concept of not having a task is effective to the activity.

Thus the concept of tasklessness is related to our need to have confidence in Intensive Interaction as a process-based activity, rather than one dominated by the achievement of a pre-specified objective. We have previously written (Hewett & Nind 1989):

> The teacher's role is to be the mediator and facilitator of the process. The process is the development of extended sequences of progressive and developmental interactive 'games' wherein fundamental learning experiences leading to the development of sociability and the foundations of communication can take place as natural, intrinsic, almost inevitable aspects of that process. At every stage, the quality of each part of the process, and its potential to provide a learning experience to the student is more important than an objective, indeed, indivisible from an objective. (p.2)

Another way of looking at it, then, is that the objective of an Intensive Interaction sequence is to get the process going. The process, operated properly, provides both the structure and the learning. Essential to the process is that there is not an emphasis on task, but rather an emphasis on the process itself.

We are not debunking the use of tasks in teaching or developmental work, nor implying here a criticism of approaches involving techniques such as skills analysis. We are simply advocating the appropriate approach to what is to be learnt. Approaches involving the setting of tasks and objectives can be fine for all sorts of learning, but not, we think, for the fundamentals of communication.

We can go further and bring together the threads of tasklessness and task. If as a practitioner, you become comfortable with working with Intensive Interaction and tasklessness, you will have developed a particular style of purposeful informality. There may be many occasions when you use other teaching approaches with a particular learner, skills analysis for instance, working through task. We suggest that your use of these approaches will be developed and enhanced by your developing knowledge of yourself as a powerful social interactor. Even in situations where you are setting a task, you can bring to the situation much of the atmosphere, the security and emotional support of Intensive Interaction, because you have become comfortable with that style. The effect will probably be to defuse the severity of the task to some extent for the learner. This interactive style of behaviour which you will bring to the situation will probably include skilful use of face and voice, of tempo, pause, burst-pause, running commentary, watching and waiting, scanning for feedback, celebrating. Our other concept of 'interactivity' relates significantly here.

Continuing to think and work along these lines will bring you to some realisations about yourself and your use of your social interaction skills in all teaching and working situations. As Tomlinson (1981) puts it, 'people are social beings in virtually every aspect of their psychological functioning' (p.267). We know, from our own experiences as teachers, that use of some teaching technologies can cause you to overlook the crucial social aspects of the activity. There can be a tendency to hand over the responsibility for the learning to the technology itself. Indeed, there are some techniques in use which ask you to remove the social aspects of the situation altogether, and behave neutrally.

Issues concerning physical contact

We are all aware that our culture is currently undergoing some trauma due to continuing revelations about sexual abuse of children and vulnerable adults in our society. This inevitably causes any teacher to give careful consideration to the extent to which they use touch in their work. We know of mainstream teachers who have said that they now completely avoid touching pupils and we know of workplaces where physical contact is banned. There has not been a great deal of interest to date, however, in the possible trauma that may be caused by denying children touch. Issues concerning physical contact are difficult ones and they can arouse deep emotional responses. We do not wish to trivialise any of this, but we do need to include some thoughts on the issues in relation to using Intensive Interaction.

When we started to use Intensive Interaction the ethics around physical contact were a big issue for us, and this continues to be an area for concern. More specifically, an issue at the outset was whether we might inadvertently cause our students to become sexually aroused because we were giving them physical contact.

We were conscious of the fact that we were working with adults, people who were sexual, but rarely aware of even the most basic of societal expectations about sexual behaviour. For some of our students, masturbation was an activity that they engaged in, alongside their stereotyped behaviours, for much of the day. We obviously would not be comfortable with basing interactive game around this activity, and perhaps because we therefore selected other behaviours to join in with and to celebrate, the masturbation became less frequent. We found also that the issue of sexual arousal never assumed the significance that we thought it might.

It was extremely rare for a student to become sexually aroused when involved in an interactive game using touch. We think that this may be because although a game may be pleasurable and involve romping and touching, we were transmitting loud and clear by the quality of our own behaviour that IT IS NOT SEX. Some students/clients of course cannot understand the subtlety of such a communication, but even so seemed to receive the nature of the message that there was no sexual signalling and no sexual atmosphere to the game. In any event, if there were any doubts that there might be sexual arousal, this was taken by the teacher as a sure signal that the interaction was not proceeding purposefully. The teacher would then modify or cease the interaction immediately. The case study of Jerry (see chapter six) gives a report of our only example of really having to tackle head on the problem of sexual arousal in response to touch.

We were in many ways prepared for problems around the issue of sexual responding which never arose. We feel confident that we would have dealt with them ethically and professionally in any event.

Most important in this is that we maintained a working atmosphere in which all staff were encouraged to discuss such issues freely. We did not try to pretend that our students, and indeed ourselves, were not sexual beings. The atmosphere was open and trusting. Also crucial

190

was that we worked in teams in classrooms where we were visible to each other, and that we had extremely careful staff selection procedures. In any event, we take the view that a student/client's apparent sexual difficulty is an aspect of the person with which we work. Some practitioners have told us that they cannot touch a certain client because he gets an erection the moment he is touched. We would say that if this is the case, then this person clearly needs to learn more about the meanings of touch – all touch. He certainly cannot learn this by not being touched. The responsibility for doing this teaching lies with the staff who work with him.

Cautious readers might wonder why we still wanted to proceed with using physical contact. Why did we not attempt to establish interactive games which did not involve touch? In answer to this we refer you back to the literature on caregiver-infant interaction (see chapter two). The literature reminds us that the interactive style which promotes child development is a whole way of being; we cannot isolate parts of this style to be used or not used. We cannot identify exactly what is taught and learned through the process of being touched, we do not fully understand this in technical terms. We do know, however, that we would not dream of denying touch to a developing infant. Touch is an irreplaceable and fundamental means of communication.

With some of our students we found it necessary to set up interactive game without using touch. To employ physical contact, to which the student consented and enjoyed, would not have been possible in the early stages. It was always our intention though, to open up at some time the powerful channel of communication which touch provides. Touch can be the most effective way of letting someone know that you are a warm and gentle person, of transmitting a mood, of communicating and receiving trust. Physical contact is also crucial for our emotional well-being, we feel better about ourselves when we are hugged, stroked, touched. Montagu's (1986) book on touch offers documentation which can help us to further understand the functions of touch. In an experiment small mammals which were given physical contact actually developed faster, with bigger brains and better cognitive performance than those without physical contact. We cannot make too many assumptions from this, but it does imply that physical contact has some cognitive, as well as emotional and communicative, significance.

We cannot deny the importance of physical contact. We can sometimes reject using touch in our work, however, due to notions of what is and what is not appropriate. Before we do this we should perhaps consider the wider cultural context. While sharing warm physical contact with other adults may be taboo in some British families, this does not make it generally inappropriate. Much of our culture is emotionally undemonstrative in comparison to other cultures and this can have a bearing on our attitudes towards activities involving physical contact. We have to say that this may only be true of many southern, white, English people such as ourselves. For many, even within British culture, sharing warm physical contact is a part of everyday life. We have given workshops in some workplaces where staff are clearly at ease with sharing chairs, leaning against each other, giving each other massage. To use physical contact in their work is not a problem. Other staff may never be fully comfortable with this. We simply recommend that you give time to discussing these issues, and that you do not deny your clients the physical contact which might be an important part of an approach that will work for them, without proper consideration.

Issues for parents

To fulfil our original intention we have had to give over much of this book to issues which affect practitioners, both teachers and workers from other disciplines. It has also been our intention though, that the book should be useful for parents of children and adults with the kinds of learning difficulties we have described. We hope that it is useful and that parents will not have felt alienated by the terminology of students/clients/learners.

Our own experience of working with parents has been limited and we are not parents ourselves. We refer you to the work of Burford (1986), however, who in developing and using the very similar approach of movement therapy (see chapter two) has worked closely and positively with parents. At Harperbury it was rare for the students to have any family contact and so we did not get into the task of explaining to parents what we were doing. Some of our workshop participants who are more likely to face this situation have expressed concern that this might be a very difficult and sensitive area. There has been concern that using an approach based on caregiver-infant inter-action could be threatening to parents; that they might interpret from this criticism of their own parenting abilities. We have had plenty of feedback to the contrary, however, in which parents have welcomed the approach as one in which they can share and contribute equally and which values and emphasises the skills present in their parenting role.

Intensive Interaction is in some senses packaged common sense. We have tried not to shroud the approach in mystery and professional jargon. We stress again that it does not involve specialist equipment and lengthy training. It requires sensitivity and a willingness to reflect and to analyse the way we interact.

The work in the United States on interventions within the family illustrates that the ways in which caregivers interact with their children can be modified to become more likely to promote development. This does not involve them in learning a new technology from the professionals, but in making subtle changes guided by watching videos and selecting processes to work on. Sometimes very little is needed to help to make interactions more reciprocal and we recommend reading the work of Fraiberg (1974). She documents how she was able to show mothers videos of their blind babies giving feedback signals, not through their eyes or faces, but through hand movements. This was enough to reconnect the mothers with their infants such that feelings of efficacy and the spiral of positive interactions were resumed. From our work we would stress that these kinds of measures can be taken by parents or other caregivers or workers, long after the years of infancy and childhood. Again we refer you to Burford's (1986) closely linked movement therapy which has been used a lot with parents of people with profound learning difficulties, including adults.

When parents have attended our workshops, or we have given sessions specifically for parents, their feedback has been highly positive. Parents have welcomed the fact that Intensive Interaction provides you with something very practical you can go away and try the next day. We have also had comments that parents have felt that continued interactions of this kind are what is needed, but that their children's schools have been urging them to move on too quickly. One set of parents we know have withdrawn their son from school in order to be able engage for a bit longer, and more frequently, in the satisfying and quality interactions they have finally been able to achieve with him. We need to know more about all this and we welcome comments from parents who read this book.

CHAPTER 6

Case Studies

Introduction

In this chapter we offer a series of case studies. Each case study relates
to a student at Harperbury Hospital School during the time when
Intensive Interaction was being developed there. We have tried to
include students with varying abilities and disabilities and those whose
story carries a particular relevance or interest. We thank the teachers
– Lindsey, Gaynor, Nikki and Lin – for their contributions to this
chapter and sometimes we will use their contributions in the first
person.

Nella, Dominic and Adrian were three of the first students with
whom we used Intensive Interaction and we were very much using our
intuitions and learning as we went along. Nella provides an interesting
case study because her behaviours were extremely challenging and
because using Intensive Interaction revealed that she could be completely different. Dominic's case study has particular relevance in
terms of getting started and in terms of working with someone with
an exclusion zone. Readers whose clients have profound and multiple
learning difficulties will be interested in the next case study, in which
we see Marion become motivated after years of being passive and
almost 'dormant'.

Adrian and Jerry were very much isolated by their complete organised self-involvement. Imitation was used when making access
with both, but with Jerry tackling the obstacle of inappropriate sexual
arousal is also part of the story. Matthew provides an example of a
student with very different problems and the case study covers the
analytical thinking the staff team had to apply in addressing his
manipulative behaviour. The problems of getting started, of overcoming inappropriate sexual behaviour and of working with someone who
tends to be very passive are again covered in Kevin's case study.

194

Betty's case study will be particularly interesting to readers working with students/clients who are verbal, but who still need help to become effective communicators. The final case studies of Georgiou and Victor relate the progress of students who were difficult to reach, up to and way beyond the initial access with them.

Readers interested in sensory impairment are directed towards the case studies of Jerry, Betty and Georgiou. We hope that the case studies draw together much of the theory and practical guidance contained within this book. We intend them to bring alive much of what we have discussed and to be enjoyed. We feel that this chapter is an appropriate conclusion to the book.

Nella

When we first started using Intensive Interaction with Nella she was a seventeen year old, with a reputation in the hospital for being very aggressive, even dangerous. The stress of working with her meant that her ward had a turnover of staff which was even higher than the norm. The main approaches to managing her on the wards included use of physical domination, restraint, exclusion and medication. At school she presented as completely non-compliant. She spent her time vomiting (without the aid of fingers down her throat) and re-eating the vomit, anal and vaginal probing, smearing faeces, playing with saliva, tearing at her skin with her teeth, scratching, pinching, hitting and biting others. On occasions we would have respite as she spent hours or days sleeping alongside the radiators; on other days she would rush frantically up and down the classroom crashing into the walls at either end and knocking down everything and everyone in her path.

As you might imagine, assessment of Nella's cognitive abilities was impossible, as was any kind of traditional work to develop such abilities. Nonetheless we had attempted to compel her to complete stacking tasks and inset puzzles; we still bear the scars! We came to recognise, however, that in many ways she was functioning at the level of an infant of a few months. She had not learned how to relate effectively to others or to her environment and her only communications were through squeals or physical attack.

Nella's behaviour in school had been managed for some years with stringent behaviour modification programmes in which she was removed to a time-out room for her various anti-social behaviours. There had been little, if any progress with this, however, and two significant problems remained: how to reward her and what to do with her when she was not in the time-out room. Use of food as a tangible reinforcer only led to her acute desire for more and with this further aggression; social reinforcers and praise were meaningless to her. She showed no interest in any equipment and although she seemed to enjoy music she almost always attacked her music therapist.

We started to use Intensive Interaction with Nella after we had enjoyed some successes with other students for whom table-work had been impossible. We were enjoying working in a way which reflected our personalities and which was pleasurable and relatively stress-free and we were feeling optimistic. We decided to change our tolerance threshold with Nella and to accept all of her behaviours, other than aggression, for which we maintained the time-out policy. As a result she was spending less of her day in the time-out room and more time in the classroom. In order to limit disruption and injury as far as possible, a member of staff was allocated to 'mind' her at all times. We rotated this role and spending time legitimately dedicated to Nella meant that we got to know her, her signals and her mood changes.

As we were beginning to use interactive game as a major teaching tool generally, it was a natural step to employ these skills when we were minding Nella. Less harsh and more playful ways were used to divert her from her persecution of her classmates. These included tickling her to lessen her grip, pulling her off others and turning the pull into a rough and tumble type swing around the room, pulling her onto our laps where we would bounce her up and down, and shouting 'reprimands' in her ear in a range of silly voices. When she was in her sleepy phases we would capitalise on these and spend time lying with her, stroking her face or being a cushion for her head, attempting to communicate warmth and convey the possible comfort and pleasure of physical contact.

Early in our experimentation with interactive games with Nella we discovered another side to her nature. She rewarded our playfulness with smiles and giggles and we were able to perceive her more positively, as baby-like. We did not lose sight of her adultness, but recognising that there was a baby-like side to her was important and useful. It helped us to perceive her behaviour pattern as the result of lack of understanding and the anxiety associated with this. Nella's signs of pleasure were compelling feedback and the games spiralled and developed effortlessly. We continued to manage her aggression with time-out as this prevented escalation of minor incidents into more serious injury, but for the first time we knew what to do in between the scratches and pinches.

The nature of Nella's day changed drastically as her time gradually became filled with warm companionship or interactive games in which she could reciprocate, take a turn, co-operate in gradually more complex signalling systems, and attend for increasingly long periods of time while anticipating the crescendo of a tension-expectancy game. She was intrinsically motivated by the activities which were matched to her very early level of development and she learned new ways of being with people other than injuring them. Alongside the active games she began to spend time on our laps in a rocking chair, where we would sing to her or where we could enjoy gentle exchanges of sound and mutual gaze.

As time went on there was a vast reduction in the frequency and severity of Nella's aggression. She continued to vomit, but her probing and her playing with saliva virtually disappeared. Her whole demeanour changed and we felt that her quality of life had vastly improved. In developmental terms, she started to use a range of speech-like sounds and through these we were able to interpret her mood. She hummed tunes and she would occasionally use her sounds or repeat part of an action to communicate her desire for 'more'. She began to use gesture and in this way she would, for example, approach staff and request that her shoes be removed or the tap turned on. She made good eye contact and she showed understanding about turn-taking and dialogue. She allowed herself to be comforted by others and she increasingly made more positive relationships with those staff who had made themselves available to her. Her increased awareness and understanding of her environment were quite tangible to us. She learned to reward others for being with her and changed from being largely aggressively rejecting of others to actually initiating social contact with us.

Nella provides us with a case-study of someone with whom we have used Intensive Interaction alongside the continuation of a time-out programme. We would regard the use of time-out as a management strategy, however, and the Intensive Interaction Teaching as the core curriculum. The time-out policy helped to prevent the escalation of aggressive incidents, but Nella's pattern of challenging behaviours could not have been successfully turned around if she had not developed new and more positive behaviours.

Dominic

Dominic was one of the first people with whom we used Intensive Interaction. Indeed the exploratory work with Dominic preceded to some extent our intellectualisation of the processes we were using. We were intuitively experimenting, trying to find a gentle and reassuring way to reach Dominic, even before we had begun to look at the literature which later guided our thoughts and activities. Dominic carried a label of autism earned by his complete isolation from others. He always sat apart from the group, cross-legged, rocking and twiddling a strip of fabric; often he hummed to himself 'Three Blind Mice'. He had what could be described as an exclusion zone – if anyone came within about three feet of him he would reach out and kick or hit them. Although considerable force was used, it was extremely rare for this to escalate further, the hit-out was hurried, powerful and almost beyond his control. It was enough to knock you over, however, and enough to keep everyone at a distance. Even at those times when we were compelling others and using a lot of dominance and physical control, we did not approach Dominic, he was left a passive observer on the sidelines. Sometimes he seemed to enjoy it when we were singing or playing tapes, but the only times when we really saw evidence of pleasure was when he was on the garden swing, where he swung so high that it was nerve-racking to watch.

In some ways the fact that we had never carried out any table work with Dominic made it easier. We didn't have any practices to alter, we were starting from afresh:

I think I began with the humming. I am not musical, but Dominic's humming was very beautiful and I used to join in while I was busy doing something else in the classroom. This joining in activity, perhaps because it was so peripheral, contained no challenge or threat. Sometimes I would glance over to him and find him watching me.

We continued humming together and I became increasingly aware that this interested him. Gradually I also became aware of other vocalisations he made and a new high-pitched, happy sound had entered his repertoire. When he made this sound, I repeated it back to him, always from across the room, but increasingly accompanied by a direct look and a smile. The exchange of vocalisations became like dialogues and we would 'chat' in this way half a dozen times during the morning. Moving nearer to Dominic was not so much planned but a natural outcome of our growing interest and confidence in each other. I was analytical enough though to know that any sudden movement or too big a step would cause him to panic and I would lose the moment.

I started to spend short periods each day sitting on the floor, cross-legged and humming. Initially I was at least six to eight feet away and I was positioned so we were not directly facing. A new kind of interactive sequence developed when Dominic began to accompany his happy vocalisations with a cheery few slaps onto the floor or a nearby chair. This gave something to imitate, to take turns with and to make into a game. By this time Dominic was accepting me face-to-face and ever nearer. I decided to vary my imitation of the slapping on the floor and I began to lean forward and slap down onto the floor in the space between us. Dominic did this too. Then he started slapping his thigh rather than the floor and I was able to reach forward and make contact with a hearty slap on his thigh also. Thus, because the activity was based on my intuitive responses to his behaviours, our first physical contact took the form of a bold, confident slap or pat on his leg. This is in direct contrast to the gentle unobtrusive touch one would have expected from a careful, aloof programme of backward chaining. By this time I was able to read his signals and know when he was beginning to get tense or worried. In this way I knew that there was no risk of him hitting out at me when I took this step.

We continued to engage in these interactions each day and to gain much pleasure from them. Games diversified to include different songs to hum, patting hands in greeting, and my swinging on the garden swing next to him, attempting to match his rhythm. Dominic's confidence in me grew and grew and he started to reach out and very gently stroke my hair. He was able to begin to share interactive games with other members of the staff team and he began to allow us to include him in group activities, though usually from a small distance away. Within a couple of months Dominic and I would share a warm embrace and a range of gentle face-to-face interactive games.

We recognised that some of what we achieved with Dominic came out of a connection of our personalities. The more relaxed classroom atmosphere also helped to set the scene. Most important though, was that we freed ourselves from anxieties of getting results and just enjoyed the process of getting to know someone through interacting with them in a way which 'felt right.' Dominic is now living successfully in the community.

Marion

Marion had lived in the hospital from early childhood and though she had attended the hospital school and had music therapy and physiotherapy, most of her reports noted regression rather than progression. She had spastic quadraplegia and her limbs were fused and flexed, her muscles wasted. She presented as largely unaware and lethargic and staff attempts to interest, stimulate and relax her had mostly failed, leading to a general feeling of despair. She suffered from epilepsy and chronic ill-health, particularly severe chest colds. Much of her time in school was spent sleeping or passively sitting with her eyes closed, her head on her chest and her fists clenched to her chest. She would sometimes grind her teeth or suck her fingers.

Marion had one spontaneous movement in which she would rhythmically rock her head from side-to-side. It was this that her teachers seized upon to join in with, celebrate and reflect back to her. They played around with the proximity of their face to hers for this activity and quickly found an optimum. This was the basis for the first games and staff were rewarded with Marion's keen interest, wide-eyed looking and occasional smiles. Using this approach staff found that motivating and stimulating Marion was not necessarily the problem.

The staff struggled instead, as is often the case with someone very passive, to chat with Marion in a burst-pause style, working hard not to take her turns for her. They also struggled with the emotional battering of working with someone who was so poorly and whose stamina was minimal. As a team they had to support each other with the finding that Marion could be responsive one day and just sleepy for the rest of the week. They learned to work towards very short bursts of quality interaction and to supplement these with holding or rocking or stroking her as she rested.

Interactive games with Marion developed such that the teacher might whisper in her ear, blow on her hands or playfully chew on her sleeve as Marion sometimes did. The teacher always exclaimed with genuine delight at Marion's response, however small that response might be. In this way Marion caused things to happen; she had a role to play in the games and this role became increasingly active and purposeful. Sometimes games would be based purely around a lively exchange of facial expressions, with Marion using her ability to turn her head away to control the pace of the game, to take time to rest, and sometimes to tease. An incredible step forward was when Marion also began to squeal with delight. There then emerged games which were a dialogue of sound-making, each person's sound changing in some way in response to the other's, reflecting each other's volume, pace or pitch and often culminating in joint laughter.

With the new approach Marion started to sit up much more, rather than her previous slumping. She looked around her much more, rather than having her eyes closed. It was as if her physical state was affected by her motivation to be social; she seemed to want to have a good viewing posture and a readiness for incidental interactions. Her limbs also became more mobile as she became more actively involved in the interactions. At times of great excitement and pleasure she would open her arms right out, swinging them in a joyous clapping motion, exposing her trunk area for the first time. Her clenched fists relaxed too and having her hands resting in her lap became a more frequent posture. Marion went on to use her body's albeit restricted movements to indicate her desire to be close to staff, turning, leaning and relaxing into them.

The changes in Marion's body seemed to be greater in these few months of Intensive Interaction than from years of physio and movement therapy. She illustrated for us so graphically the importance of motivation. With her it was like turning a switch, she changed so much and so quickly. This did require a lot of staff skill, but in some ways it felt easy. The key seemed to be in responding to Marion. Previous efforts had involved doing things to her, offering her stimuli, rather than starting from her. With the interactive games she was able to see that she was having an effect, that she could have some control over what happened. We think that this is why the passivity gave way to active involvement and engagement, because there was some point to being active.

Once staff had got it right for Marion and awoken her interest they began to question their preconceived ideas about her level of cognitive ability. This was related to a depth to her gaze and an inquiry in her facial expression. She transpired to be one of many students who led us to question our earlier judgements and the basis for making them. Marion continued to have periods of ill-health in which she would be more passive, but her apparent new outlook could no more easily be reversed than the staff's new attitude of pleasurable anticipation for Marion.

Adrian

Adrian was a young man who rarely sat down and who was always in motion. His behaviours were characterised by organised self-involvement with his stereotypies including grimaces, dropping saliva onto his hands, clapping, finger clicking, tapping parts of his body or nearby surfaces, various jerks, walks, steps and numerous hums and intonations. His moods and behaviours varied; at one extreme were distress and anger in which all his movements and sounds expressed tension, his stereotypies exaggerated and he became liable to grab others aggressively. At the other extreme he could be happy and relaxed, humming cheerfully and laughing.

Adrian could speak, although his utterings were infrequent and often unintelligible. When humming he could reproduce musical tunes with great accuracy. Opinions varied about his level of comprehension; retrospectively it seems that it was underestimated by all. When approached, Adrian might acknowledge the other person by glances and, depending on his mood, by complying with instructions. Sometimes he would approach staff, but only to request food, a recurrent obsession.

We decided to use imitation and joining in as an initial point of access, though Adrian's activities were so numerous at any one time that this was somewhat daunting. However, after strenuous attempts to imitate his entire range, we realised that it was sufficient to imitate and reflect back just those activities that were the focus of his attention. From the first session he appeared aware of being imitated. Often he seemed to check that we were imitating, by exaggerating his behaviours or by introducing another and then looking at the appropriate part of our body. Sometimes he would smile or laugh as we began to imitate him. On occasions he seemed content to continue his current behaviours and be shadowed. On other occasions he would intersperse other behaviours, some enjoyed in previous sessions, some innovative. Sometimes it felt like we were dancing around the room and in terms of a dialogue, it was like we were both talking at the same time! There was a definite atmosphere of excitement.

In individual sessions with Adrian interactions based on imitation and joining in naturally diversified into interactions in the context of activities such as looking through picture books, exploring art materials and listening to tapes. Unsuspected levels of development and potential were revealed by the Intensive Interaction, particularly in the spheres of receptive vocabulary and concepts. It became the custom for all school staff to chat, verbally or non-verbally, with Adrian whenever they encountered him.

Sometimes our interactive approaches were not responded to; like anyone else he could be unsociable at times. He was prone to ailments, which, although minor, often seemed to leave him debilitated. He also always seemed sensitive to and depressed by environmental factors and general change. At these times he would revert to jerky movements and grimaces outside the classroom door or in the school entrance hall. There were occasions during these spells when he would seem indifferent to our approaches until we went to leave, when he would refuse to let us go. At these times imitative interactions seemed to play a reassuring role.

Adrian's achievements following the start of using Intensive Interaction with him were several. Eye contact became natural. Spontaneous speech remained difficult to interpret, but emerged in a wider variety of situations with greater vocabulary and length of utterances. Facial expressions became more discernible and his posture became more upright. He started to show curiosity about others' activities and to eavesdrop and he began to display a sense of humour. The ability to really relax continued to elude him, but he came to be able to enjoy sitting on our laps and occasionally initiated this himself. We think that Adrian made this progress because we bothered to involve ourselves in his activities and his world of understanding. With a mutuality established based around his movements we could move on to explore together other ways of relating.

Jerry

It was extremely difficult to get started with Jerry. He was new in the class and we observed him for some time. He stood in one corner of the room with the top half of his body in continuous motion. He constantly swayed from the waist with both hands constantly twiddling his hair. The only variations to this were when he bent to pick up and discard fluff from the floor and when he made sudden dashes into the centre of the room to tip over furniture or to fling someone's glasses. These events were difficult to anticipate and were so fast that they always took us by surprise.

Our period of observation told us that Jerry always positioned himself such that he had maximum opportunity to keep the whole classroom and much of the corridor in view. Part of his swaying motion seemed to be to enable him to scan around. We came to realise that he had little hearing and that the visual scanning was very important to him. We also saw that although he maintained this isolation, he was interested in what was going on around him.

Our attempts to get near Jerry resulted in him grabbing our arms or hands and nibbling on them quite hard whilst masturbating furiously. This of course was part of the reason why he managed to keep a space to himself. Both staff and students were reluctant to have this treatment. Our attempts to interact with him from a distance, however, were very unrewarding. His response to verbal input was nil and face-to-face exchanges never got beyond a second's worth of acknowledgement. We instinctively felt that in order to make access with Jerry we had to get near to him. The fact that this always lead to a sexual response meant that we first had to spend some weeks talking about this and preparing ourselves. We decided to approach Jerry several times per session and that these approaches should be closely observed and documented. We ensured that our manager was aware of our reasons for involving ourselves with someone who was likely to become sexually aroused as a result. We did not pre-specify what form the approaches would take, but decided instead to leave this to the intuitions of each member of staff.

We can remember Gaynor approaching Jerry with her body curled forward slightly, making her height and body shape more like his. Her hands were just below and either side of her face in the shape of his hands as his twiddled his hair. Her facial expression communicated that she wanted to play. As expected Jerry grabbed one of her arms and nibbled it and masturbated. Gaynor twiddled her hair in imitation of his usual behaviour with the other hand. The masturbating and nibbling lasted about 60 seconds and then he pushed her away. She re-approached, this time swaying a little and laughing gently. He let her stay near and studied her for a while and then pushed her away.

We continued to make approaches, all of us choosing to use some imitation of his swaying and twiddling. The sexual behaviour never lasted more than a few seconds and after a few sessions he did not introduce this at all. Early on in our attempts at making access with Jerry he started sitting in the corner on a sofa where he would scan and sway. He then started to let us share his sofa for short periods and even began to pull us down to sit with him. He scanned us continually as we swayed and twiddled and laughed as we got dizzy. As some rapport was established we were able to introduce a game of teasingly attempting to hold his head still, in a squeaky, playful voice asking – 'What's all this for?'. Jerry's signals were very easy to read, he smiled and sometimes laughed, and pushed us out of his space when he had had enough or when he wasn't in the mood.

We became conscious of the fact that Jerry's behaviour was changing. His swaying had slowed and his twiddling was less frenzied. His sudden dashes to throw things were now rare occasions. He preferred to sit rather than stand and he liked to have company in his space in the corner of the room. The interactions gradually developed and Jerry began to explore us and our responses. He liked to twiddle with loose threads on our clothing and pick fluff from us. He liked to be teased and giggled when we pretended that we would sit on him rather than next to him. Sometimes he responded by pulling us onto his knees, turning the joke around. We were, by this time, able to share very close proximity without any sexual arousal or sexual behaviour of any kind. He did not seem to be confused about this with us, but new people had to get past what felt like a barrier in the way that we did. They were nibbled on for the first few seconds of the first few meetings and then they could get on and enjoy imitation and other interactive games.

There were times when Jerry became cross when an interaction came to an end and his previous isolation was replaced by a demand for attention. Remembering how he used to be helped us to not feel negative about this, but to develop ways of negotiating with him when we had to leave him and work with someone else. Days when he was tense, perhaps because he was unwell or because there had been an incident on the ward, were difficult. Whereas previously he might have thrown the furniture, the feelings were now directed to us. There were occasions like this when we were bitten or when we had our head grabbed and severely shaken. This was hard to bear in some ways, but we were coming to realise that Intensive Interaction awakens people's emotions and not all of these are positive. We sometimes suffered because Jerry and other students let out some of their negative emotion on us.

On the whole though, Jerry became a pleasure to be with. He enjoyed brief interactions at a distance with staff who passed by in the corridor. His limbs were rarely tensed in repetitive movement and he would sometimes be quite still. He reciprocated not just games, but friendly physical contact also. He was able to snuggle in and to return a warm squeeze. He studied our faces and shared mutual gaze as long as he could retain his position of being able to scan around the room every few seconds. He became more receptive to joining in group activities and we were able to introduce pointing and gestures and the occasional sign.

Matthew

Matthew's behaviour challenged staff in a different way to the kinds of withdrawn and stereotyped behaviour with which we were most familiar and increasingly at ease. Matthew already liked the attention of others when he joined the school in his mid-twenties. He had Down's syndrome, an appealing face and a cheeky, toothy grin. People mostly responded warmly to Matthew, probably helped by these features, and he had learned something about his powers to charm. He had also learnt, it seemed, that he could manipulate people, and that he could use his behaviours when things were not as he would like them to be. His repertoire included urinating, soiling himself and throwing furniture in order to gain attention. He would also scratch, pinch, kick and aim at people when throwing chairs.

By the time Matthew joined us we, the staff, had become increasingly reticent to use behavioural programmes and increasingly keen to find alternatives. We had become experts at reading signals of negativity and at intervening to prevent the associated negative behaviour. Many of the students no longer displayed the kinds of behaviour which might be seen to necessitate behavioural programmes. Matthew challenged us then, partly because in some ways he was an obvious candidate for behaviour modification when we would rather try a gentler, more respectful approach.

Matthew was pre-verbal, with limited communication development and problems in relating to people. In this way Intensive Interaction was seen to be relevant for him. Making access with Matthew was relatively easy. He was very responsive to imitation games, and his clapping, patting, and dramatic hand gestures made this an obvious starting point. He rewarded staff with smiles and laughter and initially it was easy not to notice that these games were totally under Matthew's control. He was active in providing actions for the game and for his interactive partners to work from. He was also rewarding and encouraging and this added to the impression that the interactions were going well. It was only when staff tried to move games on, or to introduce variations, that Matthew resisted and protested. He responded by suddenly scratching or kicking the person working with him. Staff tried to vary the games in very subtle and sensitive ways, but still Matthew became aggressive. It became apparent that he wanted to have complete control of the interactions and was trying to manipulate this.

The staff team were determined to work through this. The interactive games could not proceed purely on Matthew's terms because they then lost the essential qualities of being mutually pleasurable and reciprocal. The staff decided that at this point some behavioural action would be helpful. If Matthew became aggressive during an interaction the staff member would move away immediately which was not what he wanted to happen. He would then throw furniture and defecate but he was not given any attention as a result of this, staff merely moved the other students away. Alongside this programme staff worked hard on the interactions also. They used careful analysis to find optimum times in the flow of the interaction to introduce a change. They learned to avoid the games for which he had particularly set routines. They followed some of his cues, but never all of them. They worked to make their variations to the games potentially very enjoyable. In these ways Matthew came to allow some sharing of the control and the interactive games became more varied and more complex.

Staff were later able to identify another source of difficulty in the interactive games. Some staff were getting kicked or scratched in the middle of an interactive game much more frequently than others. The incidence of this type of response also seemed to be associated with longer interaction sessions. As part of the ongoing reflection on practice some time was spent thinking about and discussing this. It transpired that

204

Matthew could not cope with sessions above a certain length or level of intensity. Those staff getting the aggression most often were also those who were more emotionally involved and who had sessions which felt more intense. The solution was found to be greater attention to monitoring Matthew's arousal state throughout the interactions and keeping this within certain optimal limits.

The final problem which the staff team had to address was that sometimes Matthew would soil himself or hurl furniture as soon as a session finished and the member of staff moved away. This was partly solved by addressing the levels of intensity of the interactions, but staff also had to pay careful attention to the ways in which they ended the interactions. Matthew needed to be helped with what the researchers of caregiver-infant interaction referred to as cooling down, decelerating. Staff cues for this to take place had to be very explicit and they had to observe carefully to ensure that this had happened before moving away.

Some students/clients, like Matthew, can manipulate any intervention used with them. Each new member of staff who joined the team had to work through these problems with Matthew for themselves, but this was quicker and easier with the guidance of the staff who had already gained these valuable insights. We were able to succeed with Matthew, using Intensive Interaction, supplemented with some behavioural strategies, to establish a sharing of control rather than a quashing of it. Matthew gained in confidence and used more of the room rather than just his corner. He participated much more in group activities and started to be able to enjoy trips into the community. He explored with us his abilities to vocalise and to use facial expression. He became able to enjoy warm physical contact without this turning unpleasant. Perhaps most importantly though, he learned that he could use his behaviours to influence others in more positive ways, and indeed that others could positively affect him also.

Kevin

With Kevin the problem was accessing. All of us who had been working directly with Kevin over the months and years had become incredibly frustrated with him and we were having a great deal of difficulty overcoming this. Kevin's behaviour repertoire was dominated by behaviours which we primarily perceived as sexual. He had a tendency to stand with one finger hooked in his mouth making continuous short glances at people in the room. The vocalisations and facial expressions that went with this were usually reminiscent of leering; often the behaviour was accompanied by masturbation. Frequently Kevin would become fixated on one particular student or member of staff, in which case the glances became much more of a fixed leer and the masturbation became persistent. None of this made Kevin a particularly appealing person to interact with.

Adding to Kevin's difficulties in attracting our attentions was his otherwise extreme tendency towards passivity. There were stereotyped behaviours of flicking through the pages of a catalogue or fingering his neck, but otherwise he was passive. Every movement or action we wanted from him had to be physically or verbally prompted all along the way.

As a staff team we often discussed how hard we found it to find aspects of Kevin to celebrate and enjoy. We could not find in him the child-like qualities that might trigger our natural interactive abilities. Although we had succeeded in switching on these abilities with students who were adult, smelly and unattractive in other ways, Kevin's kind of leering created a revulsion posing bigger problems.

The way we found to move forward on this was to bring in Dave, who was not a regular member of our class team, and who did not have these pre-conceived ideas about Kevin. Dave knew of our difficulties, but tried to begin to make access with Kevin, using his experience and understanding of the method of Intensive Interaction. As part of his subjective observation, Dave spent several sessions in Kevin's proximity getting to know him. He found himself exploring with this proximity and noting that Kevin was interested in it. He played around with his positioning, placing his face quite close to Kevin's and moving around. He used imitation of Kevin's facial expressions and strange sniggers, managing to capture his attention while doing this. He also used a 'teasing' voice to commentate on what Kevin might be thinking and on what they were doing. At the slightest sign of interest from Kevin, Dave celebrated with a dramatic laugh.

A variation on these initial getting to know each other activities included Dave playfully imposing himself on Kevin's activity of flicking through the pages of a catalogue. Dave would teasingly intervene by examining a page or two himself or by placing his face in the line of gaze between Kevin's face and the catalogue. Kevin quickly rejected the catalogue as the focus of his interest, replacing this with the much more versatile and contingent piece of equipment that was Dave. Once this level of access was achieved, Kevin became less passive and less dominated by sexual preoccupations. We now had at least one activity identified with which we could achieve mutuality with Kevin.

The fact that Dave was not in the classroom all of the time, but came in regularly to spend time with Kevin seemed to help tremendously. Dave had not become alienated from Kevin in the way that we had and Kevin it seemed, had come to see Dave as someone with whom he behaved differently. Seeing a different side to Kevin was all that we, the class team, needed to spark off our abilities to interact with him. We were able to use ideas from Dave and Kevin's repertoire to introduce ourselves and get immediately gratifying responses. Following on from this we were able to develop interactive games and repertoires of our own.

Kevin's development was quite rapid. His limited range of strange facial expressions broadened to a wider range of expressions which were more recognisably meaningful. His looking behaviour of glances and leers also changed as he learned to make real eye contact and to give warm and interested facial regard. He started to do more for himself and to be less reliant on our continual prompts to move around the classroom, get his coat, pour drinks etc. He also surprised us on occasion by sitting down and readily completing the kind of inset puzzle it had been requiring a great deal of nagging, pointing and prodding for him to achieve. His body posture changed to become more upright and his muscle tone seemed to be less limp. He was keenly interested in the goings on in the room and he often scanned the corridors for signs of Dave.

In the time that we worked with him Kevin did not stop the behaviours which were characterised by organised self-involvement or sexual self-stimulation, but they stopped being such a problem. We learned new ways of relating to Kevin and he learned new ways of relating to us. The experience of bringing in someone different to initiate the process of Intensive Interaction was one which is worth repeating in these kinds of circumstances. Through Kevin we learnt a lot about motivating ourselves and about strategies for making access.

Betty

Betty was a woman in her forties with no sight. Though able-bodied she lived on a ward with people with profound and multiple learning difficulties and she had become very dependent – she had learned helplessness. Despite the level at which she functioned she was one of the most cognitively able students with whom we used Intensive Interaction. She was highly verbal, though what she said made little sense to the listener. She was completely locked in her own world of repeated phrases, foul language and childhood rhymes. Favourite repetitions also included wonderfully entertaining monologues of members of staff telling people off.

The staff working with Betty recognised that Intensive Interaction was as relevant for her as for their pre-verbal students. She did not use her speech to communicate and her repetitive speech had formed an effective barrier between herself and the outside world. Some days she would swear continuously and attempts to teach her to pour her own drinks, for example, or to develop some basic mobility skills, were met with shouts of abuse. She would sometimes strip herself naked and refuse to get dressed, demanding that she had a 'red dress' or 'a woolly one' to wear! Although all this was extremely exasperating, staff welcomed her as a real character in the class and they saw the potential for interactive game.

As with the demands for various types of clothing, Betty would also sometimes communicate demands for particular songs or rhymes. Although it was hard to pick out the song requests from the rest of the jumbled speech, staff seized on these genuine communications and sought to respond to them meaningfully. In more contented moods Betty would also engage in solitary word play, she would play around with the emphasis, pronunciation and sound of words. Again staff were able to employ the idea of using the learner's own behaviour, starting with what was safe and familiar for them. With Betty this meant chattering about 'who do you think you are – the Queen?', 'bugger off' and 'bouncy, bouncy gee gee'. It meant using exaggerated intonation and different tones of voices to repeat favourite nursery rhymes. Staff were confident enough in the processes to not worry about whether this might reinforce and increase

increase her inappropriate language, or about whether the rhymes were age-appropriate; Betty's language was important to her and the obvious point of access.

Staff then began to join in Betty's word play. This involved careful listening and observation to find times when Betty would be receptive and to select phrases which could be used. Just as staff had used rhythm, repetition, turn-taking, suspense and playfulness with other students with other behaviours, they brought these qualities to bear on the verbal interactions with Betty. Betty soon realised that her requests for songs and rhymes were responded to and a favourite game involved Betty providing a first line for someone to continue on. This soon became a game in which the lines were alternated in jovial turn-taking – 'my mother said' . . . 'I never should', with the staff member using burst and pause to create the anticipation of Betty's response. She enjoyed this, leaving expectant gaps also, and together staff and Betty diversified the rhymes, sometimes messing up the last line in some way, rushing it, squeaking it or shouting it.

As well as using the word games, staff used intentionality with Betty. They were able to pick out bits of what she said and respond to them as if they were intentional communications. At snack times she refused at first to make verbal choices. She would instead chatter on at other times making oblique references to 'a lovely cup of tea'; such references were treated as genuine communications. She started to become aware of where her language was having an effect. Sometimes though, she would be obstinate and would just repeat the string of choices offered to her. In these instances the choice offered to her would not automatically be the one that staff knew she preferred. In time she gained the abilities and motivation to use her speech communicatively to express food and drink choices.

With the increasing recognition of her ability to have an effect on others she began to call out the names of members of staff across the room, enjoying their calls back to her. She would check out who was present in the room and staff would let her know where missing people were. She sometimes teased by deliberately asking for people who weren't around. There were gentle interactions as well as the more lively, playful ones. On occasions she would relax and enjoy the closeness of someone familiar singing a range of her various songs.

There continued to be times when Betty was angry and when she would shout and swear and strip. These occasions became less frequent, however, and less prolonged. Staff became increasingly skilled at diverting her and cheering her up at the first signs of this. There were times though, when they knew that all they could do was respect her need to have some time and space for a good rant.

Betty had isolated herself, perhaps as her way of coping with life. She responded to the playful coaxing to be social and she could not resist being communicative when staff made everything right for this. She came to enjoy her time in school and to develop some warm and fun relationships. There were, however, other aspects of the curriculum which were

·important for her, and the aims for Betty went beyond the realms of communication and sociability. Staff were able to use the rapport and trust they developed with her to encourage her to move around independently, to put out her hands to feel what was in front of her, to trail her way along the corridor to the toilets. This was a long process and was helped along by the improved communications and by the games that could cheer her up if she had a bump. Making access with Betty using Intensive Interaction opened up a range of opportunities for her. She now lives in the community.

Georgiou

Georgiou was a student at the school when the old-style curriculum was in place. He was a young man with Down's syndrome who was visually impaired with bilateral cataracts. The hospital was his sixth placement and he had been resident there since the age of five. His behaviours were stereotyped and ritualistic and his repertoire included rocking, rhythmic vocalising, turning on the spot, rubbing his palms together, rubbing his palms on his head and poking his fingers in his eyes. Predominantly he rhythmically shook and banged and mouthed things and his response to the activities available at that time had been to treat all equipment presented to him in this way. He was unresponsive to staff, self-absorbed and withdrawn. He had made no progress in a number of years and his school place was terminated.

Later when we became involved with developing the new style of working and excited by the possibilities being demonstrated by using Intensive Interaction, we felt that we knew what we should have been doing with Georgiou. We re-opened his school place and instead of offering him sand and water, bricks and toys, we offered him ourselves and our new sensitivities. To start with we simply observed him, but not from a distance, from the perspective of joining in with his rhythms, getting some feel for what it was like to be him.

We joined with Georgiou in his rocking and involved ourselves in aspects of his organised self-involvement. This was actually quite easy because when he came across our hands, for example, he simply took them up, shook them, mouthed them and banged them as he would any other object. At this stage he did not seem to perceive us as people – something different from objects. With his attention on our hands we could make them responsive to him, we could intersperse his activity with our activity, we could bring a new dimension of interest to our hands. Most of the sequences at this time centred around rubbing palms, patting, pushing against each other's weight and clapping. We incorporated into this his rhythms, exaggerated rhythms and sequences of burst and pause.

As this proceeded we saw Georgiou move on from the exploration with touch and rhythms which was safe and familiar and barely exploratory at all. He began to experiment with what happens if . . . and to visually explore. Thus when we deliberately brought the two pairs of hands up to near our faces we brought his gaze with them. Again with the deliberate intent of progression we worked hard to use our faces to gain his attention. How we did this was based on his activity as we focussed in on the rhythmic movements of his mouth that usually accompanied his other stereotypies. We imitated these rhythmic movements, sometimes imitating the sounds too if they were there, sometimes silently. On reflection these variations in the games were almost completely intuitive. We changed the pace of the movements, made the sounds softer and louder, left our mouths wide open in moments of exaggerated pause, all the while scanning him for feedback signalling his interest. He was interested, he seemed to think this was great and soon he was varying his own stereotypies also.

He started to explore our faces with his hands and his eyes and when we shared moments of laughter his attention was drawn to the whole face and to our eyes. Somewhere around this time eye contact started, it was warm and intensely encouraging; it seemed to us that he had begun to see us as people, not just objects. On one significant occasion he put down the ever-present spoon (his favourite thing to be mouthed, shaken and banged) in order to free his hands to place them on his teacher's face. He just held her still for a while, studying her, and then commenced to see what would happen if he pulled on her ears and twisted her nose, laughing uproariously at the exaggerated squeals which resulted.

The interactive games with Georgiou diversified so that each member of the four staff had their own repertoire. He knew us as different people and offered different contributions to the games accordingly. He enjoyed rough and tumble games, games built around being pushed on the garden swing, tension expectancy games where we could hide our hands behind our backs and playfully make them reappear and many more. On arrival in class his first move was no longer to seek out a spoon or bells to mouth, but to seek a member of staff and climb onto their back or pull them to the floor to play. He became someone who could, and wanted to, initiate and sustain social interaction, albeit at his basic playful level.

The interactive games we played with Georgiou were based on mutual activity and mutual regard. The possibilities they gave for variations were endless and we rarely had to think about how to move things on. We greatly enjoyed these interactions, he rewarded us superbly for our presence and we were practically queuing up to play! Contributing to the attractiveness of these interactions must have been the fact that Georgiou was small, had child-like features, big eyes and smile and an infectious laugh. Once we had reached him, he taught us how to behave to get the best from him; he also taught us a lot about strategies we could use with students whose personal qualities were less likely to trigger in us the use of our intuitive abilities.

Victor

Victor, a young man with a diagnosis of autism and severe learning difficulties, had lived in the institution from the age of six, but even then it was his thirteenth placement. Victor was a challenging person to work with and to care for, partly because he was hyperactive and partly because he

210

was very obsessive. He displayed a range of ritualistic behaviours including at various times repeatedly flushing the toilet, screeching, and scrib-
bling on the floor and urinating on the marks. He was also an opportunist
and acutely aware of his surroundings to the extent of noting when new
staff were around, when routines were different, and where keys were left,
capitalising on opportunities to abscond.

Staff working with Victor were familiar with his bouts of spinning objects,
ripping fabric, thumping people on the back, masturbating on rubbery
surfaces, playing with his nipples, and repetitive activity with sand. What
was particularly troublesome in the classroom context though, was his
behaviour of filling a particular beaker with water and running with it
(spilling some) to a particular window from which he poured it onto a
particular spot. For about six months he did this to the virtual exclusion of
everything else. At this time, as always, he was remote and restless,
completely unable or unwilling to give eye contact.

Previous approaches to working with Victor had involved, in the ward
context the use of a range of medication, and in the school context the use
of behaviour modification. Interventions were based on the premise that
Vic had to be made to slow down and to stop his behaviours before further
work could be done with him. Intensive Interaction, however, challenged
this premise and gave other philosophical and practical alternatives. The
combination of the new approach together with a member of staff who
really warmed to Vic meant that after many years some mutuality was
achieved with him.

The initial breakthrough was made with the blending of two personalities. Victor's teacher, Lindsey, did not seek to stop the water-pouring
activity, but instead used it to reach him. Vic was active and lively and a
gentle approach would not have touched him. Instead Lindsey used an
approach of playful intrusion, intercepting his water-pouring at various
points. She would seek to catch the water he poured, to tip his beaker
before his desired destination, to jog his arm, all with very playful voice
and body language. Vic would never have let her take or share control of
this activity, but he did show signs of being amused, of anticipating and
enjoying her interference.

Responding to Victor's feedback, other intrusions with a similar lively,
playful feel were tried. Vic began to diversify in his obsessions again and
his teacher had to be flexible; when he poured sand she had to develop
playful intrusions into this, when he spun objects she had to snatch a turn
to spin for herself. There was often some nominal resistance to these
games, but because of the constant and sensitive scanning for feedback,
she was able to know when her games were welcomed. Her teasing voice
and face set the tone of what it was all about. Nonetheless other students
might have responded very differently to such approaches.

With increasing confidence built between them, Lindsey used what she
had learned about the tempo and type of contact which Victor responded
to best as a basis for new games. Doing Intensive Interaction 'on the move'
she would chase him or intercept him on his roamings, ruffle his hair, pat

or tickle him quite firmly, give him a bear hug. Victor did not give eye contact yet, but he rewarded her with happy vocalisations and broad grins.

Victor was known as a difficult and unresponsive student, but other staff were able to see him responding and being playful. With time there was generalisation of his new abilities to include new games and more staff. He enjoyed being pushed down onto a beanbag or mattress and staff found that they could pin him to a spot for a while to enjoy a game. Significantly he would also choose to be still in order to give his attention fully to the interactions. He started to reciprocate much more, holding onto the teacher's wrists in a nose-tweaking game for example, taking some control for the tempo and communicating his desire for more.

Along the way Victor lost interest in water-pouring and gained interest in the potential of other people and of interactive game. When he spun objects or attempted to abscond, he did so whilst looking around him to see who would join him or stop him or play. He developed the ability to be still, to be involved in periods of joint focus and to be engaged. Most significant, however, and most startling for all concerned was that he started to make eye contact and this came in quite long bursts with a warm or teasing quality.

Glossary

Accessing A term to describe the two-way process of the initial stage of establishing interactive sequences between student/client and staff member(s).

Arousal A heightened intellectual or emotional state.

Availability The ability to assume a posture, body language and facial signalling which indicates willingness to indulge in interaction.

Engagement A state of mutual focus in which both parties are intellectually or emotionally aroused.

Facial regard Looking at a face. The main purpose of this term is to distinguish looking at a face from eye contact.

Intentionality The process of behaving toward students/clients as if their behaviour is meaningful and communicative, even before it is.

Interaction sequence A series of related games, activities or episodes, which develop or follow on from one another, and which make up a continuous session.

Interactive behaviour Behaviour which is directed toward another person and which has the potential to initiate, sustain, or spiral a positive interaction.

Interactive game A playful interaction, without formal rules, in which both participants are experiencing pleasure.

Interactivity The ability to use interaction principles to general effect in activities other than interaction sessions.

Intervention A structured procedure designed to change the environment or course of development for an individual or group of individuals.

Joint focus Two people attending simultaneously to the same stimulus. Implied here, too, is a degree of awareness from both people that this is happening.

Motherese A language style use by carers in communicative interactions with their infants.

Mutuality Two people sharing similar experiences and/or emotional states. Implied here is a degree of engagement which stimulated the shared emotional state. There is overlap in definition with 'joint focus'.

Practitioner A worker from any discipline who carries out face-to-face work with students/clients.

Proximity Being near or close by. The term which describes geographical placement of people in relation to each other.

Reciprocity The term for the concept of mutual give and take exchanges in which influences are two-way.

Repertoire An established array of interactive games and activities. 'Established' implies that the student/client has ready memory and knowledge of these games and activities.

Sociability The motivation and ability to relate to others in a mutually rewarding and reciprocal fashion.

Bibliography

Affleck, G., McGrade, B.J., McQueeney, M. and Allen, D. (1982) 'Promise of relationship-focused early intervention in developmental disabilities', *Journal of Special Education*, **16**, 413–30.

Arco, C.M.B. and McCluskey, K.A. (1981) 'Change of pace: an investigation of the salience of maternal temporal style in mother-infant play', *Child Development*, **52**, 941–49.

Argyle, M. (1975) *Bodily Communication* (London: Methuen & Co Ltd).

Beckwith, L., Cohen, S., Kopp, C., Parmalee, A. and Macy, D. (1976) 'Caregiver-infant interaction and early cognitive development in preterm infants', *Child Development*, **47**, 579–85.

Beebe, B. (1985) 'Interpersonal timing: the application of an adult dialogue model to mother-infant vocal and kinesic interactions', in Field, T.M. and Fox, N.A. (eds) *Social Perception in Infants* (Norwood: Ablex).

Bell, R.Q. (1968) 'A reinterpretation of the direction of effects in studies of socialization', *Psychological Review*, **75**, 81–95.

Beveridge, M.C. and Berry, P. (1977) 'Observing interactions in severely mentally handicapped children', *Research in Education*, **17**, 13–22.

Beveridge, M. and Hurrell, P. (1979) 'Teachers' responses to severely mentally handicapped children's initiations in the classroom', *Journal of Child Psychiatry*, **21**, 175–81.

Beveridge, S. (1989) 'Parents as teachers of children with special educational needs', in Sugden, D. (ed) *Cognitive Approaches in Special Education* (London: Falmer Press).

Billinge, R. (1987) 'The objectives model of curriculum development – a creaking bandwagon', *Mental Handicap*, **16**, 26–29.

214

Bray, A., MacArthur, J. and Ballard, K.D. (1988) 'Education for pupils with profound disabilities: Issues of policy, curriculum, teaching methods and evaluation', *European Journal of Special Needs Education*, 3, 207–24.

Brazelton, T.B. (1984) *Neonatal Behavioural Assessment Scale*, 2nd edn. (London: Heinemann Medical Books).

Brazelton, T.B., Koslowski, B. and Main, M. (1974) 'The origins of reciprocity: the early mother-infant interaction', in Lewis, M. and Rosenblum, L.A. (eds) *The Effect of the Infant on its Caregiver* (New York: Wiley).

Brinker, R.P. and Goldbart, J. (1981) 'The problem of reliability in the study of early communication skills', *British Journal of Psychology*, 72, 27–41.

Brinker, R.P. and Lewis, M. (1982) 'Discovering the competent handicapped infant: a process approach to assessment and intervention', *Topics in Early Childhood Special Education*, 2, 1–16.

Bromwich, R.M. (1981) *Working with Parents and Infants: An Interactional Approach* (Baltimore: University Park Press).

Bruner, J. (1975) 'The ontogenesis of speech acts', *Journal of Child Language*, 2, 1–19.

Bruner, J. (1983) *Child's Talk: Learning to Use Language* (New York: Oxford University Press).

Bull, P. (1983) *Body Movement and Interpersonal Communication* (Chichester: John Wiley and Sons).

Bullowa, M. (1979) 'Pre-linguistic communication: a field for scientific research', in Bullowa, M. (ed) *Before Speech* (Cambridge: Cambridge University Press).

Burford, B., (1986) 'Communication through movement', in Shanley, E. (ed) *Mental Handicap – A Handbook of Care* (Edinburgh: Churchill Livingstone).

Burford, B. (1988) 'Action cycles: Rhythmic actions for engagement with children and young adults with profound mental handicap', *European Journal of Special Needs Education*, 3, 189–206.

Calhoun, M.L. and Rose, T.L. (1988) 'Early social reciprocity interventions for infants with severe retardation: current findings and implications for the future', *Education and Training in Mental Retardation*, 23, 340–43.

Carlson, L. and Bricker, D.D. (1982) 'Dyadic and contingent aspects of early communicative intervention', in Bricker, D.D. (ed) *Interventions with At-Risk and Handicapped Infants* (Baltimore: University Park Press).

216

Christie, P. and Wimpory, D. (1986) 'Recent research into the development of communicative competence and its implications for the teaching of autistic children', *Communication*, **20**, 4–7.

Clare, I. and Clements, J. (1990) 'Social cognition and impaired social interaction in people with severe learning difficulties', *Journal of Mental Defiency Research*, **34**, 309–24.

Clark, G.N. and Seifer, R. (1983) 'Facilitating mother-infant communication: a treatment model for high-risk and developmentally delayed children', *Infant Mental Health Journal*, **4**, 67–81.

Corbett, J. and Barton, L. (1992) *A Struggle for Choice: Students with Special Needs in Transition to Adulthood* (London: Routledge).

Crawford, N. (1980) *Curriculum Planning for the ESN(S) Child* (Kidderminster: BIMH).

Cunningham, C.E., Reuler, E., Blackwell, J. and Deck, J. (1981) 'Behavioural and linguistic development in the interactions of normal and retarded children with their mothers', *Child Development*, **52**, 62–70.

Davis, M. (1985) 'The usefulness of an interactive approach to the education of severely and profoundly handicapped individuals', Unpublished dissertation, (Hertfordshire College of Higher Education, now University of Hertfordshire, Department of Education).

Donellan, A.M., Mirenda, P.L., Mesaros, R.A. and Fassbender, L.L. (1984) 'Analyzing the communicative functions of aberrant behaviour', *Journal of the Association for Persons with Severe Handicaps*, **9**, 201–12.

Duchan, J.F. (1983) 'Autistic children are non-communicative: or so we say', *Seminars in Speech and Language*, **4**, 53–61.

Dunham, P. and Dunham, F. (1990) 'Effects of mother-infant social interactions on infants' subsequent contingency task performance', *Child Development*, **61**, 785–93.

Dunst, C.J. and Trivette, C.M. (1986) 'Looking beyond the parent-child dyad for the determinants of maternal styles of interaction', *Infant Mental Health Journal*, **7**, 69–80.

Durand, M.V. and Carr, E.G. (1985) 'Self-injurious behaviour: motivating conditions and guidelines for treatment', *School Psychology Review*, **14**, 171–76.

Eheart, B.K. (1982) 'Mother-child interactions with non-retarded and mentally retarded preschoolers', *American Journal of Mental Deficiency*, 20–25.

Emerson, G. (1992) 'What is Normalisation?' in Brown, H. and Smith,

H. *Normalisation: A Reader for the Nineties* (London: Tavistock/Routledge).

Ephraim, G.W.E. (1979) 'Developmental Process in Mental Handicap: A Generative Structure Approach', Unpublished PhD thesis (Uxbridge: Brunel University Department of Psychology).

Evans, P. and Ware, J. (1987) *'Special Care' Provision: The Education of Children with Profound and Multiple Learning Difficulties* (Windsor: NFER-Nelson).

Exline, R.V. and Fehr, B.J. (1982) 'The assessment of gaze and mutual gaze' in Scherer, K. and Ekman, P. (eds) *Handbook of Methods in Nonverbal Behaviour Research* (Cambridge: Cambridge University Press).

Ferguson, L.R. (1971) 'Origins of social development in infancy', *Merrill-Palmer Quarterly*, **17**, 119–39.

Field, T.M. (1977) 'Effects of early separation, interactive deficits, and experimental manipulations on infant-mother face-to-face interaction', *Child Development*, **48**, 763–71.

Field, T.M. (1978) 'The three R's of infant-adult interactions: rhythm, repertoires and responsivity', *Journal of Pediatric Psychology*, **3**, 131–36.

Field, T.M. (1979) 'Games parents play with normal and high-risk infants', *Child Psychiatry and Human Development*, **10**, 41–48.

Field, T.M., Healy, B.T., Goldstein, S. and Guthertz, M. (1990) 'Behaviour-state matching and synchrony in mother-infant interactions of nondepressed vs depressed dyads', *Developmental Psychology*, **26**, 7–14.

Fogel, A. (1982) 'Affect dynamics in early infancy: affective tolerance' in Field, T.M. and Fogel, A. (eds) *Emotion and Early Interaction* (New Jersey: Lawrence Erlbaum Associates).

Fraiberg, S. (1974) 'Blind infants and their mothers: an examination of the sign system' in Lewis, M. and Rosenblum, L.A. (eds) *The Effect of the Infant on its Caregiver* (London: John Wiley).

Frye, D. (1989) 'Social and cognitive development in infancy', *European Journal of Psychology of Education*, **4**, 129–39.

Fyfe, R. (1980) 'The Foundations of Communication', unpublished dissertation, (Hertfordshire College of Higher Education, now University of Hertfordshire, Department of Education).

Garfin, D.G. and Lord, C. (1976) 'Communication as a social problem in autism' in Schopler, E. and Mesibov, G.B. (eds) *Social Behaviour in Autism* (New York: Plenum Press).

Gardner, J. and Crawford, N. (1983) *The Skills Analysis Model* (Kidderminster: BIMH).

Gleason, J.J. (1989) *Special Education in Context: An Ethological Study of Persons with Developmental Disabilities* (Cambridge: Cambridge University Press).

Goldberg, S. (1977) 'Social competence in infancy: a model of parent-infant interaction', *Merrill-Palmer Quarterly*, **23**, 163–77.

Green, J.A., Gustafson, G. and West, M. (1980) 'Effects of infant development on mother-infant interactions', *Child Development*, **51**, 199–207.

Guralnick, M.J. and Bennett, F.C. (1987) 'Early intervention for at-risk and handicapped children: current and future perspectives', in Guralnick, M.J. and Bennett, F.C. (eds) *The Effectiveness of Early Intervention for At-Risk and Handicapped Children* (London: Academic Press).

Guralnick, M.J. and Bricker, D. (1987) 'The effectiveness of early intervention for children with cognitive and general developmental delays', in Guralnick, M.J. and Bennett, F.C. (eds) *The Effectiveness of Early Intervention for At-Risk and Handicapped Children* (London: Academic Press).

Hanzlik, J.R. and Stevenson, M.B. (1986) 'Interactions of mothers with their infants who are mentally retarded, retarded with cerebral palsy, or nonretarded', *American Journal of Mental Defiency*, **90**, 513–20.

Harding, C.G. (1983) 'Setting the Stage for Language Acquisition: Communication Development in the First Year of Life', in Golinkoff, R.M. (ed) *The Transition from Pre-Linguistic to Linguistic Communication* (Hillsdale NJ: LEA).

Hanzlik, J.R. (1989) 'Interactions between mothers and their infants with developmental disabilities: analysis and review', *Physical and Occupational Therapy in Pediatrics*, **9**, 33–47.

Harrison, J.A., Lombardino, L.J. and Stapell, J.B. (1987) 'The development of early communication: using developmental literature for selecting communication goals', *Journal of Special Education*, **20**, 463–73.

Hart, V. (1990) 'Handicapped infants', in Wang, M.C., Reynolds, M.C. and Walberg, H.J. (eds) *Special Education: Research and Practice, Synthesis of Findings* (Oxford: Pergamon Press).

Hess, R.D. and Shipman, V. (1976) 'Cognitive Elements in Maternal Behaviour', in Hill, J.P. (ed) *Minnesota Symposium on Child Psychology,* **1** (Minneapolis: University of Minnesota Press).

Hewett, D. (1985) 'The implications of studies in mother-infant inter-action for teaching strategies with young people with profound and complex learning difficulties', Unpublished dissertation (Cambridge Institute of Education).

Hewett, D. (1986) 'Towards a general theory of interactive teaching for pupils with severe and complex learning difficulties: a study of a project involving imitative interactions', Unpublished dissertation (Cambridge Institute of Education).

Hewett, D. (1989) 'The most severe learning difficulties: does your curriculum 'go back far enough'?', in Ainscow, M. (ed) *Special Education in Change* (London: David Fulton).

Hewett, D. (in progress) 'Towards a general theory of Intensive Interaction', unpublished PhD thesis (Cambridge Institute of Education).

Hewett, D. and Nind, M. (1989) 'Developing an interactive curriculum for pupils with severe and complex learning difficulties: a classroom process', in Smith, B. (ed) *Interactive Approaches to the Education of Children with Severe Learning Difficulties* (Birmingham: Westhill College).

Hewett, D. and Nind, M. (1989) 'Intensive Interaction: Draft Curriculum for use with students with very severe/fundamental learning difficulties' (Harperbury School: privately published and circulated).

Hewett, D. and Nind, M. (1992) 'Returning to the basics: a curriculum at Harperbury Hospital School', in Booth, T., Swann, W., Masterton, M. and Potts, P. (eds) *Learning for All 1: Curricula for Diversity in Education* (London: Routledge in association with O.U.).

Hodapp, R.M. and Goldfield, E.C. (1983) 'The use of mother-infant games with delayed children', *Early Child Development and Care*, **13**, 17–32.

Hodapp, R.M., Goldfield, E.C. and Boyatzis, C.J. (1984) 'The use and effectiveness of maternal scaffolding in mother-infant games', *Child Development*, 55, 772–81.

Hogg, J. and Sebba, J. (1986) *Profound Retardation and Multiple Impairment, Volume I: Development and Learning* (London: Croom Helm).

Hogg, J. and Sebba, J. 1986 *Profound Retardation and Multiple Impairment, Volume II: Education and Therapy, London, Croom Helm.*

Hoffman, M.L. (1981) 'Perspectives on the difference between understanding people and understanding things: the role of affect', in Flavell, J.H. and Ross, L. (eds) *Social Cognitive Development:*

Frontiers and Possible Futures (Cambridge: Cambridge University Press).

Holmberg, M.C. (1980) 'The development of social interchange patterns from twelve to forty-two months', *Child Development*, **51**, 448–56.

Howlin, P. (1986) 'An overview of social behaviour in autism', in Schopler, E. and Mesibov, G.B. (eds) *Social Behaviour in Autism* (New York: Plenum Press).

Jones, M. (1981) 'Environment and communication: a review', *Special Education Forward Trends*, **8**, 22–24.

Jones, O.H.M. (1977) 'Mother-child communication with pre-linguistic Down's Syndrome and normal infants', in Schaffer, H.R. (ed) *Studies in Mother-Infant Interaction* (London: Academic Press).

Kaye, K. (1977) 'Toward the origin of dialogue' in Schaffer, H.R. (ed) *Studies in Mother-Infant Interaction* (London: Academic Press).

Kaye, K. (1979) 'Thickening the thin data: the maternal role in developing communication and language', in Bullowa, M. (ed) *Before Speech* (Cambridge: Cambridge University Press).

Kaye, K. and Fogel, A. (1980) 'The temporal structure of face-to-face communication between mothers and infants', *Developmental Psychology*, **5**, 454–64.

Kiernan, C., Jordan, R. and Saunders, C. (1978) *Starting Off* (London: Souvenir Press).

Kiernan, C. and Reid, B. (1987) *Pre-Verbal Communication Schedule* (Windsor: NFER-Nelson).

Kitzinger, S. and Kitzinger, C. (1989) *Talking with Children: About Things That Matter* (London: Pandora).

Klein, M.D. and Briggs, M.H. (1987) 'Facilitating mother-infant communicative interaction in mothers of high-risk infants', *Journal of Childhood Communication Disorders*, **10**, 95–106.

Knight, C. and Watson, J. (1990) *Intensive Interaction Teaching at Gogarburn School, Edinburgh* (Moray House College).

Knoblock, P. (1983) *Teaching Emotionally Disturbed Children* (Boston, Houghton Mifflin).

Koegel, R.L. and Koegel, L.K. (1990) 'Extended reductions in stereotypic behaviour of students with autism through a self-management treatment package', *Journal of Applied Behaviour Analysis*, **23**, 119–27.

Kogan, K.L., Tyler, N. and Turner, P. (1974) 'The process of interpersonal adaptation between mothers and their cerebral palsied children', *Developmental Medicine and Child Neurology*, **16**, 518–27.

Kysela, G.M. and Marfo, K. (1983) 'Mother-child interactions and early intervention programmes for handicapped infants and young children', *Educational Psychology*, 3, 201–12.

Langley, M.B. and Lombardino, L.J. (1987) 'Application of a normal developmental model for understanding the communicative behaviours of students with severe handicaps', *European Journal of Special Needs Education*, 2, 161–76.

Lewis, M. (1986) 'The role of emotion in development' in Curry, N.E. (ed) *The Feeling Child: Affective Development Reconsidered* (Haworth Press).

Lewis, M. and Coates, L. (1980) 'Mother-infant interaction and cognitive development in twelve-week-old infants', *Infant Behaviour and Development*, 3, 95–105.

Lewis, M. and Goldberg, S. (1969) 'Perceptual-cognitive development in infancy: a generalized expectancy model as a function of the mother-infant interaction' *Merrill-Palmer Quarterly*, 15, 81–100.

Lewis, M. and Rosenblum, L.A. (eds) (1974) *The Effect of the Infant on its Caregiver* (New York: Wiley).

Lock, A. (1978) *Action, Gesture and Symbol* (London: Academic Press).

Mahoney, G. (1988) 'Maternal communication style with mentally retarded children', *American Journal of Mental Deficiency*, 92, 341–48.

Mahoney, G., Finger, I. and Powell, A. (1985) 'Relationship of maternal behavioral style to the development of organically impaired mentally retarded infants', *American Journal of Mental Deficiency*, 90, 296–302.

Mahoney, G. and Powell, A. (1988) 'Modifying parent-child interaction: enhancing the development of handicapped children', *Journal of Special Education*, 22, 82–96.

Marsh, P. (1988) *Eye to Eye: How People Interact* (Dorchester-on-Thames: Andromeda Oxford Ltd).

Mayer, N.K. and Tronick, E.Z. (1985) 'Mothers' turn-giving signals and infant turn-taking in mother-infant interaction', in Field, T.M. and Fox, N.A. (eds) *Social Perception in Infants* (New Jersey: Ablex).

McConachie, H. (1986) *Parents and Young Mentally Handicapped Children* (London: Croom Helm).

McConkey, R. (1981) 'Education without understanding', *Special Education Forward Trends* 8, 8–11.

McConkey, R. (1989) 'Interaction; the name of the game', in Smith,

222

B. (ed) *Interactive Approaches to the Education of Children with Severe Learning Difficulties* (Birmingham: Westhill College).

McCollum, J.A. (1984) 'Social interaction between parents and babies: validation of an intervention procedure', *Child: Care, Health and Development*, **10**, 301–15.

McCormick, L. and Noonan, M.J. (1984) 'A responsive curriculum for severely handicapped preschoolers', *Topics in Early Childhood Special Education*, **4**, 79–96.

McGee, J.J. Menolascino, F.J., Hobbs, D.C. and Menousek, P.E. (1987) *Gentle Teaching: A Nonaversive Approach for Helping Persons with Mental Retardation* (New York: Human Science Press).

Miller, A. (1986) *The Drama of Being a Child* (London: Virago).

Miller, A. (1991) *Banished Knowledge: Facing Childhood Injuries* (London: Virago).

Miller, L. and Ephraim, G. (1988) 'The role of "augmented mothering" in teacher education in special needs', *Mental Handicap*, **16**, 108–11.

Molony, H. and Taplin, J. (1988) 'Deinstitutionalization of people with developmental disability', *Australia and New Zealand Journal of Developmental Disabilities*, **14**, 109–22.

Montagu, A. (1971) *Touching: The Human Significance of the Skin* (New York: Columbia).

Newson, J. and Newson, E. (1974) 'Cultural aspects of Childrearing in the English-Speaking World', in Richards, P.M. (ed.) *The Integration of a Child into a Social World* (Cambridge: Cambridge University Press).

Newson, J. (1979a) 'The growth of shared understandings between infant and caregiver', in Bullowa, M. (ed) *Before Speech* (Cambridge: Cambridge University Press).

Newson, J. (1979b) 'Intentional behaviour in the young infant', in Shaffer, D. and Dunn, J. (eds) *The First Year of Life* (New York: Wiley).

Nind, M. (1986) 'The importance of body awareness teaching to deaf-blind young people with profound learning difficulties', *British Journal of Special Education, Research Exchange*, **6**, 11–12.

Nind, M. and Hewett, D. (1988) 'Interaction as Curriculum: A process method in a school for pupils with severe learning difficulties', *British Journal of Special Education*, **15**, 55–57.

Nind, M. and Hewett, D. (1989) 'Teaching pupils with very severe learning difficulties by means of Intensive Interaction', in Maunder, S. (ed) *Portage – Into the Nineties*, National Portage Association 1989 Conference papers.

Nind, M. (1993) 'Access to Communication: Efficacy of Intensive Interaction Teaching for People with Severe Developmental Disabilities Who Demonstrate Ritualistic Behaviours', unpublished Ph.D thesis (Cambridge Institute of Education).

Nirje, B. (1976) 'The Normalization Principle', in Kugel, R. and Shearer, A. (eds), *The Principle of Normalization in Human Services* (Toronto: National Institute on Mental Retardation).

Norris, J.A. (1991) 'Providing Developmentally Appropriate Intervention to Infants and Young children with Handicaps', *Topics in Early Childhood Special Education* 11, 21–35.

Odem, S.L., Yoder, P. and Hill, G. (1988) 'Developmental intervention for infants with handicaps: purposes and programs', *Journal of Special Education*, 22, 11–24.

O'Hagan, K. (1993) *Emotional and Psychological Abuse of Children* (Buckingham: Open University Press).

Olley, J.G. (1985) 'Social aspects of communication in children with autism' in Schopler, E. and Mesibov, G. (eds) *Communication Problems in Autism* (New York: Plenum Press).

Olson, S.L., Bates, J.E. and Bayles, K. (1984) 'Mother-infant interaction and the development of individual differences in children's cognitive competence', *Developmental Psychology*, 20, 166–79.

Ouvry, C. (1987) *Educating Children with Profound Handicaps* (Worcester: BIMH).

Pawlby, S.J. (1977) 'Imitative interaction' in Schaffer, H.R. (ed) *Studies in Mother-Infant Interaction* (London: Academic Press).

Perrin, B. and Nirje, B. (1985) 'Setting the Record Straight: A Critique of Some Frequent Misconceptions of the Normalization Principle', *Australia and New Zealand Journal of Developmental Disabilities*, 11, (2), 69–74.

Piaget, J. (1952) *The Origins of Intelligence in Children* (New York: International Universities Press).

Price, P. and Bochner, S. 1991 'Mother-child interactions and early language intervention', in Mitchell, D. and Brown, R.I. (eds) *Early Intervention Studies for Young Children with Special Needs* (London: Chapman and Hall).

Rogers-Warren, A.K. and Warren, S.F. (1984) 'The social basis of language and communciation in severely handicapped pre-schoolers', *Topics in Early Childhood Special Education*, 4, 57–72.

Rosenberg, S. and Robinson, C. (1985) 'Enhancement of mothers' interactional skills in an infant education program', *Education and Training of the Mentally Retarded*, 20, 163–69.

Sailor, W., Gee, K., Goetz, L. and Graham, N. (1988) 'Progress in educating students with the most severe learning disabilities; is there any?', *Journal of the Association for Persons with Severe Handicaps*, **13**, 87–99.

Sameroff, A. (1975) 'Transactional models in early social interactions', *Human Development*, **18**, 65–79.

Schaffer, H.R. (1971) *The Growth of Sociability* (Harmondsworth: Penguin).

Schaffer, H.R. (1977a) *Studies in Mother-Infant Interaction* (London: Academic Press).

Schaffer, H.R. (1977b) 'Early interactive development', in Schaffer, H.R. (ed) *Studies in Mother-Infant Interaction* (London: Academic Press).

Schaffer, H.R. (1984) *The Child's Entry into a Social World* (New York: Academic Press).

Schaffer, H.R. and Emerson, P.E. (1964) 'Patterns of response to physical contact in early human development', *Journal of Child Psychology and Psychiatry*, **5**, 1–13.

Schweigert, P. (1989) 'Use of microswitch technology to facilitate social contingency awareness as a basis for early communication skills', *Augmentative and Alternative Communication*, **5**, 192–98.

Seigal-Causey, E. and Guess, D. (1989) *Enhancing Nonsymbolic Communication Interactions among Learners with Severe Disabilities* (Baltimore: Paul Brookes).

Smith, B. (1989) 'Which approach? the education of pupils with SLD', *Mental Handicap*, **17**, 111–15.

Smith, B., Moore, Y. and Phillips, C.J. (1983) 'Education with understanding', *Special Education Forward Trends*, **10**, 21–24.

Snow, C.E. (1977) 'The development of conversation between mothers and babies', *Journal of Child Language*, **4**, 1–22.

Stern, D.N. (1974) 'Mother and infant at play: the dyadic interaction involving facial, vocal, and gaze behaviours', in Lewis, M. and Rosenblum, L.A. (eds) *The Effect of the Infant on its Caregiver* (New York: Wiley).

Stern, D.N., Beebe, B., Jaffe, J. and Bennett, S.L. (1977) 'The infants' stimulus world during social interaction: a study of caregiver behaviours with particular reference to repetition and timing', in Schaffer, H.R. (ed) *Studies in Mother-Infant Interaction* (London: Academic Press).

Stern, D.N. and Gibbon, J. (1979) 'Temporal expectancies of social behaviours in mother-infant play', in Thoman, E.B. (ed) *Origins of the Infant's Social Responsiveness* (New Jersey: Lawrence Erlbaum).

Stern, G.G. (1974) 'A factor analytic study of the mother-infant dyad', in Stone, L.J., Smith, H.T. and Murphy, L.B. (eds) *The Competent Infant* (London: Tavistock).

Sternberg, L. and Owens, A. (1985) 'Establishing pre-language signalling behaviour with profoundly mentally handicapped students: a preliminary investigation', *Journal of Mental Deficiency Research*, **29**, 81–93.

Stevenson, M.B. and Lamb, M.E. (1979) 'Effects of infant sociability and the caretaking environment on infant cognitive performance', *Child Development*, **50**, 340–49.

Szivos, S.E. and Griffiths, E. (1990) 'Consciousness Raising and Social Identity Theory: A Challenge to Normalization', *Clinical Psychology Forum*, August 1990, 11–15.

Thoman, E.B. (1975) 'The role of the infant in early transfer of information', *Biological Psychiatry*, **10**, 161–69.

Tiegerman, E. and Primavera, L. (1984) 'Imitating the autistic child: facilitating communicative gaze behaviour', *Journal of Autism and Developmental Disorders*, **14**, 27–38.

Tomlinson, P. (1981) *Understanding Teaching: Interactive Educational Psychology* (Maidenhead: McGraw-Hill).

Trevarthen, C. (1974) 'Conversations with a two-month old', *New Scientist*, 230–35.

Trevarthen, C. (1979) 'Communication and cooperation in early infancy: a description of primary intersubjectivity', in Bullowa, M. (ed) *Before Speech* (Cambridge: Cambridge University Press).

Tronick, E., Als, H. and Adamson, L. (1979) 'Structure of early face-to-face communicative interactions', in Bullowa, M. (ed) *Before Speech* (Cambridge: Cambridge University Press).

Vitagliano, J. and Purdy, S. (1987) 'Mother-infant activities: the inital step in language development in the deaf-blind child', *Journal of Rehabilitation of the Deaf*, **21**, 33–36.

Walker, J.A. (1982) 'Social interactions of handicapped infant', in Bricker, D.D. (ed) *Interventions with At-Risk and Handicapped Infants* (Baltimore: University Park Press).

Wang, M.C. (1990) 'Learning characteristics of students with special needs and the provision of effective schooling', in Wang, M.C., Reynolds, M.C. & Walberg, H.J. (eds) *Special Education: Research and Practice* (Oxford: Pergamon).

Ware, J. (1989) 'Designing appropriate environments for people with

226

PMLD', in Fraser, W. (ed) *Key Issues in Mental Retardation Research* (London: Methuen).

Ware, J. and Evans, P. (1987) 'Room management is not enough', *British Journal of Special Education*, **14**, 78–80.

Warren, S.F. and Rogers-Warren, A. (1984) 'The social basis of language and communication in severely handicapped preschoolers', *Topics in Early Childhood Special Education*, **4**, 57–72.

Watson, J.S. (1985) 'Contingency perception in early social development', in Field, T.M. and Fox, A. (eds) *Social Perception in Infants* (New Jersey: Ablex).

Weistuch, L. and Byers-Brown, B. (1987) 'Motherese as therapy: a programme and its dissemination', *Child Language Teaching and Therapy*, **3**, 57–71.

Welch, M. (1983) 'Retrieval from autism through mother-child holding therapy', in Tinbergen, N. and Tinbergen, E.A. *'Autistic' Children – New Hope for a Cure* (London: George Allen and Unwin).

White, M. and East, K. (1986) 'Selecting early language objectives', *Educational Psychology in Practice*, **2**, 15–23.

Wolfensburger, W. (1980) 'The Definition of Normalization: Update, Problems, Disagreements, and Misunderstandings', in Flynn, R.J. and Nitsch, K.E. *Normalization, Social Integration and Community Services* (Baltimore: University Park Press).

Wolfensburger, W. (1983) 'Social Role Valorisation: A Proposed New Term for the Principle of Normalization', *Mental Retardation*, **21**(6), 234–39.

Wood, S. and Shears, B. (1986) *Teaching Children with Severe Learning Difficulties: A Radical Reappraisal* (London: Croom Helm).

Yoder, P.J. (1990) 'The theoretical and empirical basis of early amelioration of developmental disabilities: implications for future research', *Journal of Early Intervention*, **14**, 27–42.

Yoder, P.J. and Feagans, L. (1988) 'Mothers' attributions of communication to prelinguistic behaviour of developmentally delayed and mentally retarded infants', *American Journal of Mental Deficiency*, **93**, 36–43.

Yoder, P.J. and Kaiser, A.P. (1989) 'Alternative explanations for the relationship between maternal verbal interaction style and child language development', *Journal of Child Language*, **16**, 141–60.

Author Index

Adamson, L. 23
Affleck, G. 18, 36
Allen, D. 18, 36
Als, H. 23
Arco, C.M.B. 23
Argyle, M. 97
Bakeman, R. 31, 32
Ballard, K.D. 37, 38
Barton, L. 171, 172
Bates, J.E. 29, 43
Bateson, M.C. 21
Bayles, K. 29, 43
Beckwith, L. 29
Beebe, B. 23, 24
Bell, R.Q. 19
Bennett, F.C. 38
Bennett, S.L. 23
Berry, P. 35, 38
Beveridge, M.C. 35, 38
Beveridge, S. 33
Billinge, R. 38
Blackwell, J. 32
Bochner, S. 19
Bray, A. 37, 38
Brazelton, T.B. 18, 23, 165
Bricker, D.D. 18, 24, 29, 30, 32
Briggs, M.H. 29, 31, 32
Brinker, R.P. 18, 32, 38
Bromwich, R.M. 18, 19, 29, 36
Brown, J.V. 31, 32
Bruner, J. 18, 23, 27, 29, 36
Bull, P. 97
Bullowa, M. 29
Burford, B. 34, 42, 191, 192
Byers-Brown, B. 21

Calhoun, M.L. 21, 35, 36
Carlson, L. 18, 24, 30, 32
Carr, E.G. 40
Christie, P. 41
Clare, I. 41
Clark, G.N. 3, 21, 24, 29, 31, 33, 36
Clements, J. 41
Coates, L. 24, 29
Cohen, S. 29
Corbett, J. 171, 172
Coupe, J. 159
Crawford, N. 5
Cunningham, C.E. 32,
Davis, M. 8, 43
Deck, J. 32
Donellan, A.M. 40
Duchan, J.F. 41
Dunham, F. 29
Dunham, P. 29
Dunst, C.J. 33
Durand, M.V. 40
East, K. 38
Eheart, B.K. 18
Emerson, G. 173
Emerson, P.E. 27
Ephraim, G.W.E. 6, 19, 43
Evans, P. 35, 37
Exline, R.V. &
Fassbender, L.L. 40
Ferguson, L.R. 20, 27
Field, T.M. 20, 23, 26, 31
Finger, I. 27
Fogel, A. 21, 27, 36
Fraiberg, S. 192
Frye, D. 19

228

Fyfe, R. 43
Gardner, J. 5
Garfin, D.G. 41
Gee, K. 37
Gibbon, J. 37
Gleason, J.J. 35
Goetz, L. 37
Goldbart, J. 159
Goldberg, S. 19, 24, 31
Goldfield, E.C. 19
Graham, N. 37
Green, J.A. 27
Griffiths, E. 173
Guess, D. 42
Guralnick, M.J. 35, 38
Gustafson, G. 27
Hanzlik, J.R. 18, 29
Harding, C.G. 27
Harrison, J.A. 42
Hart, V. 38
Hess, R.D. 29
Hewett, D. 4, 6, 8, 9, 10, 11, 43, 187
Hill, G. 18, 27, 36
Hobbs, D.C. 16, 40, 42
Hodapp, R.M. 19
Hoffman, M.L. 29
Hogg, J. 19, 38
Holmberg, M.C. 27
Howlin, P. 41
Hurrell, P. 38
Jaffe, J. 23
Jones, M. 39
Jones, O.H.M. 32
Jordan, R. 5
Kaye, K. 21, 26
Kiernan, C. 5, 159
Kitzinger, C. 175
Kitzinger, S. 175
Klein, M.D. 29, 31, 32
Knight, C. 43
Knoblock, P. 41
Koegel, L.K. 40
Koegel, R.L. 40
Kogan, K.L. 31, 32
Kopp, C. 29
Koslowski, B. 18, 23
Kysela, G.M. 18, 36
Lamb, M.E. 29
Langley, M.B. 18
Lewis, M. 18, 19, 24, 29, 30, 32, 38
Lock, A. 22
Lombardino, L.J. 18, 42
Lord, C. 41

MacArthur, J. 37, 38
Macy, D. 29
Mahoney, G. 18, 27, 31, 36
Main, M. 18, 23
Marfo, K. 18, 36
Marsh, P. 97
Mayer, N.K. 26
McCluskey, K.A. 23
McCollum, J.A. 31
McConachie, H. 29, 34
McConkey, R. 19, 168
McCormick, L. 37, 38
McGee, J.J. 16, 40, 42
McGrade, B.J., 18, 36
McQueeney, M. 18, 36
Menolascino, F.J. 16, 40, 42
Menousek, P.E. 19, 40, 42
Mesaros, R.A. 40
Miller, A. 86, 90, 175
Miller, L. 43
Mirenda, P.L. 40
Molony, H. 40
Montagu, A. 27, 190
Moore, Y. 38
Newson, E. 6, 18, 22, 175
Newson, J. 6, 18, 19, 22, 175
Nind, M. 4, 6, 8, 9, 10, 11, 41, 43, 158, 159, 187
Nirje, B. 173
Noonan, M.J. 37, 38
Norris, J.A. 176
O'Hagan, K. 175
Odom, S.L. 18, 27, 36
Olley, J.G. 40
Olson, S.L. 29, 43
Ouvry, C. 39
Owens, A. 38
Parmalee, A. 29
Pawlby, S.J. 26, 27
Perrin, B. 173
Phillips, C.J. 38
Piaget, J. 19
Powell, A. 18, 27, 36
Price, P. 19
Primavera, L. 40
Purdy, S. 29, 42
Reid, B. 165, 159
Reuler, E. 32
Robinson, C. 36
Rogers-Warren, A.K. 18, 32, 33
Rose, T.L. 21, 35, 36
Rosenberg, S. 36
Sailor, W. 37, 38

Sameroff, A. 19, 36
Saunders, C. 5
Schaffer, H.R. 6, 18, 21, 23, 26, 27, 29, 30
Schweigert, P. 38
Sebba, J. 19, 38
Seifer, R. 3, 21, 24 , 29, 31, 33, 36
Seigal-Causey, E. 42
Shears, B. 38
Shipman, V. 29
Smith, B. 24, 38
Snow, C.E. 21
Stapell, J.B. 42
Stern, G.G. 20
Stern, D.N. 23, 36
Sternberg, L. 38
Stevenson, M.B. 18, 29
Szivos, S.E. 173
Taplin, J. 40
Thoman, E.B. 32
Tiegerman, E. 40

Tomlinson, P. 188
Trevarthen, C. 18, 23
Trivette, C.M. 33
Tronick, E.Z. 23, 26
Turner, P. 32
Tyler, N. 32
Vitagliano, J. 29, 46
Walker, J.A. 18, 32
Wang, M.C. 37
Ware, J. 35, 37, 38, 40
Warren, S.F. 18, 32, 33
Watson, J. 43
Watson, J.S. 24
Weistuch, L. 21
West, M. 27
White, M. 38
Wimpory, D. 41
Wolfensburger, W. 173, 176
Wood, S. 38
Yoder, P. 18, 33, 35, 36

Subject Index

Accessing
examples/method 85, 89–91, 197, 198, 199, 200, 202, 203, 204, 205, 206, 210
giving time 84–85, 87, 92
meaning of 89–90
timescale 91, 147, 164, 166, 199
accountability of teacher 154
age-appropriateness 15–16, 75, 100–101, 119, 206
aggression 194, 195, 196, 199, 203
during interaction sequence 203–204
apprenticeship 69, 181
arousal
emotional/affective 32, 62, 63, 199, 204
intellectual 32
optimum level 33, 204
assessments, formal 83, 158–159
attention-seeking behaviour 202, 203
autism 13, 39–41, 196, 209–211

Basic care activities 131–132
behavioural approaches 5, 13, 154–155, 177, 194, 203, 210
and autism 40, 210
and PMLD 38
inadequacy for teaching communication 6, 38
behavioural objectives 37, 154–155, 186
blind learners 206–208
body language/movement 60, 85, 86, 91, 93, 95, 97–99, 110, 119, 129, 130, 201, 210

body language-teacher 'available' look 91, 97–99, 123, 124
burst-pause 57, 74, 94, 198, 207

Capitalising on learner behaviours 9, 46, 51, 52–53, 56–57, 59–60, 61–62, 84, 92, 94, 101, 113, 129, 196–197, 198, 199–200, 201, 203, 205, 206–207, 208, 210
caregiver errors 32
caregiver role, 29, 50, 166
cause and effect 63, 68, 109, 198, 199, 204, 207, 209
celebrating learner behaviours 49, 52, 74, 84, 95, 98, 101, 103, 104, 114, 121, 124, 126, 134, 140, 179, 205
challenging behaviour 7, 13, 39, 76, 83–84, 86, 104, 139, 161–162, 180–181, 194, 195, 196, 199, 201, 202–203, 206, 210
chiming in 121–122, 134,
cognitive development 81, 196, 205–206
communication development 81, 165, 166–167, 196, 198–199, 200, 202, 205, 207, 211
communication rehearsal 26, 66, 177
communication teaching 38–39, 40, 42, 144
concentration span 69, 195
contingent responding 24, 27, 68, 199
contingent responding lack of in classrooms 35
curriculum for people with learning difficulties 4, 5, 37–39

process/product 13–14, 15, 38, 76, 186, 187–188
theory 7, 103

Deaf-blind learners 42
dominance and compulsion
  in classrooms 76, 150, 196
  lack of 64, 70
Down's Syndrome 32, 202, 208
dramatisations 46–47, 51, 57, 59, 62, 69, 107, 115–116, 195, 205, 207

Effectiveness feelings of 24
ethics 6,
eye contact 63, 86, 89, 91, 94, 103, 106, 110, 119, 127, 129, 140, 200, 205, 209
  people with autism 211
  people with Down's Syndrome 32

Face, use of face 109, 111–112
facial expression 8, 9, 50–51, 66, 89, 91, 106–107, 110, 111, 114, 119, 198, 200, 201, 205
facial regard 95, 110, 127, 164, 165
following the learner's lead 24, 32, 46, 52–53, 134, 209

Gaze 20, 195, 202, 209
gentle running commentary 92, 94, 100, 127, 128

Harperbury Hospital School 4, 15, 139, 153, 155, 156, 161, 163–164, 166–167, 179, 180
hearing impaired learners 201
Holding Therapy 15,
hyperactive learners 194, 199, 209

Imitation/modified reflecting 26, 28, 40, 50, 126, 127, 179, 197, 198, 199–200, 201, 205, 207, 209,
infant-focussed interventions 1, 35–37
infant development 19, 24, 29, 45,
  cognitive 81
  communication 81
  equal partners 19
  infant active in own development 19, 60–61, 73, 76
  lack of boundaries 71
  language 29, 39
  link with interaction 29, 35, 73, 80
  social 29, 70

infant elicited behaviours 21, 22
inner 'switch' 96–97
institutional living environment 4, 38
intellectualisation 153, 186, 203, 205
intensive interaction
  attitudes 83
  background 4–8, 18, 80, 163–164, 180, 194–195, 196
  content 9, 79, 165, 167
  definition 8–10
  effectiveness/results of 163–165, 179, 180, 195–196, 197, 198, 199, 200, 202, 204, 205, 208, 209, 211
  environment for 11, 48, 150
  ethical issues 6, 180, 189
  ethos and atmosphere 83, 137, 197, 200
  fit with other approaches 13–14, 152–153, 162
  generalisability 11–12,
  getting started 85, 89–91, 197, 198, 199, 200, 201, 203, 204, 205, 206, 210
  learner engagement 164–165, 199, 211
  method 167–168
  natural momentum 138, 139, 143
  natural momentum plateaux and problems 141, 142
  observation phase 82–89, 200–201, 205, 206, 208
  organisation of 105, 145–159
  physical characteristics of the learner 84, 96–97, 204–205
  interaction planning 154–156
  preparation 201
  principles 87, 167, 172
  progression 10, 27, 28, 138, 165–168, 197, 198, 200, 202, 204, 205, 208–209, 211
  purposes/aims 11–12, 15, 81–82, 84, 103, 165, 180, 181
  structure 13, 154–155, 165–166, 187
  teamwork 97, 142, 146–148, 151, 156–157, 162, 189–190, 203–204, 205
  values/philosophy 14–16, 84, 180, 210
  who for 11–13, 167, 180, 203, 206
intentionality 21–22, 55, 67, 74, 120–121, 207
interaction 'coaching' 35–36
interactive 'fit' 32–33, 166, 167

interactive games/sequences
  arousal levels 123, 134–135, 136
  atmosphere 11,
  breakdown 31, 73–76, 142, 203
  burst-pause use of 57, 74, 94, 198, 207
  content 9, 197, 198, 205, 207, 208
  different intensities 149, 195, 198, 204, 207
  establishing 95–96, 131,
  face to face 48, 63, 88, 197, 198, 205
  finishing 9, 62, 64, 135–136, 201, 202, 204
  flexibility of focus/content 113–114, 168
  guiding 140,
  imitation, use of 26, 28, 40, 50, 126, 127, 197, 198, 199–200, 201, 205, 207, 209
  incidentally occuring 139,
  infants with disabilities 31
  initiating 19–20, 38, 41, 107, 139, 140, 207, 209
  intentionality use of 21–22, 55, 67, 74, 207,
  length of 9, 147–149, 198, 203
  'more' signals 94, 113
  objects, use of 56, 62, 71, 205
  OSI, use of 178, 209, 210
  pauses, use of 23, 50, 74, 88, 100, 106, 116–117, 118, 122–124, 198,
  peaks 62, 199
  physical contact, use of 7, 9, 27, 88, 195, 197, 201, 204, 210,
  playfulness 195, 202, 205, 207, 210
  repertoires 103, 114, 126, 140–141
  repetition 9, 62, 139, 141, 207
  rhythm, use of 56, 88, 179, 198, 207, 208–209
  rough and tumble 9, 88, 94, 130, 195, 209
  speech in 88, 200, 201, 205, 207
  teacher doing too little 160
  teacher doing too much 92, 93, 134
  teasing 198, 202, 205, 207, 210
  tempo 92, 138
  tension-expectancy 9, 94, 108, 117–120, 209
  timing/flow 23, 88, 198, 202, 203, 210
  turn-taking 88, 94, 197, 198, 207
  variation 209
  variety/type 9, 103
  vocalisations 94, 197, 198, 209
  watching and waiting 23
  where to do them 11, 99
interactive style 27, 28–30, 51, 52
  and autism 41
  changing 36–37, 85, 166
  controlling 31, 33, 35, 37
  in classrooms 35, 37, 72, 76, 80
  optimal 29, 35, 36–37, 85
  summary 65
  variations 34, 166
interactivity 143–144, 152, 171
interpersonal behaviours 20–21
intuitive/rational 96, 156, 203, 205
intuitive abilities 8, 11, 30, 37, 72, 197, 201, 209
intuitive responding/judgements 8, 10, 11, 96, 128, 129,

Jiggling 9, 88, 132, 141
joining student/client in own world 48, 75, 94, 99, 100, 101, 102, 150, 196–197, 199, 200, 206–207, 208
joint focus 8, 111, 179, 198, 200, 211

Language development 29, 39, 200, 207
learner's own terms/point of view 16, 83, 85, 90, 92, 99, 103, 134–135
learner safety/security 89, 99, 100
learning principles learner active participant 19, 60–61, 73, 76, 199

Masturbation 102, 189, 201, 204, 210
mixed ability groups 153–154
modifications voice, face, body 5, 8, 58, 90, 116, 206, 209
motherese 21
mothering 6, 19
motivation 29, 66–67, 70, 75, 78, 195, 198, 199, 205–206, 207
motivation of teacher 74, 75, 206
movement 42, 198–199, 199–200, 202
movement therapy 34, 42
mutual enjoyment 19, 49, 70, 84, 200, 209
mutual pleasure 8, 16, 23, 25, 104, 195, 197, 198, 202
  lack of 31
mutuality 8, 20, 179, 200, 205, 209, 210

National Curriculum 92,
negotiation 16,
non-confrontation 7, 77, 144
normalisation 169, 171–174

Objects/things rather than people 91, 100
observation 82–89, 147